THE
PACKWOOD
REPORT

THE

PACKWOOD

REPORT

The Senate Ethics Counsel

FOREWORD BY HELEN DEWAR
OF *The Washington Post*

TIMES BOOKS

RANDOM HOUSE

Publisher's Note:
This book contains the entire text of
the Senate Ethics Counsel Report to the
Select Committee on Ethics, released on
September 7, 1995.
No copyright is claimed in the text of this
official Government document.
Foreword copyright © 1995 by Helen Dewar
ISBN: 0-8129-2782-6
Manufactured in the United States of America

SELECT COMMITTEE ON ETHICS
MITCH McCONNELL, Kentucky, *Chairman*
RICHARD H. BRYAN, Nevada, *Vice Chairman*

BOB SMITH, New Hampshire   BARBARA A. MIKULSKI, Maryland
LARRY E. CRAIG, Idaho   BYRON L. DORGAN, North Dakota

VICTOR McEVER BAIRD, *Staff Director and Chief Counsel*
LINDA S. CHAPMAN, *Counsel*
DAVID M. FEITEL, *Counsel*
HOUSTON R. FULLER, *Investigator*

MEMBERS' STAFF

MELISSA PATACK, Office of Senator McConnell
JEAN NEAL, Office of Senator Bryan
PATRICK PETTEY, Office of Senator Smith
GREGORY CASEY, Office of Senator Craig
STEPHANIE FOSTER, Office of Senator Mikulski
MARY HAWKINS, Office of Senator Dorgan

ETHICS COMMITTEE STAFF

ELIZABETH RYAN, *Counsel*
ADAM BRAMWELL, *Counsel*
MARIE MULLIS, *Professional Staff Member*
ANNETTE GILLIS, *Chief Clerk*
PAUL LEGRADY, *Special Assistant for Financial Disclosure*
DAWNE VERNON, *Staff Assistant*
KIMBERLY ECKHARDT, *Staff Assistant*
MARCIE PHILLIP, *Staff Assistant*

Foreword
by Helen Dewar

IN EARLY OCTOBER 1992, *The Washington Post* began looking into rumors that had been circulating on Capitol Hill for years: that Republican Senator Bob Packwood of Oregon, a prominent champion of women's rights, was also a womanizer who made unwanted sexual advances to women staffers and others during his nearly quarter century in the Senate.

Just short of three years later, Packwood—at the moment that he expected to play the greatest role of his career as chairman of the Senate Finance Committee during Congress' struggles over taxes, Medicare and welfare—stood tearfully before his colleagues to announce his resignation from the Senate.

He faced a unanimous recommendation from the Senate ethics committee, issued just the day before, that he be expelled for improper sexual conduct, for soliciting jobs for his wife from lobbyists and for tampering with evidence in the case. He would have been the first senator expelled since fourteen southerners were tossed out for supporting rebellion during the Civil War. As it was, Packwood became only the fifth senator in more than two centuries of congressional history to relinquish his seat to avoid expulsion.

It was, he said, the only "honorable thing to do for the country, for the Senate."

Between the start of *The Post*'s investigation and the end of Packwood's political career was a story filled with moments of high drama and moments that seemed made for a soap opera, a story of sex, power and pathos that often seemed as though it would never end.

But it was not just a story of official corruption or sexual excess or the folly of keeping diaries.

It was an account of an enormously talented man who was victimized by his own arrogance, loneliness, binge drinking and compulsive need to prove his sexual as well as political prowess. When he came to the Senate in 1969, he was seen as a 36-year-old boy wonder, the giant killer who brought down the venerable Senator Wayne Morse. But by now his wife had left him; he was estranged from his children; he was nearly broke; he had even sold the unoccupied trailer outside of Portland that he had called his official "residence" in Oregon. "His whole life had been politics and the Senate," said Craig Berkman, a former chairman of the Oregon Republican Party. And now that was gone, too.

There was a bizarre, even pathetic quality to the sexual exploits that he recounted in his diaries, conducted everywhere from parking lots and hotel bars to his Senate office. At one point, he refers to "the 22 staff members I'd made love to and probably 75 others I've had a passionate relationship with." At another point, he suggests it was his "Christian duty" to have sex with a woman he thought was deprived of it. He tells of lying naked on the floor of his office after engaging in sex with a staffer, with other staffers sitting just outside the locked door, apparently well aware of what was going on.

The allegations against Packwood came to light only after the all-male Senate Judiciary Committee's hearings on Anita F. Hill's allegations of harassment by Supreme Court nominee Clarence Thomas in 1991 created a national uproar and helped propel a record number of women into races for public office, including the Senate.

The Committee—and by extension the Senate—was widely criticized for underestimating the gravity of Hill's allegations, badgering Hill during the hearings, allowing the proceedings to be turned into a circus and confirming Thomas in spite of doubts among many senators about who was telling the truth.

Despite its reluctance to judge its own, the Senate was not about to let this happen again. Through its ethics committee, it signaled that it believed at least seventeen of the more than two dozen women who accused Packwood of groping, grabbing and kissing them between 1969 and 1990 and was prepared to hand down the severest of all sanctions: expulsion.

Part of the reason was the nature of the allegations against Packwood, which seemed to grow more serious at every major turn in the investigation. But another important part was the change in the Senate itself in the four years since the Thomas-Hill hearings.

In the 1992 elections, four new women senators were elected to join the two already serving in the Senate. Not only were there more female voices speaking out for women's concerns, but male members had only to look around the chamber—its sea of gray suits suddenly enlivened by dashes of vivid linen and silk—for daily reminders of the power of the women's vote. Few failed to get the message. As a result, the Democrats' senior woman member, Barbara A. Mikulski of Maryland, was put in the Democratic leadership and on the ethics committee, where she became a force for stern discipline in the Packwood case. Outside the committee, Democratic Senator Barbara Boxer of California, one of the newcomers, was Packwood's most relentless critic.

Senator Richard H. Bryan of Nevada, Democratic vice chairman of the ethics committee, may have been right when he said that Packwood's behavior would have been "unacceptable at the time Columbus discovered America," but it would have been hard to imagine a similar outcome in the Senate even a decade ago. Even though many of the incidents in the Packwood case occurred before the mid-1980s, none of the women filed a complaint until after *The Post* published its first story in November 1992. And the ethics committee had never even considered a sexual misconduct case, let alone contemplated expulsion for it.

The Packwood case also threw new light on the insidious, all-too-cozy relationships between some lawmakers and the influence peddlers who are always ready with a campaign contribution, a favor or an expensive dinner, along with suggestions for legislation. Aides become lobbyists; lobbyists become friends. Some senators draw a line and keep it; others do not.

The issue at hand was Packwood's solicitations of jobs for his estranged wife from lobbyists and others with an interest in legislation before Congress, an effort that was clearly aimed at reducing his alimony payments. But the record showed that Packwood's job hustling was part of a broader Washington subculture that is dominated by money, booze and power.

Describing his 1989 meeting over beers with lobbyist-friend Steve Saunders, a former Packwood employee who was a registered foreign agent for Mitsubishi Electric Corp., Packwood asked Saunders if he could put his wife Georgia on a retainer. "He says, 'How much?' I said, '$7,500 a year.' he said, 'Consider it done.' Another lobbyist offered $37,500 for five years of part-time work and added, "If you're chairman of the Finance Committee, I can probably double that." Packwood was not unaware of the risks. "Boy, I'm skating on thin ice here," he wrote in late January 1990.

Ironically, the case came to a head just as congressional leaders were dawdling over legislation to reform campaign finance laws by curbing the influence of special interest money. With the Packwood case hovering in the wings, the Senate approved legislation this year to tighten lobbyist registration rules and severely limit gifts to senators from lobbyists and others. But House leaders indicated they were in no hurry to act on the lobbyist constraints.

Lastly, the story was another chapter in the saga of hubris on the part of politicians who think they can defy the rules, especially the one that was made famous by President Richard M. Nixon: it's the cover-up that will really do you in.

When Packwood realized that the ethics committee would want his diaries, he set about altering them to remove some of the most damning and embarrassing entries, ignoring the virtual inevitability that his diary-tampering would somehow come to the ethics committee's attention. He said he was only doing so to keep some of the excerpts from falling into the hands of the tabloid journalists; the ethics committee concluded it was the intended victim of the deception.

For the committee, this was not only obstruction of justice in violation of federal law but, far worse in the eyes of senators, a crime against the Senate itself.

All the evidence leading to the committee's conclusions—covering the sexual advances, job solicitations and diary tampering—is distilled and summarized in the official report of the Ethics Counsel to the Senate. The report, published here in its entirety, covers the origins of the allegations, testimony of witnesses, Packwood's response and an account of the probe as it moved from the committee's highly secure meeting room to the Senate floor, to the Supreme Court and back to the committee's guarded, windowless room on the fourth floor of the Capitol. It also includes the committee counsel's findings on each of the counts that the committee examined and the committee's own conclusions.

The Packwood case broke records of all kinds for congressional ethics investigations.

The Senate thought it had seen it all when it spent two years in the early 1990s investigating five senators' involvement with failed savings and loan executive Charles H. Keating, Jr., resulting in a nationally televised public hearing, boxes full of documents and an assortment of rebukes for the "Keating Five" senators. But the Packwood case was entering its 34th month when it ended, setting a new record for length. In addition to being its first case involving sexual misconduct, it was the first in which the ethics committee had to subpoena evidence from a reluctant senator or go all the way up to the Supreme Court to force a senator to cooperate. The committee interviewed or took testimony from more than 260 witnesses, conducted 111 depositions, reviewed more than 16,000 pages of documents, served 44 subpoenas, reviewed 2,600 pages of diary transcripts and 350 audio tapes and sent questionnaires to 293 women who had worked for Packwood, two-thirds of whom responded.

The case was also rich with ironies.

Not only had Packwood been a hero to the women's movement in his support for abortion rights and other of its causes, but, at 62, halfway into his fifth term in the Senate, he was at the peak of his powers in the shaping of fiscal legislation.

As chairman of the powerful Finance Committee, he was poised to play a pivotal role in what was expected to be the biggest fight of the first session of the 104th Congress: the huge budget "reconciliation" bill that included tax cuts, overhaul of Medicare and spending cuts designed to put the federal budget on track toward balance within seven years. As finance chairman, he was also floor manager for the bill to revamp the nation's welfare system, holding center stage on the Senate floor until the day that he announced his resignation. The day after he resigned, he appeared ready to lead the charge again, until the Democrats cried foul and Majority Leader Robert Dole quickly sent in replacement forces.

The case itself was a study in delays, most of them engineered by Packwood and his lawyers, that often obscured what turned out to be a relentless march toward disgrace.

Packwood, a candidate for reelection in 1992, denied the women's allegations when first confronted by them in the fall of that year, and *The Post* did not publish its story until after the election. He checked into an alcoholic treatment center, emerging to say he had stopped drinking and was sorry if he had offended anyone.

But he was in trouble both at home and in Washington. In Oregon, former supporters turned against him, and critics circulated petitions for his removal. He made few trips home, and, when he did, he created "stealth events" so hecklers would not know where to go. In Washington, the women started filing their allegations, and the ethics committee began its probe.

Everything seemed to be moving along slowly but smoothly until October 1993, when Packwood mentioned his diaries to the committee and it began reviewing them. Packwood abruptly called a halt to the diary-reading when the committee's counsel discovered references to the job solicitations and sought copies of these excerpts.

This led to a committee subpoena for the rest of the diaries, a Packwood refusal and an unprecedented fight in the federal courts—ultimately all the way to the Supreme Court—over the constitutionality of the committee's demand for access to the diaries. Packwood tried to keep them from the committee on grounds of privacy and protection against self-incrimination but lost at every step of the way.

At one point during the court proceedings, the committee learned from Cathy Wagner Cormack, Packwood's longtime secretary and transcriber of his diaries, that he had altered them, apparently in anticipation of a subpoena. The committee then broadened its probe to include the tampering issue.

At another point, shortly after the Senate approved the subpoenas, Packwood offered to resign, withdrawing the offer after the Justice Department issued a subpoena of its own for a probe of the job offers. The department never prosecuted on the jobs issue but is already looking into the tampering evidence.

The court fight, coupled with an elaborate court-ordered process for committee review of the diary tapes and transcripts, caused nearly a year's delay in the committee's work. In the meantime, Packwood endeavored, both in Oregon and in Washington, to rehabilitate himself, stressing his role on important and popular legislation.

With the Republican takeover of the Senate in the 1994 elections, he became chairman of the Finance Committee; his prominence—and the illusion of his survival—grew by the day. But it was only an illusion. In May, the committee concluded its probe and found "substantial credible evidence" on the sex, jobs and tampering issues, releasing a devastating bill of particulars that vividly described eighteen incidents of sexual misbehavior.

But the committee, composed of three Republicans and three Democrats, became hopelessly divided along party lines over whether to order public hearings after Packwood waived his right to them. Boxer tried to force the Senate itself to order hearings, failing by only a couple of votes.

A bombshell was waiting for the committee when it returned to its deliberations the next day. Two more women, including one who was a seventeen-year-old former Packwood intern at the time of the alleged incident, had filed charges with the committee. For the first time, a minor was involved. The Senate was clearly getting more disturbed—and Packwood more concerned.

Then, while the Senate was home for its August recess, Packwood made a desperate and ill-fated move: he changed his mind and asked for hearings, leaving Republican loyalists who had stuck with him in the vote against hearings to hang out to dry. Among them were the three Republicans on the ethics committee, including the prickly Republican Senator Mitch McConnell, who had previously been urging colleagues to settle for censure and stripping Packwood of his committee chairmanship. McConnell later said he saw the request as a delaying tactic.

Before the committee reconvened September 6, Bryan told McConnell he was prepared to recommend expulsion. But McConnell beat him to the punch at the meeting, and the vote was 6 to 0. Using words like "reprehensible" and "contemptuous," the committee said Packwood was guilty of abuse of power and had brought discredit on the Senate. In the case of the tampering charge, it said, he was guilty of a "crime against the Senate."

Packwood raced to the cameras to accuse the committee of acting like the Inquisition and said he would not resign, a vow that seemed to get stronger as he appeared on television talk shows later that night and the next morning.

But it was all over, McConnell and Bryan excoriated Packwood at a news conference and released the 10,000 pages of documents accumulated in the case, which seemed certain to bury him. As excerpts from the infamous diaries floated across television screens, Senators Alan K. Simpson of Wyoming and John McCain of Arizona, who had remained close to him during his ordeal, finally met with Packwood to tell him it was time to go. Dole, joining the group at the end, agreed. Packwood went back to his office to tell his staff.

Shortly afterward, the staff filed into the VIP gallery above the Senate floor, looking grim and shaken. Senators began drifting in; an awkward calm settled over the chamber. As he sat down,

Packwood was embraced by Oregon's senior senator, Mark O. Hatfield. His voice quavering and breaking at times, Packwood said he was "aware of the dishonor that has befallen me in the last three years" and did not want to burden the Senate with any more of it. "I leave this institution, not with malice, but with love," he said. It was a rare moment of grace for a man that had exhibited so little of it.

Key Events in Packwood Case:
A Chronology

■ **Background:** *Sen. Bob Pack-wood (R-Ore.), 63, has served in the U.S. Senate since 1969 and was elected to a fifth term in 1992.*

■ **Committees:** *Finance (chairman); Commerce, Science and Technology.*

■ **Joint committee:** *Taxation (vice chairman)*

■ **Family:** *Divorced, two children*

1992
■ **Oct. 29–31:** *Washington Post* reporters present Packwood with allegations of uninvited sexual advances. He denies them and provides statements intended to undercut the women's credibility.

■ **Nov. 3:** Packwood is reelected with 52 percent of vote.

■ **Nov. 22:** *The Washington Post* reports allegations by 10 women of sexual misconduct. Packwood says he is sorry if

he caused "any individual discomfort or embarrassment."

■ **Nov. 27:** Packwood checks into an alcoholism diagnostic and treatment program for five days.

■ **Dec. 1:** Senate ethics committee begins inquiry into allegations of sexual misconduct.

■ **Dec. 10:** Packwood says at news conference: "My actions were just plain wrong . . . I just didn't get it. I do now."

1993
■ **Oct 6:** In deposition before committee staff, Packwood refers to his personal diaries, leading to a battle over access to the journals.

■ **Oct. 21:** Senate ethics committee unanimously votes to seek Packwood's diaries.

■ **Nov. 1:** Ethics Chairman Richard H. Bryan (D-Nev.) says the diaries indicate possible criminal misconduct relating to jobs lobbyists offered Packwood's ex-wife.

- **Nov. 2:** After two days of debate, Senate votes 94 to 6 to allow ethics committee to go to court to enforce a subpoena for Packwood's diaries.

- **Nov. 17–19:** Packwood offers to resign. He withdraws offer after Justice Department subpoenas the diaries to investigate whether Packwood's job solicitations violated criminal laws against obstruction of justice.

- **Nov. 22:** Ethics panel files suit to enforce subpoena.

- **Dec. 14:** Senate lawyers ask federal judge to seize diaries immediately, saying Packwood altered them.

1994

- **Jan. 24:** U.S. District Judge Thomas Penfield Jackson rules that the committee is entitled to the diaries.

- **March 2:** Chief Justice William Rehnquist denies Packwood's final effort to keep his diaries.

- **March 11:** Packwood says the ethics panel offered in November 1993 to drop its investigation if he would resign. The committee said he offered to resign to end the investigation after being rebuffed in efforts to plead no contest.

- **March 30:** Ethics committee begins receiving copies of the diary transcripts, putting the inquiry back on track. Audiotapes become available in October.

1995

- **Jan. 17–21:** The committee resumes taking Packwood's deposition.

- **May 17:** The committee finds "substantial credible evidence" that Packwood may have violated Senate rules by the sexual encounters, job solicitations and diary tampering and describes 18 instances of allegedly improper sexual conduct.

- **June 22–29:** Packwood appears before the committee to respond.

- **June 28:** Justice Department says it won't prosecute Packwood on allegation regarding his ex-wife.

- **July 5:** Packwood declines public hearings.

- **July 31:** Committee rejects public hearings but agrees to release all evidence in the case.

- **Aug. 2:** In 52 to 48 vote, Senate upholds ethics committee decision.

- **Aug. 3:** Committee says two more women, including one who was 17 at the time, have brought sexual misconduct allegations.

- **Aug. 25:** Packwood reverses himself and says he wants public hearings.

- **Sept. 6:** Ethics committee votes unanimously to recom-mend Packwood's expulsion from the Senate.

- **Sept. 7:** Packwood announces he will resign.

- **Sept. 8:** Packwood resigns immediately as Finance Committee chairman and agrees to leave the Senate Oct. 1.

SOURCES: Staff reports, Congressional Staff Directory, "Almanac of American Politics 1994," Associated Press. From *The Washington Post*. Used by permission.

Contents

THE
PACKWOOD
REPORT

I

Introduction

Senate Ethics Counsel submits this Report in the matter of Senator Bob Packwood pursuant to Rule 5(f)(1) of the Supplementary Procedural Rules of the United States Senate Select Committee on Ethics (the "Committee"). This Report contains findings based upon the evidence gathered during the course of the Committee's proceedings in this matter.

Initially, the Report reviews the procedural background of the matters which are the subject of the Committee's Investigation. The Report then addresses the scope of the Committee's authority to investigate and sanction misconduct of Members, and discusses Senate precedents.

The Report then discusses in detail the evidence gathered by the Committee with respect to each of the matters under Investigation. Based upon this evidence, Counsel makes findings of improper conduct with respect to each of the three charges contained in the Committee's Resolution of May 16, 1995.

Procedural Background

SEXUAL MISCONDUCT

Origin of Allegations

ON NOVEMBER 22, 1992, the *Washington Post* published a story detailing allegations against Senator Packwood of sexual harassment and misconduct by Senator Packwood by seven women, five of whom were named in the article, and two of whom were anonymous.

By a letter received at the Committee November 30, 1992, the Women's Equal Rights Legal Defense and Education Fund (WERLDEF), filed a complaint against Senator Packwood, and requested an investigation of the sexual harassment and misconduct allegations that had been made against him. By letter dated December 1, 1992, the Committee notified Senator Packwood of the complaint, and that the Committee had decided to conduct a preliminary inquiry into the allegations.

On December 10, 1992, Senator Packwood held a press conference, in which he read a statement saying, *inter alia,* that he took full responsibility for his conduct, that all of his past record was clouded because of incidents in which his actions were unwelcomed and offensive to the women involved, and justifiably so; that his past actions were not just inappropriate, that what he had done was not just stupid or boorish, but his actions were just plain wrong. He stated that he "didn't get it", but that he did now. Without getting into specific allegations, he admitted his mistake, and apologized to the women involved.[1]

---

[1] At his deposition in January 1995, Senator Packwood disavowed any intent by this statement to admit to any specific conduct; he only meant to say that *if* the conduct had occurred, he was sorry.

On December 21, 1992, the Committee received a sworn complaint, in which a woman alleged that Senator Packwood had made an improper advance toward her, and asked that the Committee investigate his behavior. Her attorney also requested the Committee to conduct an inquiry into the pattern of Senator Packwood's conduct over a period of years with regard to other women.

The Committee received numerous letters from other groups and private citizens urging that the Committee investigate the allegations of sexual harassment and misconduct.

On February 4, 1993, the Committee announced that it was expanding the scope of its inquiry to include allegations of attempts to intimidate and discredit the alleged victims, and misuse of official staff in attempts to intimidate and discredit.

How the Investigation Was Conducted

The staff took sworn depositions or statements from twenty-two women who made allegations of sexual harassment or misconduct against Senator Packwood. The staff also interviewed or deposed witnesses who corroborated the allegations made by some of the women accusers, by virtue of the fact that the women had told them about the incident, although not always in great detail, either shortly after it occurred, or well before the allegations were published by the *Post*.

The staff also mailed a letter and questionnaire to 293 female former Packwood staff members, asking if they had information relevant to the Committee's inquiry. 194 questionnaires were returned.[2] 39 signed returned receipt cards were returned, but no corresponding questionnaires were returned.[3] 47 of the questionnaires were returned as undeliverable.[4] Thus, out of the 293

---

[2] Three of the persons to whom the questionnaire was directed were deceased.

[3] Some of the return receipts were not signed by the addressee. The staff interviewed three of these persons independently of the questionnaire.

[4] The staff interviewed two of these persons independently of the questionnaire.

questionnaires originally sent, 280 have been accounted for, either by the questionnaire being returned, by the return receipt card being returned, indicating that the questionnaire was delivered but the addressee did not wish to respond, or by the questionnaire being returned as undeliverable.

The bulk of the persons responding to the questionnaire (approximately 122) had no relevant information[5]; approximately 34 did not wish to become involved in the Committee's inquiry.[6] Approximately 35 women responded that they had relevant information; most of these women provided (by a written statement accompanying their questionnaire, by a telephone interview, or both) statements of support for the Senator, generally stating that they had a wonderful experience working for him, that they had neither experienced nor heard of any type of sexual misconduct by the Senator, and that they viewed the Senator as a gentleman who was genuinely interested in advancing women and women's causes. A few of these women provided information about misconduct involving women who have not chosen to come forward, some of which corroborated information the staff had already uncovered. Two persons who responded to the Committee's questionnaire have come forward with allegations of sexual misconduct.

The staff also attempted to contact and interview or depose every person who the staff had reason to believe, by virtue of other testimony or information, might have knowledge either implicating Senator Packwood in unwanted sexual behavior toward his staff, or tending to exonerate him of such accusations.

---

[5] Two of these persons were interviewed by the staff independently of the questionnaire.

[6] One of these persons was interviewed by the staff independently of the Committee's questionnaire.

The staff also took the depositions of Jack Faust, Senator Packwood's longtime friend, campaign adviser, and attorney, and Elaine Franklin, Senator Packwood's chief of staff.

Senator Packwood was served with two separate document requests, on March 29 and July 16, 1993, asking for virtually every document that dealt with the allegations of sexual misconduct, or the women who were making the allegations. His chief of staff, Elaine Franklin, was also served with a document request, and Jack Faust was served with a subpoena for documents.

Senator Packwood appeared for his deposition by the Committee staff on Tuesday, October 5, 1993. During questioning by the staff, Senator Packwood testified that he had kept detailed diaries from the time he had taken office, which he dictated and then had transcribed by a staff member. Senator Packwood testified that he had reviewed some portions of the diaries and scanned others, and that the diaries contained some entries that were relevant to the complaints that had been made against him.[7]

At that point, the deposition was halted. An agreement was reached for review of the diaries by Committee counsel and counsel immediately began that review. After counsel discovered entries in the diaries that appeared to implicate Senator Packwood in other conduct that was arguably improper, Senator Packwood refused to allow further review of his diaries. The Committee voted unanimously to subpoena Senator Packwood for production of his diaries. When he did not comply, the Committee intro-

---

[7] Senator Packwood stated that he had reviewed his diaries, but that on the advice of his counsel, he had not reviewed them for the purposes of preparing for his deposition. Senator Packwood's counsel was under the mistaken impression that if Senator Packwood reviewed the diaries in preparation for his deposition, Committee counsel would demand to see the diaries pursuant to the Federal Rules of Evidence, which provide that the opposing party may review any documents that a witness has used to refresh his recollection in preparation for testimony.

duced a resolution on the floor of the Senate to authorize the Senate legal counsel to file suit in Federal District Court to enforce the subpoena. The resolution was approved by a vote of 94 to 6.

The Committee's application to enforce the subpoena was filed on November 22, 1993, and was heard by the Hon. Thomas Penfield Jackson on December 16, 1993. On January 24, 1994, Judge Jackson granted the Committee's application, and after consulting with the parties, on February 4, 1994, established guidelines for the Committee's review of the diaries. The Committee received Senator Packwood's diary transcripts from March 1994 through April 1994, and the diary tapes from October 1994 through February 1995. Senator Packwood's deposition was concluded in January 1995.

ALTERATION OF EVIDENCE

The Committee's Pursuit of the Diaries
The Committee's Document Requests

The two document requests issued to Senator Packwood by the Committee in March and July 1993 required him to produce *all* documents of any kind, including personal records, regarding, related to, communicating with, or memorializing communications with a wide range of identified individuals, or referring or relating to a set of identified events, within the scope of the Committee's inquiry. The second request specifically stated that "[t]he Committee expects that you will conduct a reasonable and thorough search of your Senate office files, your personal files, campaign committee files, and other files that are within your possession, custody, and control, or otherwise would be available to you, in order . . . to ensure full compliance" with the Committee's document requests.

As defined in the requests, the word "document" included any information stored on audio or videotape, or by any other electromagnetic or electronic means.

The existence of diaries kept by Senator Packwood was known to the staff, through a press report and a reference to them in another document produced by Senator Packwood. Although Senator Packwood produced a number of documents pursuant to these requests, he produced no portions of his diaries. Further, although the Senator informed the Committee that he was asserting the attorney-client or work-product privilege with respect to the production of more than 100 documents and disclosed the existence of the documents that he was withholding on that ground, the Senator never disclosed that he was withholding, or asserting a privilege from producing, diaries responsive to the Committee's document requests.[8]

The staff assumed in good faith that Senator Packwood had complied with the two document requests, and had identified *all* material that was responsive to the Committee's requests, either by turning it over to the Committee, or disclosing its existence but withholding it on grounds of privilege. Because no entries

---

[8] The privilege log provided to the Committee by Senator Packwood's attorneys listed 112 memoranda that were being withheld on the grounds of either attorney-client or work-product privilege, and identified them by date, author, recipient(s), and the name of the complainant or potential complainant who was discussed in the memorandum. The privilege log did *not* disclose that attached to many of the memoranda were excerpts from Senator Packwood's diary pages, some of which referred to women who had made claims of misconduct against Senator Packwood. At his deposition, Jim Fitzpatrick, one of Senator Packwood's attorneys at the law firm of Arnold & Porter, testified that they viewed some of the diary entries as falling outside the scope of the Committee's request, and some of them as falling within the scope; to the extent that they fell within the scope of the request, he stated that they were adequately identified on the privilege log. Six of the memoranda identified on the privilege log pre-dated the November 1992 election. Mr. Fitzpatrick testified that their representation of Senator Packwood began just after that election.

from Senator Packwood's diaries were ever produced, nor was the Committee advised that Senator Packwood was withholding them on the basis of any privilege, the staff assumed that the diaries contained no material responsive to the Committee's document requests.

The Committee Learns of the Existence of Relevant Diary Entries

At his first deposition in October 1993, Senator Packwood testified under oath that he had scanned more than ten years of his diaries in connection with the Committee's inquiry, and that his diaries contained materials concerning persons and events that were the subject of the Committee's inquiry. He gave no explanation for his failure to produce these materials in response to the Committee's request, despite the fact that he testified that they included relevant information.[9]

At that point, the staff requested that Senator Packwood provide his diaries to the Committee so that the staff could examine them before completing his deposition. The staff began negotiations with Senator Packwood's attorneys for access to the diaries. The Committee agreed to allow Senator Packwood to produce diaries covering specific years (the last period of which terminated with the then-present date, October 6, 1993), and to mask with opaque tape passages covered by the attorney-client privilege, the physician-patient privilege, or that referred solely to personal, private family matters. The Committee permitted Senator Packwood to mask entries dealing with personal, private

---

[9] Also for the first time, Senator Packwood disclosed the existence of daily records of events, which he had kept for over twenty years, and travel records, neither of which had been provided to the Committee in response to its requests. Senator Packwood provided those records to the Committee within a few days after his deposition.

family matters, despite the fact that such entries were not protected by any recognized evidentiary privilege, to accomodate Senator Packwood's concerns about the private nature of diary entries about his family. However, the Committee did not accede to Senator Packwood's request that he be allowed to mask entries dealing with consensual sexual relationships, because such matters would likely bear on the potential bias of witnesses before the Committee, and because consent was at the heart of the issues before the Committee. Senator Packwood's attorney specifically advised the staff that the Senator had agreed to produce his diaries under these conditions.

Before the staff began reviewing the diaries, Senator Packwood's attorneys asked whether the staff would agree that if, while reviewing the diaries, the staff identified passages raising issues within the Committee's jurisdiction, but beyond the scope of its inquiry into alleged sexual misconduct and witness intimidation, the staff would not require copies of those entries, but would set aside those additional issues for later consideration. The staff refused to make such a commitment.

On October 12, 1993, Senator Packwood began providing his masked diaries for review.[10] Over the next four days, four Committee counsel reviewed an estimated 3,000 to 4,000 pages spanning 1969 through 1983, and identified 115 pages or portions of pages that contained relevant material. Senator Packwood provided photocopies of those pages to the Committee.

As agreed, the diaries were reviewed by the staff only in the presence of Senator Packwood's attorneys. Staff did not take any notes, make any copies, or take custody of any of the diaries.

---

[10] The diaries requested by the Committee on October 6, 1993, which were to be reviewed under the agreement were for the following periods: January 1969 through December 1972; January 1975 through December 1977; September 1978 through December 1986; and August 1989 through October 6, 1993.

Staff marked for photocopying those entries it determined had some relevance to the Committee's inquiry, with the understanding that Senator Packwood's attorneys would provide copies of these passages. As agreed, if there were disputes about the relevance of any particular passages that the staff requested be photocopied, which could not be resolved at the staff level, Senator Packwood had the right to press his objection before the Committee leadership, and ultimately before the full Committee, for a ruling.

On October 14, while the staff continued to review the diaries, Senator Packwood requested, by way of a letter addressed to the Committee, that he be allowed to mask entries relating to his consensual intimate activities during the years since 1989. He suggested that Kenneth Starr be retained to review any such masking to ensure that it dealt only with consensual activity. The Committee rejected Senator Packwood's request, because such material could be probative of potential witness bias and could bear directly on one of the key factual issues that the Committee would ultimately need to resolve, namely, whether particular conduct was or was not consensual. Senator Packwood continued to produce his diaries in accordance with the previous agreement.

Committee counsel continued to review Senator Packwood's diaries over the weekend of October 16 and 17, examining an additional estimated 1,000 to 2,000 pages, and marking approximately 170 pages or portions of pages for photocopying.[11]

---

[11] On at least two occasions during the Committee's review of the diaries, the Senator's attorneys informed staff that particular passages had been masked that did not fall within the agreed-upon categories, but which related to extremely personal information about third parties, and were in no way relevant to matters under inquiry. Staff declined an offer to examine this material, and consented to its masking.

The Committee's Review of the Diaries
Comes to a Halt

On Sunday, October 17, Committee counsel came across two passages from 1989 that indicated possible misconduct in areas unrelated to the Committee's pending inquiry into sexual misconduct and witness intimidation.

These entries raised questions whether Senator Packwood may have improperly solicited financial support for his wife from individuals with interests in legislation and whether such solicitations may have been linked to his performance of official acts. The entries implicated possible violations of federal laws, as well as rules and standards of the Senate.

These entries appeared in the diaries on November 3 and November 6, 1989. At that time, as reflected in the diaries, Senator Packwood was contemplating divorce from his wife, and was worried about the amount of support that he would have to pay as part of the divorce settlement. The November 3 entry stated that Senator Packwood had met with Steve Saunders, and had asked him to put the Senator's wife on "retainer" for $7500 per year; the individual agreed, expressing relief that the figure was an annual, and not a monthly, amount. The entry also reflects that Senator Packwood had approached two other individuals with similar requests.

A diary entry on November 6, 1989, three days after the meeting with Steve Saunders, reflected that Senator Packwood attended a meeting or hearing of the Senate Committee on Finance, of which Senator Packwood was the ranking Republican member. Senator Packwood recorded that he had raised questions or suggested legislative language of some sort for Mr. Saunders.

Senator Packwood's handwritten calendars, which he turned over to the Committee after their existence was discovered during his deposition, also confirm the November 3 meeting with

Mr. Saunders, and that on November 6, Senator Packwood went to "Finance for Saunders."

Committee counsel marked these entries in the diary for photocopying, and on October 18, Victor Baird, Chief Counsel for the Committee, advised the Committee leadership of the discovery of the entries.

On Monday, October 18, Senator Packwood's attorney failed to deliver the next series of diaries for review[12] under the agreement. When Victor Baird inquired of Senator Packwood's attorney when the diaries would arrive, Senator Packwood's attorney expressed concern over one of the two passages that had been marked for photocopying, claiming that it was not relevant to the Committee's inquiry, and asking why it had been marked. He was advised that the entry raised new issues of potential misconduct, and was cited to specific laws, Senate rules, and standards that might apply. The Senator's attorney asked if these new issues could be treated as a separate matter, and not acted upon until the Committee's current preliminary inquiry was concluded. Mr. Baird informed him that he could not agree to that, and that it was the Committee's decision as to whether any new issues would be treated separately. Mr. Baird reminded the Senator's attorney that he had earlier raised this question, and that Mr. Baird had made it clear that the Committee was obligated to follow up on any information of potential misconduct within its jurisdiction that came to its attention.

Later that day, one diary volume was produced for review by the staff counsel. When Mr. Baird telephoned Senator Packwood's attorneys to ask when additional diaries would be pro-

[12] Senator Packwood also refused to provide the Committee with copies of these November 3 and November 6 entries, or of any of the entries designated for copying over the weekend of October 16 and 17.

duced, he was told that the next diaries in sequence for review were in the process of undergoing additional masking in light of the Committee's discovery of the new materials. Senator Packwood's attorney explicitly confirmed that not only was he now masking additional material based upon the Committee's discovery of information relating to potential misconduct in new areas, but that additional material had been masked in the single diary volume that had been delivered for review by the Committee earlier that afternoon. Senator Packwood's attorney was told that additional masking was unacceptable, and if the Senator was not willing to produce his diaries pursuant to the original agreement, the Committee would need to consider subpoenaing them. At that point, Senator Packwood broke off all further cooperation under the agreement, refusing to provide copies of any of the approximately 170 pages or portions of pages from 1984 through early 1990 that Committee counsel had already reviewed and determined to be relevant.

The Committee Insists on Completing
its Review of the Diaries

The Committee requested that Senator Packwood immediately complete his production of the remaining diaries. The Committee proposed that the Senator deliver them, after masking them in the three categories previously agreed upon, to Kenneth Starr, who would review the masked material to ensure that it complied with the agreement, and then forward the masked diaries to the Committee counsel for review. Counsel would review only the unmasked material, identify entries relevant to matters within the Committee's jurisdiction for copying, and return the originals to Mr. Starr for safekeeping.

Senator Packwood refused to accept this proposal, or to resume abiding by his original agreement with the Committee.

Instead, he insisted on masking additional materials, including all "entries which relate to political, campaign, staff or similar activities and are wholly unrelated to the sexual misconduct/intimidation issues."[13] He further demanded that the Committee agree not to pursue at that time either the new matters its counsel had discovered, or any other matters outside the scope of the preliminary inquiry. The Committee rejected the Senator's proposal.

The Committee Votes to Issue a Subpoena

On October 20, after advising the Senator's attorneys that continued recalcitrance would lead to a subpoena, the Committee voted unanimously to issue a subpoena to Senator Packwood, requiring him to produce his diaries from January 1, 1989 to the present, by delivering them to Mr. Starr. The subpoena required production forthwith of:

> All diaries, journals, or other documents, including tape recordings and materials stored by computer or electronic means, in his possession, custody, or control, which were prepared by him or at his direction, recording or describing his daily activities for January 1, 1989 through the present.

Senator Packwood's attorneys were informed that he would still be permitted to mask attorney-client and physician-patient material, and information relating to personal, private family matters, subject to Mr. Starr's review. The subpoena was served on Senator Packwood on the morning of October 21. The Committee informed Senator Packwood that, unless he complied with the subpoena, the Committee intended to meet later that day to con-

---

[13] Letter from James Fitzpatrick and Daniel Rezneck to Senators Richard H. Bryan and Mitch McConnell, October 20, 1993.

sider reporting a resolution to the full Senate seeking authority to initiate a civil action to enforce the subpoena. Senator Packwood sought additional time to respond, and repeated his attorneys' earlier proposal that the Committee defer attempting to obtain information related to newly discovered matters and limit its request to the sexual misconduct and witness intimidation issues.

The Committee unanimously voted to report a resolution to the Senate to seek civil enforcement of its subpoena unless Senator Packwood produced the diaries immediately. Upon receiving no response from Senator Packwood, on the evening of October 21, the Committee reported the enforcement resolution to the Senate.

The Senate Debates Enforcement of the Subpoena

The Senate took up consideration of the resolution on November 1. The Senate debated the resolution for approximately fifteen hours on November 1 and 2.

At the request of Senator Packwood and his attorneys, the Committee leadership and Committee counsel met with Senator Packwood and his attorneys on the evening of November 1. In response to Senator Packwood's claim that he did not know what new matters in the diaries had drawn the Committee's attention, Victor Baird again set forth, as he had done earlier to Senator Packwood's attorneys, the precise provisions of federal law, Senate rules, and standards that were potentially implicated by particular entries in the diaries.

Senator Packwood then offered to produce all diary entries that he judged to be relevant to either the initial matters under Committee inquiry, or the new matters that had come to the Committee's attention regarding solicitation of income for his wife. He proposed that Mr. Starr (who was not aware of this proposal) review the completeness of his production, but on the condition that he not divulge any evidence he found of potential new violations. The Committee met and unanimously rejected Senator Packwood's proposal, and informed him that it had the duty to investigate all credible information relating to potential misconduct of a Senator, and could not erect a barrier deliberately to screen itself from potential evidence of wrongdoing.

After extensive debate, the Senate voted 94 to 6 to adopt the Committee's proposed resolution to authorize the Senate Legal Counsel to enforce the Committee's subpoena.

The Committee Proposes a Process for Review of the Diaries

The Committee then wrote to Senator Packwood, to clarify the procedures for complying with the subpoena and to respond to questions that Senator Packwood had raised.[14] The Committee made it clear that the subpoena required production of only Senator Packwood's diaries and no other documents, and that the Committee would cut off production under the subpoena at July 16, 1993, the date of its second document request to him. The Committee also reemphasized that Senator Packwood could continue to mask the three categories agreed upon earlier. The Committee repeated that Mr. Starr would verify the appropriateness of all masking, and that the Senator would still have the opportunity to object to the Committee on the relevance of any materials selected and copied from his diaries by Committee counsel.

Senator Packwood Offers to Resign

On November 17, 1993, Senator Packwood wrote to Senators Bryan and McConnell, stating that he did not choose to fight on, and that he was "emotionally, physically, and financially ex-

---

[14] Letter from Senators Richard H. Bryan and Mitch McConnell to Senator Bob Packwood, November 9, 1993.

hausted." He asked that the Committee accept his plea of *nolo contendere* to the charges involving sexual misconduct and intimidation. The Committee met on November 18, and discussed the letter over several hours. It was unclear from the letter, for example, what Senator Packwood meant by his wish to "put this matter behind me, without further proceedings," or what would be encompassed in a plea of *nolo contendere;* it was decided that staff would meet with Senator Packwood's attorneys to discuss these issues.[15]

By the time of this Committee meeting on November 18, the Justice Department had already notified the Committee that it intended to open an inquiry into possible solicitation of employment by Senator Packwood for his spouse, and had asked about the possibility of Committee staff meeting with the Department to discuss coordination of the separate inquiries, as the Department did not wish to interfere with the Committee's inquiry.

At some time during November 18, Senator Packwood contacted Senator McConnell and during the course of their conversation indicated that he wanted a "window of opportunity" between the termination of the Committee's proceeding and Justice Department action so that he could destroy his diaries. Senator McConnell immediately conveyed this information to the Chairman and the Committee staff.

During the evening and early morning hours of November 18 and 19, an agreement was reached that Senators Bryan and McConnell would meet with Senator Packwood in the presence of staff counsel and attorneys for Senator Packwood. At around 11:00 a.m. on November 19 the meeting took place, with Senators Bryan, McConnell, Packwood, staff counsel, Jim Fitzpatrick, and Bill Diefenderfer, as a "friend" of Senator Packwood. It

---

[15] The attorneys met with the staff, but there was a very brief discussion with little or no elaboration on the proposal being advanced by Senator Packwood.

became clear early on in the meeting that it would likely be impossible for a resolution of the case to be agreed upon in the absence of delivery of the diaries. Senator Packwood asked that he and his attorney be excused, and Mr. Diefenderfer presented a proposal on behalf of the Senator: Senator Packwood would resign, the Committee would terminate the preliminary inquiry and cease all discovery and subpoena enforcement activity, and the subpoena would be withdrawn.[16] During this discussion with Mr. Diefenderfer, Senator Bryan specifically mentioned the Committee's concern about document preservation; Mr. Diefenderfer stated that he did not believe that the Senator had any intention of destroying the diaries. Mr. Diefenderfer agreed to give the Committee an hour to respond to this proposal.

In view of the earlier notification from the Department of Justice of their interest in the matter, and the concerns raised by Senator Packwood's comments to Senator McConnell about a "window of opportunity" to destroy the diaries, it was agreed that communication with the Justice Department was required, in order to preserve the Department's opportunity for access to the diaries. Michael Davidson, Senate Legal Counsel, joined the discussion, and agreed that it was appropriate to contact the Department of Justice. Mr. Davidson contacted Jack Keeney, Deputy Assistant Attorney General of the Criminal Division, Department of Justice, and inquired about the Department's intentions with respect to the diaries in the event that the Committee withdrew its subpoena. Mr. Keeney informed Mr. Davidson that the Department would immediately subpoena the diaries from Senator Packwood.

The Committee met again at about 1:30 p.m. and agreed to Senator Packwood's proposal to resign. Mr. Diefenderfer was

---

[16] Informally, the Committee would not seek to curtail the Senator's pension, an action which was not within the Committee's power in any event.

notified, and the proposal was reduced to writing in the form of a letter which was signed by Senators Bryan and McConnell. Before this letter could be delivered to Senator Packwood for his signature, Mr. Diefenderfer contacted Senator McConnell and told him that Senator Packwood had been served with a subpoena for his diaries by the Department of Justice, and that he no longer intended to resign. The Committee met later that afternoon, and was so informed.

The Committee Goes to Court to Enforce the Subpoena

On November 22, 1993, Senate Legal Counsel filed an application to Enforce the Subpoena in the United States District Court for the District of Columbia. Senator Packwood's attorneys responded, claiming that the diaries were protected from production by the Fourth and Fifth Amendments to the Constitution. A hearing was held on December 16, 1993, and argument was presented by both sides.[17] On January 24, 1994, Judge Jackson issued his ruling, finding that the Committee was entitled to production of the diaries. On February 7, 1994, Judge Jackson issued a further ruling, setting out the procedures for review by Kenneth Starr, and incorporating the categories for masking of material that had been suggested by the Committee in its November 19, 1993 letter to Senator Packwood.

Evidence of Possible Alteration

During the time that the Committee was seeking access to Senator Packwood's diaries, news accounts and public statements by Senator Packwood raised questions about how his former secretary, Cathy Wagner Cormack, had been paid to transcribe his diaries. The staff took Ms. Cormack's deposition in order to

[17] By this time, Senator Packwood had retained different attorneys, the firm of Stein, Mitchell & Mezines, who continue to represent him in this matter.

determine whether she was paid from Senate or campaign funds, as opposed to Senator Packwood's personal funds, for transcription of the diaries.

After her deposition was transcribed and she had an opportunity to review it, Ms. Cormack provided a sworn affidavit to the Committee, indicating that after the initiation of the Ethics Committee investigation, Senator Packwood had taken back from her some tapes that he already had given her to transcribe, and that at a later time it appeared to her that he may have made some revisions to those tapes. She also stated that Senator Packwood confirmed to her that he had made changes to the tapes. Based on this information, Ms. Cormack's deposition was taken a second time, on December 15, 1993, and she confirmed the information she had included in her affidavit.

That Senator Packwood's diaries may have been altered was set forth in a December 7, 1993 letter provided to the Chairman of the Committee by Senator Packwood's attorney, which stated, *inter alia,* that:

> With what may be a few or possibly no exceptions, the originals of these tapes (the diaries) are among the materials now held by Arnold & Porter. . . . In discrete instances, the transcripts depart from the original tapes. Based on a recounting of events, it is unlikely such transcripts were among the transcripts examined by the Senate Ethics Committee staff.[18]

---

[18] On December 10, 1993, Michael Davidson, Senate Legal Counsel, wrote to Senator Packwood's attorneys, stating, *inter alia:*

> [i]t would be helpful and appreciated if you could advise us of the dates of the transcripts that depart from the original tapes, and also provide us with any other specific information that could shed light on the integrity of the tapes and transcripts.

Senator Packwood's attorney responded that his letter of December 10, 1993, "must stand without comment."

The information indicating possible alteration of the diaries was provided to Judge Jackson, who, at the hearing on December 16, 1993, ordered that all diaries, including transcripts and audiotapes, be immediately deposited with the Court for safe-keeping pending the Court's decision on the Committee's application to enforce the subpoena.

Procedure for Production of Diaries to the Committee, and the Committee's Review of the Diaries

The Court's Order

On February 7, 1994, after conducting a status conference with the parties to discuss procedures to implement the Court's January 24, 1994 Order granting the Committee's application to enforce its subpoena, the Court issued an Order setting out procedures under which the Committee would obtain Senator Packwood's diaries.[19]

Kenneth Starr was appointed Special Master[20], and the tapes and transcripts that had been turned over to the Court as a result of the December 16, 1993 hearing were transferred to him. Mr. Starr was instructed to provide the transcripts and tapes to the Federal Bureau of Investigation for duplication, with copies to be provided to Mr. Starr, Senator Packwood, and the Clerk of the Court. The original transcripts and tapes were returned to Mr. Starr for possible later forensic examination to determine

---

[19] Senator Packwood petitioned the District Court for a stay of its Orders of January 24 and February 7, 1994, while he appealed those Orders to the Court of Appeals. The District Court denied this motion. Senator Packwood's appeal for a stay was also denied by the Court of Appeals on February 18, 1994. On March 2, 1994, Chief Justice Rehnquist denied Senator Packwood's request for a stay, and Senator Packwood subsequently withdrew his appeal of the Orders themselves.

[20] Mr. Starr also continued to act as the Committee's Hearing Examiner.

the nature and extent of any alterations, if requested by the Committee.

The Court's Order provided that Senator Packwood would have a reasonable opportunity to mask portions of the transcripts and audiotapes, according to the criteria for masking allowed by the Committee.[21] Mr. Starr would then review the masking to determine if it met these criteria, unmasking any portions that did not, and provide a copy to the Committee.

Production of the Diaries to the Committee

DIARY TRANSCRIPTS

The Committee began receiving copies of diary transcripts[22] that had been masked by Senator Packwood on March 30, 1994. Although these copies had not yet been reviewed by Mr. Starr to determine if they had been properly masked, they were provided to the Committee in an attempt to avoid unnecessary delay in the Committee's review of the diaries. The Cormack transcripts were designated as "Q 1 through Q 10," with each "Q" representing six months of entries. As Mr. Starr reviewed the Cormack transcripts, he provided the Committee with entries that he had determined did not meet the criteria for masking. This process continued through April 29, 1994, when the Committee received the last of the Cormack transcripts.

DIARY TAPES

The Court's Order of February 7, 1994, contemplated that Senator Packwood would have the right to mask the audiotapes that

---

[21] These criteria were the same as set out in the November 9, 1993 letter from the Committee to Senator Packwood.

[22] To avoid confusion, the written diary transcripts that were provided to the Committee by Senator Packwood, through Mr. Starr, will be referred to as the "Cormack transcripts."

corresponded to the Cormack transcripts. It also provided that Mr. Starr could reassess his judgment about the propriety of any masking, if he discovered alterations in the Cormack transcript or the audiotape.

Shortly after Senator Packwood began designating portions of the audiotapes that should be masked, Mr. Starr informed the parties that the audiotapes and the Cormack transcripts were different in several respects. There were portions of the audiotapes that did not appear on the Cormack transcript, and portions of the Cormack transcript that did not appear on the audiotapes. There were also entries on the audiotape that were captured on the Cormack transcript, but in a different, or paraphrased, form. Senator Packwood maintained that he had a right to mask portions of the audiotape that fit the criteria allowed for masking by the Committee, *even if* those portions did not correspond to the Cormack transcript. The Committee made clear its position that any entries on the audiotape that did not match entries on the Cormack transcript, or vice versa, constituted possible evidence of alteration, and could not be masked by Senator Packwood. It appears that Mr. Starr permitted further masking where he deemed it appropriate.

The Committee began receiving audiotapes that had been masked and reviewed by Mr. Starr in October 1994. Because the testimony from Ms. Cormack indicated that changes to the diary were most likely made in 1992 and 1993, the Committee had requested that it be provided with the tapes for these years first. As the Committee received the tapes for 1992 and 1993, it had them transcribed by a reporting service. The diaries thus transcribed were compared to the Cormack transcripts. For the years 1989 through 1991, the staff listened and compared the audiotapes themselves to the Cormack transcript.

The last of the audiotapes corresponding to Q 1 through Q 10 were received by the Committee on January 13, 1995. A final delivery of ten tapes occurred on February 27, 1995.

EMPLOYMENT OPPORTUNITIES
FOR MRS. PACKWOOD

Origin of Allegations

The allegations involving inappropriate linkage of personal financial gain to Senator Packwood's official position by soliciting or otherwise encouraging offers of financial assistance from persons having a particular interest in legislation or issues that Senator Packwood could influence are based on a number of the Senator's diary entries from the years 1989 through 1991.

How the Investigation Was Conducted

Committee staff took sworn depositions from ten persons referenced in the diary as possibly having some involvement in extending employment opportunities to Mrs. Packwood. The Committee also took the sworn deposition of Senator Packwood's former wife and received sworn testimony from Senator Packwood. In total, thirteen persons were deposed on this subject.

In addition, the Committee subpoenaed documents from each of the individuals mentioned above. The subpoena called for all documents referring or relating to either Senator or Mrs. Packwood. The Committee also subpoenaed documents from Mrs. Packwood and from Senator Packwood. In response to these subpoenas, the Committee received in excess of four thousand pages of documents.

3

The Committee's Authority
to Investigate and Sanction
Misconduct of Members

AUTHORITY OF THE CONGRESS
TO DISCIPLINE ITS MEMBERS

THE UNITED STATES CONSTITUTION confers on each House of Congress the power to punish and expel its Members. Article I provides:

> "Each House may determine the Rules of its Proceedings, punish its Members for disorderly Behavior, and, with the Concurrence of two thirds, expel a Member."[1]

Pursuant to this authority, in 1964, the Senate adopted Senate Resolution 338, which created the Select Committee on Standards and Conduct, and delegated to it the authority to "receive complaints and investigate allegations of improper conduct which may reflect upon the Senate, violations of law, and violations of rules and regulations of the Senate, relating to the conduct of individuals in the performance of their duties as Members of the Senate."[2]

[1] U.S. Const. art. I, § 5, cl. 2.
[2] S. Res. 338, § 2(a)(1), 88th Cong., 2d Sess. (1964).

In those situations where the violations are sufficiently serious to warrant sanctions, the Committee is authorized to recommend to the Senate by report or resolution appropriate disciplinary action.[3]

The Senate has disciplined Members for conduct that it has deemed unethical or improper, regardless of whether it violated any law or Senate rule or regulation.[4] As it adopted new rules governing Members' conduct, the Senate has recognized that the rules did not "replace that great body of unwritten but generally accepted standards that will, of course, continue in effect."[5]

PRIVATE VERSUS OFFICIAL CONDUCT

The Senate or House may discipline a Member for any misconduct, including conduct or activity which does not directly relate to official duties, when such conduct unfavorably reflects on the institution as a whole.[6] In his historic work on the Constitution, Justice Joseph Story noted in 1833 that Congress' disciplinary authority for "expulsion and any other punishment" is apparently unqualified as to "the time, place or nature of the offense."[7] Moreover, the Supreme Court has consistently declared that the Senate has far-reaching discretion in disciplinary

---

[3] *Id.*, amended by S. Res. 110, 95th Cong., 1st Sess. (1977), § 2(a)(2).

[4] *Senate Election, Expulsion and Censure Cases From 1793 to 1972*, S. Doc. No. 7, 92d Cong., 1st Sess. 127, 157 (1972).

[5] 114 Cong. Rec. 6833 (1968) (comments of Senator John Stennis).

[6] S. Rep. 2508, 83d Cong., 2d Sess. 20,22 (1954); H.R. Rep. No. 27, 90th Cong., 1st Sess. 24 (1969).

[7] Joseph Story, *Commentaries on the Constitution of the United States,* Volume II, § 836, (Boston 1833, De Capo Press Reprint Edition, 1970).

matters.[8] Precedent within both the House and Senate has reaffirmed this broad authority. In the censure of Senator Joseph McCarthy, the Select Committee to Study the Censure Charges in the 83rd Congress reported:

"It seems clear that if a Senator should be guilty of reprehensible conduct unconnected with his official duties and position, but which conduct brings the Senate into disrepute, the Senate has the power to censure."[9]

Additionally, in the report on Representative Adam Clayton Powell from the House Judiciary Committee, which recommended that Powell be censured for misconduct, the Committee noted that the conduct for which punishment may be imposed is not limited to acts relating to the Member's official duties.[10]

In proposing a permanent standing committee on ethics in the Senate, Senator John Sherman Cooper expressly referred to the select committee that investigated the censure charges of Senator Joseph McCarthy as a model—a committee that had unambigu-

[8] See, e.g., In re Chapman, 166 U.S. 661, 670 (1897) (in upholding the authority of the Senate to require by subpoena testimony of private persons in an investigation of Senatorial misconduct, the Court noted the expulsion of former Senator Blount as an example of Congress's broad authority: "It was not a statutable offense nor was it committed in his official character, nor was it committed during the session of Congress, nor at the seat of government."); United States v. Brewster, 408 U.S. 501 (1972) (in dicta, the Court observed, "The process of disciplining a Member of Congress . . . is not surrounded with the panoply of protective shields that are present in a criminal case. An accused Member is judged by no specifically articulated standards, and is at the mercy of an almost unbridled discretion of the charging body . . . from whose decisions there is no established right of review.").

[9] Report of the Select Committee to Study Censure Charges pursuant to S. Res. 301 and amendments, S. Rep. 2508, 83rd Cong., 2d Sess. 20,22 (1954) (a resolution to censure the Senator from Wisconsin, Mr. McCarthy).

[10] H.R. Rep. No. 27, 90th Cong., 1st Sess. 24 (1969).

ously asserted its authority to investigate conduct "unconnected with [a Member's] official duties and position." Senator Cooper and supporters of the resolution emphasized that the Select Committee was intended "to be free to investigate anything which, in its judgment, seemed worthy, deserving, and requiring investigation"[11] and "would not be limited to alleged violations of Senate rules, but it would take into account all improper conduct of any kind whatever."[12]

It appears that the intent of the Senate in adopting S. Res. 338 was to convey to the Ethics Committee the authority to investigate and make recommendations to the full Senate on misconduct of Members over which the institution has jurisdiction. Nowhere in the legislative history of this resolution was there language which expressed or implied any intent to reserve some authority only in the full Senate, or to limit the authority of the Committee to investigate and report to the full Senate concerning any misconduct of a Member within the jurisdiction of the institution.

Improper Conduct Reflecting Upon the Senate

The Senate did not attempt to delineate all the types of conduct or the guidelines which the Committee should follow in determining which actions by a Member would constitute "improper conduct" reflecting on the Senate.[13] It appears that the standards and guidelines of what would be deemed proper or improper conduct for a Member would change and evolve, both

[11] 110 Cong. Rec. 16,933, (1964).

[12] Id.

[13] When asked about the types of misconduct the committee might investigate, Senator Cooper explained as follows: "I cannot foresee every case . . . I believe one of the great duties of such a committee would be to have the judgment to know what it should investigate and what it should not, after looking into a question." Id.

as to the perception of the general public as well as for those within the legislature itself.[14] The drafters of the resolution in 1964 intended that "improper conduct" would be cognizable by the Senate when it was so notorious or reprehensible that it could discredit the institution as a whole, not just the individual, thereby invoking the Senate's inherent and constitutional right to protect its own integrity and reputation.[15]

Senate Resolution 338, as amended, which establishes and sets forth the responsibilities of the Select Committee on Ethics, provides, in part:

> Sec. 2(a) It should be the duty of the Select Committee to—
>   (1) "receive complaints and investigate allegations of *improper conduct which may reflect upon the Senate,* violations of law, violations of the Senate Code of Official Conduct, and

[14] *See, e.g.,* Jack Maskell, Congressional Research Service Confidential Report to the Select Committee on Ethics, *Jurisdiction and Authority of the Senate Select Committee on Ethics Over What Might be Characterized as "Personal" or "Private" Misconduct of a Senator* (not published, March 3, 1993).

[15] In the censure of Senator Joseph McCarthy of Wisconsin, the Select Committee to Study the Censure Charges reported to the Senate:

"It seems clear that if a Senator should be guilty of reprehensible conduct unconnected with his official duties and position, but which conduct brings the Senate into disrepute, the Senate has the power to censure."

S. Rep. No. 2508, *supra,* note 6, at 22.

The House of Representatives has held a similar view. In the report on Representative Adam Clayton Powell from the House Judiciary Committee, which recommended that Powell be seated, and then censured for his misconduct, the Committee noted that: "Nor is the conduct for which punishment may be imposed limited to acts relating to the Member's official duties." *In Re Adam Clayton Powell* H.R. Rep. No. 27, 90th Cong., 1st Sess. 24 (1967).

See also, for examples of recommendations for discipline for conduct which brings "the Senate into dishonor and disrepute": S. Rep. No. 382, 101st Cong., 2d Sess. 14 (1990); S. Rep. No. 337, 96th Cong., 1st Sess. 18 (1979); S. Rep. No. 193, 90th Cong., 1st Sess. (S. Res. 112, 90th Cong.) (1967); note discussion in S. Rep. No. 2508, 83rd Cong., 2d Sess. 20–23 (1954); S. Res. 146, 71st Cong., 1st Sess. (1929).

violations of rules and regulations of the Senate, relating to the conduct of individuals in the performance of their duties as Members of the Senate, or as officers or employees of the Senate, and to make appropriate findings of fact and conclusions with respect thereto . . ."[16] (emphasis added)

S. Res. 338 gives the Committee the authority to investigate Members who engage in "improper conduct which may reflect upon the Senate," regardless of whether such conduct violates a specific statute, Senate Rule, or regulation. Indeed, the original Rules Committee proposal, rejected by the Senate, would have given the Committee the authority to investigate only alleged violations of the rules of the Senate.[17] In offering the amendment containing the language adopted by the Senate[18], Senator Cooper described his amendment as authorizing the new committee "to receive complaints of unethical, improper, illegal conduct of members."[19] Senator Case, in discussing this amendment, noted that the Committee "would not be limited to alleged violations of Senate rules, but it would take into account *all improper conduct of any kind whatsoever.*"[20]

Historical Context of Improper Conduct and Committee Precedent

The phrase "improper conduct" as used by S. Res. 338 can be given meaning by reference to generally accepted standards of

---

[16] S. Res. 338, 88th Cong., 2d. Sess. (1964), as amended by S. Res. 110, 95th Cong., 1st Sess. (1977).

[17] S. Rep. No. 1147, 88th Cong., 2d Sess. 1 (1964).

[18] S. Res. 338, § 2(a)(1) (1964); 110 Cong. Rec. 16939 (1964) (emphasis added).

[19] S. Rep. No. 1125, 88th Cong., 2d Sess. 13 (1964).

[20] 110 Cong. Rec. 16933 (1964) (emphasis added).

conduct, the letter and spirit of laws and Rules[21], and by reference to past cases where the Senate has disciplined its Members for conduct that was deemed improper, regardless of whether it violated any law or Senate rule or regulation.

As early as 1797, Senator William Blount was expelled from the Senate for inciting Native Americans against the government, despite the fact that he had committed no crime, and neither acted in his official capacity nor during a session of Congress.[22] In 1811, the Senate censured Senator Thomas Pickering for reading a confidential communication on the Senate floor, despite the fact that there was no written rule prohibiting such conduct.[23] In 1873, a Senate Committee also recommended the expulsion of Senator James Patterson, for accepting stock at a reduced price knowing that the offeror intended to influence him in his official duties, for giving a false account of the transaction, suppressing material facts, and denying the existence of material facts which must have been known to him.[24]

In 1929, the Senate condemned Senator Hiram Bingham for placing an employee of a trade association with a direct interest in tariff legislation then pending on the Senate payroll. In 1954, the Senate condemned Senator Joseph McCarthy for his lack of cooperation with and abuse of two Senate committees that investigated his conduct.

---

[21] In a report of a 1964 investigation into certain activities undertaken by Robert Baker, then Secretary to the Majority of the Senate, the Committee on Rules and Administration stated: "It is possible for anyone to follow the 'letter of the law' and avoid being indicted for a criminal act, but in the case of employees of the Senate, they are expected, and rightly so, to follow not only the 'letter' but also the 'spirit' of the law." S. Rep. No. 1175, 88th Cong., 2d Sess. 5(1964).

[22] See In Re Chapman, 166 U.S. 661, 669–670 (1897).

[23] S. Doc. No. 7, 92d Cong., 1st Sess. 6 (1972) (Expulsion and Censure Cases).

[24] The Senate decided not to act on the Committee's recommendation before the end of the session, and Senator Patterson left the Senate at the end of his term. S. Rep. No. 519, 42d Cong., 3rd Sess. VIII–X (1873).

None of these cases involved conduct that was found to violate any law, rule, or regulation, but in each case, the conduct was deemed to violate accepted standards and values controlling Senators' conduct.

After the passage of S. Res. 338 establishing the Select Committee on Standards and Conduct, the next case involving a finding of improper conduct was the investigation of Senator Thomas Dodd. The Committee investigated allegations of unethical conduct concerning the Senator's relationship with a private businessman with overseas interests; the conversion of campaign contributions to personal use; the free use of loaned automobiles; and the acceptance of reimbursements from both the Senate and private sources. Although no Senate rule or law prohibited the use of campaign funds for personal use at that time, the Committee found that the testimonial dinners investigated were political in character, and thus the proceeds should not have been used for personal use.[25]

The Committee recommended, and the Senate adopted, a resolution censuring Senator Dodd for having engaged in a course of conduct

"exercising the influence and power of his office as a United States Senator . . . to obtain, and use for his personal benefit, funds from the public through political testimonials and a political campaign."

Such conduct, although not violative of any specific law or Senate rule in force at that time, was found to be "contrary to accepted morals, derogates from the public trust expected of a Senator, and tends to bring the Senate into dishonor and disrepute."[26]

[25] S. Rep. No. 193, 90th Cong., 1st Sess. (1967).
[26] S. Res. 112, 90th Cong., 1st Sess. (1967).

In 1966, pursuant to S. Res. 338, the Select Committee on Standards and Conduct began to develop recommendations for rules and regulations regarding Senators' conduct. The Committee ultimately proposed S. Res. 266, the Senate Code of Official Conduct, which addressed outside employment, disclosure of financial interests, and campaign contributions. The floor debate on this resolution demonstrates that the Rules were not intended to be a comprehensive code of conduct for Senators, but were targeted at a limited area of activity, and more importantly, that they were not intended to displace generally accepted norms of conduct. During that debate, the Committee's Chairman, Senator John Stennis, stated:

"We do not try to write a full code of regulations. . . . [O]ur effort is merely to add rules and not to replace that great body of unwritten but generally accepted standards that will, of course, continue in effect."[27]

In addition, the Committee's Vice Chairman, Senator Wallace Bennett, stated that it was impossible to develop written rules that address every possible area of misconduct.[28]

In 1990, upon the recommendation of the Committee, the Senate denounced Senator David Durenberger, in part based on his financial arrangements in connection with a condominium in Minneapolis, finding that his conduct was deemed to have "brought discredit upon the United States Senate" by a "pattern of improper conduct," although the Committee did not find that any law or rule had been violated in connection with the condominium.[29] However, the Committee Chairman noted that the

[27] 114 Cong. Rec. 6833 (1968).
[28] Id. at 6842.
[29] S. Rep. No. 382, 101st Cong., 2d Sess. 14 (1990).

Senator's conduct violated the spirit of 18 U.S.C. § 431, which generally prohibits a Member from benefitting from a contract with the federal government.[30]

Most recently, in 1991 the Committee concluded that Senator Alan Cranston engaged in improper conduct which reflected on the Senate by engaging in an impermissible pattern of conduct in which fund raising and official activities were substantially linked. The Committee found that for about two years, Senator Cranston had personally or through his staff contacted the Federal Home Loan Bank Board on behalf of Lincoln Savings and Loan during a period when he was soliciting and accepting substantial contributions from Mr. Keating or his affiliates, and that Senator Cranston's office practices further evidenced an impermissible pattern of conduct in which fund raising and official activities were substantially linked. The Committee specifically found that none of the activities of Senator Cranston violated any law or Senate rule. Nonetheless, the Committee found that his impermissible pattern of conduct

> "violated established norms of behavior in the Senate, and was improper conduct that reflects upon the Senate, as contemplated in Section 2(a)(1) of S. Res. 338, 88th Congress, as amended."[31]

The Committee found that Senator Cranston's conduct was improper and repugnant, and that it deserved the "fullest, strongest, and most severe sanction which the Committee has the authority to impose." The Committee issued a strong and severe reprimand of Senator Cranston.[32]

---

[30] 136 Cong. Rec. 510,560 (daily ed. July 25, 1990) (statement of Senator Heflin).
[31] S. Rep. No. 223, 102d Cong., 1st Sess. 36 (1991).
[32] Id.

S. Res. 266 and the Code of Ethics
for Government Service

Part III of the Select Committee's Rules of Procedure sets out the sources of the Committee's subject matter jurisdiction, which include, in addition to those set out in S. Res. 338, the Preamble to S. Res. 266, and the Code of Ethics for Government Service. The Preamble to S. Res. 266, by which the Senate Code of Official Conduct was first adopted, provides that

"(a) The ideal concept of public office, expressed by the words, "A public office is a public trust," signifies that the officer has been entrusted with public power by the people; that the officer holds this power in trust to be used only for their benefit and never for the benefit of himself or of a few; and that the officer must never conduct his own affairs so as to infringe on the public interest. All official conduct of Members of the Senate should be guided by this paramount concept of public office.

(b) These rules, as the written expression of certain standards of conduct, complement the body of unwritten but generally accepted standards that continue to apply to the Senate."[33]

Thus, in this Preamble, specifically set out as a source of jurisdiction for the Committee under S. Res. 338, the Senate has recognized that it has the authority to discipline its Members for conduct that may not necessarily violate a law, or Senate rule or regulation, but that is unethical, improper, or violates unwritten

---

[33] Preamble to S. Res. 266, 90th Cong., 2d. Sess. (1968).

but generally accepted standards of conduct that apply to the Senate.[34]

The Code of Ethics for Government Service, passed by House Resolution on July 11, 1958, with the Senate concurring, is also specifically listed in the Committee's Rules as a source of jurisdiction for the Committee under S. Res. 338. It sets out ten broadly-worded standards of conduct that should be adhered to by all government employees, including office-holders. The first and last of these standards state that any person in government service should:

> "Put loyalty to the highest moral principles and to country above loyalty to persons, party, or Government department.
>
> Uphold these principles, ever conscious that public office is a public trust."[35]

Again, these standards of conduct generally encompass conduct that may not violate a specific law, rule, or regulation, but that is not consistent with "loyalty to the highest moral principles."[36]

---

[34] The Committee has never relied specifically on the Preamble as an enforceable standard, but prior to adoption of S. Res. 266, its predecessor Committee on Standards and Conduct had recommended censure for Senator Thomas Dodd in part because it found his conduct "derogates from the public trust expected of a Senator." S. Rep. No. 193, 90th Cong., 1st Sess. (1967). The Preamble continues as a Standing Order of the Senate. See Senate Manual, paragraph 79.6.

[35] The Code of Ethics for Government Service, H. Con. Res. 175, 85th Cong., 1st Sess. (1957).

[36] Although the House of Representatives has used the broad standards set out in the Code of Ethics for Government Service as a disciplinary standard in investigations of misconduct, the Senate has never done so. See In The Matter Of Representative Austin J. Murphy, H. Rep. No. 485, 100th Cong., 1st Sess. 4 (1987); 133 Cong. Rec. H11686–96 (1987) (Member permitted official resources to be diverted to his former law partner); In The Matter Of A Complaint against Representative Robert L. F. Sikes, H. Rep. No. 1364, 94th Cong., 2d Sess. 3 (1976) (debate and reprimand of Member on charges concerning use of official position for financial gain, and receipt of benefits under circumstances that might have been construed as influencing official duties).

TIME LIMITATIONS

Historical Context

The United States Constitution which grants the Senate the express authority to discipline its own Members contains no apparent time limitation on this authority.[37] Thus, the Supreme Court, in 1897, implied an unqualified authority of each House of Congress to discipline a Member for misconduct, regardless of the specific timing of the offense.[38] The Court cited the case of the expulsion of Senator Blount by the Senate as support for the constitutional authority of either House of Congress to punish a Member for conduct which, in the judgment of the House or Senate, "is inconsistent with the trust and duty of a member" even if such conduct was "not a statutable offense nor was it committed during the session of Congress, nor at the seat of government."[39]

The Senate Select Committee on Standards of Conduct, predecessor of the current Committee, noted in a matter before it in 1967, that the procedural rules for disciplining a Member is a matter within the Senate's discretion, as long as the institution abides by the basic guarantees of due process within the Constitution.[40] Since discipline of its own Members is a power and authority expressly committed to the Senate in the Constitution, the Senate may establish or choose its own time limitations for investigations and disciplinary proceedings, or may choose not to attach any specific limitations on such actions.

[37] U.S. Const., art. I, § 5, cl. 1.

[38] *In re Chapman*, at 669.

[39] *Id.* at 670; *see,* II Hinds' Precedents of the House of Representatives, § 1263.

[40] Report of the Select Committee on Standards and Conduct, United States Senate on the Investigation of Senator Thomas J. Dodd of Connecticut, S. Rep. No. 193, 90th Cong., 1st Sess., 11 (1967).

The specific procedure adopted and followed by the Senate for its own internal disciplinary actions would most likely not be subject to judicial review because of the non-justiciability of the issue.[41]

Historically, neither House of Congress has abdicated its ability to punish a Member in the form of *censure* for conduct which occurred in a Congress prior to a Member's re-election to the current Congress. In the censure of Senator Joseph McCarthy of Wisconsin, the Select Committee to Study the Censure Charges in the 83rd Congress, after consideration of the fact that the Senate is a continuing body, reported:

"It seems clear that if a Senator should be guilty of reprehensible conduct unconnected with his official duties and position, but which conduct brings the Senate into disrepute, the Senate has the power to censure. The power to censure must be independent, therefore, of the power to punish for contempt. A Member may be censured even after he has resigned (2 Hinds' Precedents 1239,1273, 1275 (1907)). . . . While it may be the law that one who is not a Member of the Senate may not be punished for contempt of the Senate at a preceding session, this is not a basis for declaring that the Senate may not censure one of its own Members for conduct antedating that session, and no controlling authority or precedent has been cited for such a position."[42]

There have been indications that the Senate, in an *expulsion* case, might not exercise its disciplinary discretion with regard to con-

---

[41] *U.S. v. Brewster,* 408 U.S. 501, 519 (1972).
[42] S. Rep. 2508, 83rd. Cong., 2d Sess. 20–21, 22 (1954).

duct in which an individual had engaged before the time he or she had been a Member.[43]

Limitations Applicable to S. Res. 338 and the Senate Code of Conduct

The Senate does *not* have a rule which would limit an inquiry into, or disciplinary action taken, within the jurisdiction of the Select Committee on Ethics. However, the Senate may not conduct an initial review or investigation of any alleged violation of law, the Senate Code of Official Conduct, or rule or regulation that was not in effect at the time of the alleged violation.[44] It should be noted that the House of Representatives recently amended its own internal rules of discipline to institute a "statue of limitations" on internal disciplinary matters which would restrict inquiries into conduct which occurred before the three previous Congresses.[45]

Finally, the Senate Ethics Study Commission of the 103rd Congress (which included the members of this Committee) recommended in its Report to the Senate that:

---

[43] In the expulsion case of Senator John Smith, Senator John Quincy Adams, reporting for the committee, noted that the power of expulsion is "discretionary" and is "without any limitation other than that which requires a concurrence of two-thirds of the votes to give it effect." *See* II Hinds' Precedents § 1264, at 817–18. Although the power was described broadly, Hinds' Precedents notes that the charge that Smith made an oath of allegiance to a foreign king, was not acted upon since it was to have been taken previously to the election of Mr. Smith.

[44] S. Res. 338, as amended by § 202 of S. Res. 110 (1977).

[45] P.L. 101–194, § 803, amending, under the House's rulemaking authority, House Rule X, Clause 4(e)(2)(C), to provide: "nor shall any investigation be undertaken by the committee of any alleged violation which occurred before the third previous Congress unless the committee determines that the alleged violation is directly related to any alleged violation which occurred in a more recent Congress."

The Senate should not adopt a fixed statute of limitations, but should continue its practice of balancing on a case-by-case basis potentially relevant considerations, such as fairness, staleness, integrity of evidence, reasons for delay, and seriousness of alleged misconduct, in evaluating the timeliness of allegations of misconduct. High ethical standards should be maintained throughout the period of service within the Senate, and technical rules should not be used to avoid the Senate's responsibility to redress serious misconduct.

The Report further stated, in part:

Under current practice, in determining what action to take in response to an allegation of potential misconduct, the Ethics Committee has discretion to take into consideration the interval of time since the conduct allegedly occurred. A number of factors may play a role in the Committee's determination of its course of action, including the fairness in investigating the allegations, the staleness of the charges, the availability and integrity of relevant evidence, the reasons the allegations were not presented earlier, the seriousness of the alleged behavior, and whether continuing effects from the alleged misconduct persisted well after the conduct, among others.

4

Evidence Regarding the Allegations
of Sexual Misconduct

THE FOLLOWING IS a discussion of the evidence regarding the eighteen incidents outlined in the Committee's Resolution of May 16, 1995. Senate Ethics Counsel finds that these incidents, taken collectively, reflect an abuse of his United States Senate Office by Senator Packwood, and that this conduct is of such a nature as to bring discredit upon the United States Senate.

PACKWOOD STAFF MEMBER[1]

Testimony by Staff Member

This staff member was hired in March 1990 by Senator Packwood as the press secretary for the Senate Finance Committee minority staff. In August 1991, she was hired as Senator Packwood's personal press secretary; she left that job on July 26, 1992 to take a job in Oregon.

Around July of 1990, the Senator learned that the staffer loved old music, movies, and books, which were also interests of Senator Packwood. Senator Packwood and the staffer frequently exchanged music tapes, and Senator Packwood occasionally invited her to his office to listen to music with other staff members, or to look at his antique book collection. They also had long discussions

[1] This staff member is designated "C-1" in the Committee Exhibits.

about politics and history. According to the staffer, it was typical for Senator Packwood to have wine available when she and others were in his office. Senator Packwood and the staffer exchanged notes, usually accompanying the tapes. Senator Packwood often let the staffer know that he thought she was talented and creative, and he singled her out in staff meetings for compliments.

In the early fall of 1990, perhaps in September, about 5:00 p.m., Senator Packwood called the staffer at the Finance Committee offices and asked her to come to his office to listen to a tape of songs by Erroll Garner and George Shearing. When she arrived, Senator Packwood had a box of wine on his desk and was getting out two glasses. This was the first time that the staffer had been alone with Senator Packwood in his office. Within moments of the staffer's arrival, Senator Packwood was called to a vote; he told her to stay until he returned. As the staffer waited in Senator Packwood's office, his secretary, Pam Fulton, told her that she (the staffer) was new in the office, and Ms. Fulton wanted to warn her that she should not be there when the Senator returned.[2] The staffer left the office before Senator Packwood returned.

About this same time, the tone of the notes that Senator Packwood sent her with the tapes changed, and seemed to the staffer to become more "sentimental." She began to feel that Senator Packwood wanted an "emotional" type of friendship with her, of the type that she was not used to having with a supervisor.

Toward the end of October 1990, possibly October 30, Senator Packwood invited several staff members from the Finance

---

[2] During an interview, Ms. Fulton stated that she had asked the staffer not to hang around the office in the evenings, because if someone was around to drink and talk with the Senator, he would stay instead of going home. Ms. Fulton was worried about his drinking, and felt that the staffer gave him an excuse to stay at the office and drink.

Committee, including the staffer, to join him at the Irish Times bar to celebrate approval of the 1990 budget agreement. He wanted to buy drinks to thank the staff for the long hours they had put in during the preceding weeks. Senator Packwood sat next to the staffer at the bar. Toward the end of the evening, Senator Packwood yelled to her, over the music, that they needed to find some way to "do this" without letting Elaine Franklin, his chief of staff, know. He kept staring at her, and repeated that they needed to pursue this, but that Ms. Franklin could not come after her. The staffer finally realized that Senator Packwood seemed to think that they were about to start a relationship, and she began to feel very nervous. She excused herself to go to the ladies room, and tried to telephone her boyfriend (now her husband).

After the group had been at the bar for several hours, Senator Packwood asked another staffer, Lindy Paull, and her husband to drive him and the staffer back to his office. He told them that he had something he wanted to show the staffer.

When they got to the office, Senator Packwood asked Ms. Paull and her husband to go to one of the adjoining suites down the hall, because he had something he wanted to show the staffer. Senator Packwood then started showing the staffer cards in a card file that detailed the long relationships he had with national labor leaders. Each time he showed her a card, he asked her, "Does Peter DeFazio know about this friendship?" The staffer's boyfriend was the legislative director for Rep. Peter DeFazio of Oregon, who was considering running against Senator Packwood in the next election.

The staffer asked the Senator why he was doing this, and told him that she was loyal, that she was not going to go to Rep. DeFazio and tell him things about Senator Packwood.

Senator Packwood then grabbed the staffer by the shoulders with both hands, exclaimed "God, you're great!" and kissed her fully on the lips. The staffer was stunned. She did not want the Senator to go any further, but at the same time, she did not want to anger him. She made an excuse that she had to go to the bathroom, and ran down the hall to another office. She called her boyfriend and asked him to pick her up right away, left the building, and waited for him to arrive.

The staffer avoided the Senator for a month or so. She made sure that she was always the first one to leave a meeting, and that she left in a crowd. She did not tape any more music for Senator Packwood. Senator Packwood no longer singled her out or paid her special compliments in staff meetings.

In August 1991, the staffer was promoted to press secretary for Senator Packwood's personal staff, with a salary increase.

Near the end of April 1992, the staffer learned from her former roommate that a free-lance reporter was working on a story about sexual harassment in the Senate. The staffer felt that it was her duty as Senator Packwood's press secretary to share that information with him. She did not have any intention of telling the reporter about her incident with Senator Packwood.

When the staffer told Senator Packwood about the reporter, he seemed frightened, and perplexed or confused about whether he had harassed anyone, and about what exactly constituted sexual harassment. The staffer pointed out to Senator Packwood that if she did not respect him so much, she could claim that he had harassed her 18 months earlier. Elaine Franklin was called in, and she quizzed the staffer about how she knew about the story, and which friend had told her about the story. The staffer refused to say who had told her about the story, but gave Senator Packwood and Ms. Franklin the name and phone number of the reporter.

After the staffer told Senator Packwood and Ms. Franklin about the story that was being written, the staffer was left out of campaign meetings and strategy sessions. She felt that there was a lack of trust in her, either because of the story or because she had married her boyfriend, who worked for Rep. DeFazio. Eventually, she decided to leave the office. When she did so, in July 1992, Senator Packwood and Elaine Franklin provided excellent recommendations to her current employer.

After the staffer told Senator Packwood and Elaine Franklin about the story, Ms. Franklin pressed her repeatedly for the names of others whom she told about the incident between herself and Senator Packwood. The staffer told Ms. Franklin that she had told no one, although she had told her husband and her roommate; she was afraid that Ms. Franklin would hound them if she knew that the staffer had told them about the incident. Before the staffer left for her new job, Ms. Franklin warned her not to say anything about the incident to her new employers, or to any women's groups. Ms. Franklin continued to call the staffer through the fall, pressing her for information about whom she had told about the incident, and accusing her of lying when she denied telling anyone.

Corroborating Witnesses

Committee counsel deposed or interviewed four witnesses, including the staffer's husband and her roommate at the time of the incident, who recall the staffer telling them that Senator Packwood had kissed her in his office one evening after hours. The staffer's husband and her roommate recall that she told them about the incident almost immediately after it happened.[3] Her husband testified that the staffer was so hysterical when he

---

[3] The recollections of the staffer and her roommate are slightly different regarding the timing of when she told her roommate about the incident. The staffer recalls that she told her roommate about the incident the next day. Her roommate recalls that the staffer came home the evening of the incident, upset and crying, told her what had happened, and that she then went to her boyfriend's apartment. Nevertheless, the staffer's roommate remembers specific details of the incident as described to her by the staffer.

picked her up that evening that he thought at first that she might have been raped.

Another witness stated that the staffer told her in the summer of 1991 that Senator Packwood had tried to kiss her several times, once in his office after hours.

In addition, nine members of Senator Packwood's staff, including his chief of staff, have testified that the staffer told them that Senator Packwood had "crossed the line," or made an inappropriate advance, or kissed her, before word began spreading about the anticipated *Washington Post* article. Several of these persons indicated that the staffer did not seem to take the incident all that seriously. Elaine Franklin testified that when she heard from another staffer about the incident, she spoke with the staffer, and the staffer indicated that she was not concerned about it.

Several members of Senator Packwood's staff have stated in depositions or interviews that when the rumors first started surfacing about the proposed story on Senator Packwood, there was much speculation in the office about whether the staffer would be one of the accusers, since she had told people about an incident before the possibility of an article came up.

Senator Packwood's Response

Senator Packwood testified at his deposition that he recalled the staffer very well. He claimed that the staff, both from the Finance Committee and his personal office, almost to a person intensely disliked and distrusted her, and advised him that she was unreliable and should be excluded from meetings.[4] However, he could not remember the name of any person who had so advised him. He described it as the "collective wisdom" of the office, and as the staffer's "general reputation" in the office.

[4] Senator Packwood testified that Lindy Paull had told Elaine Franklin that she would not come to any meetings with the staffer, but he could not recall whether he learned this while the staffer worked for him, or after she left.

Nor could Senator Packwood recall when he had first heard complaints about the staffer, or even who had made the first complaint. He described the complaints as rather serious: that she lied, fantasized, and leaked information to the Democrats.[5] He did not know if any of these complaints had ever been documented in writing, nor did he produce anything to indicate that they had been. He himself did not instruct anyone to do so. During an interview with *Washington Post* reporters in October 1992 about the allegation, Elaine Franklin had told the reporters that she would look for office records that reflected the staffer's poor performance. Senator Packwood did not know if there were any such records, or if Ms. Franklin had found any, or even if they kept such records. He stated that he did not know what Ms. Franklin was talking about, but that as far as he knew, there were no such files.

Senator Packwood disclaimed responsibility for making the decision to bring the staffer from the Finance Committee staff to his personal staff, although he did concede that he was aware of the decision, and that he had the power to veto it. He stated that even if he were aware of the problems she had on the Finance Committee staff at the time, he would have approved her move to the personal staff, because he would assume that whoever made that decision knew about the problems too, and he did not feel strongly enough to veto that decision.

Senator Packwood's records indicate that the staffer received raises while on the Finance Committee, and that she received a small raise while she worked on his personal staff. Senator Pack-

[5] The staffer's fiancé, later her husband, worked for Rep. DeFazio, a Democrat from Oregon. Entries in Senator Packwood's diaries indicate that he attempted to capitalize on this fact by feeding misleading information to the staffer's husband, in the hopes that he would pass it on to his boss, and by using the staffer as a "mole" in the DeFazio camp. When he was shown these entries, however, Senator Packwood could not remember if he took advantage of the staffer's relationship with her boyfriend to pass misinformation on to Rep. DeFazio.

wood would not concede that he approved this raise, or even knew about it, saying that it could have been done without his knowledge, if someone just gave him a list of proposed raises which he signed without reviewing.[6]

Senator Packwood claimed that once she was on the personal staff, the staffer caused problems with everyone who came in contact with her. He stated that she was a topic of common complaint—that she was indiscreet, that she fantasized, that she lied, and that she was not to be trusted—but again, he could not remember any specific staff members who told him of these complaints.

Senator Packwood was referred to three entries in his diary where he reviewed the performance of his staff, something he did periodically throughout his diaries. Senator Packwood stated that these reviews reflected his judgments about his staff members at the time, although he was sometimes wrong in those judgments.[7] His staff reviews dated August 3 and November 5, 1990, do not mention the staffer, although he did not hesitate to make unfavorable comments about several other staffers. His staff review dated March 16, 1992 indicates that the Senator viewed the staffer as "okay," but immature; he testified that by "immature," he meant that she was a "torrent of indiscretion."[8] However, Senator Packwood did not mince words when describing the performance of other staffers in this entry.

---

[6] Senator Packwood stated that he did not know if his signature was even necessary to activate a pay raise, and it was possible that people got pay raises without his knowledge or approval.

[7] Senator Packwood would not say whether he attempted to accurately record his thoughts and impressions of his staffers—he said that he was "not going to get into that." Nor could he vouch for the accuracy or inaccuracy of these entries at the time he recorded them; he would not say whether he intended these entries to be accurate.

In fact, there are a number of references to the staffer in Senator Packwood's diary during the time she worked for the Finance Committee and on his personal staff. There is no indication that she was causing any problems, or that her conduct was as described by Senator Packwood in his deposition. In fact, various entries indicate that it was good to have the staffer taking control of the press (May 10, 1991); that she continued to be the bright light—bold, imaginative, forward, and sassy (July 29, 1991); that the staffer made Senator Packwood believe (July 31, 1991); and that now that he was not thinking of running for President, Senator Packwood would bring her down as his press secretary once the election was over (July 31, 1991).[9]

Senator Packwood testified that he liked the staffer, and tried to ignore the complaints for a long time. They exchanged friendly notes, and tapes of music they both enjoyed. The staffer invited him to attend a Mel Torme concert, he assumed as part of a group. He testified that he later heard from another staffer (he did not recall who) that the staffer had intended to go to the concert alone with him, but that the other staffer had reprimanded her. Senator Packwood did attend the concert, with a group that included the staffer's boyfriend, a reporter for the

---

[8] In a diary entry dated May 12, 1992, in which Senator Packwood records a conversation with Elaine Franklin about the possible Vanity Fair article, he records Ms. Franklin's comment that this was another example of the staffer blowing things out of proportion; he also records Pam Fulton's opinion that the staffer was indiscreet, because she told Ms. Fulton that she felt that she had to stay around and drink with the Senator.

[9] An April 1, 1992 diary entry records that the staffer is a liar, *after* Senator Packwood learned that she had some complaint about him making sexual advances toward her. There is also an entry in the Cormack transcript for February 5, 1993, in which Senator Packwood recorded that the staffer was a "habitual liar;" however, this entry does not appear in the original diary tape. Senator Packwood testified that he added it in late July or early August 1993. Another diary entry in Senator Packwood's diary that indicates that the staffer was a liar appears in July of 1993.

Oregonian and her companion, Senator Packwood's companion, and perhaps a fourth couple.[10]

Senator Packwood stated that the staffer often hung around his office after work until he invited her in for a glass of wine; she had wine with him more frequently than any other staffer.

Senator Packwood testified that he has had to piece together the events of the evening at the Irish Times.[11] He had a dim recollection that a number of the staff went to the Irish Times one evening, where they drank heavily. He recalled that he and the staffer did some heavy drinking; another staffer who was present told him later that they shared three large pitchers of beer; others who were present told him that after this other staffer left, the Senator and the staffer continued drinking. He testified that he talked with the staffer about labor leaders, and which ones would be supportive of him in the campaign; he may have intended for her to pass the information on to the Democrats through her boyfriend.

---

[10] Julia Brim-Edwards, a Packwood staffer, in a statement she prepared for the *Post* in the fall of 1992, claimed that the staffer did not intend to ask anyone else to the Mel Torme concert, and that a week or so before the concert, she told the staffer that she thought it was inappropriate that she had asked the Senator to go to the concert. She claimed that the staffer agreed, and tried to round up others to go; although there was not a lot of interest, she finally was able to find others to attend.

Senator Packwood's diary, however, has an entry several weeks before the concert reflecting that the reporter who attended the concert had been in his office that day, and that she was one of the persons who would be attending the Mel Torme concert.

[11] Although Senator Packwood claimed that he had been drinking heavily that evening, and that he did not recall returning to his office with the staffer, his diary contains an entry noting that he had taken the staff to dinner at the Irish Times, that he had "pushed a little hard" on the staffer, wanting her to be "a mole and a spy into the DeFazio organization because of her relationship with the guy she goes with," and noting that the staffer talked about Rep. DeFazio's support from the unions. Senator Packwood would not say if this entry was accurate, and stated that he could have totally made up the part of the entry discussing the conversation about labor unions. However, this account of their conversation is consistent with the staffer's recollection of the evening.

Senator Packwood recalled "next to nothing" about what happened after he left the Irish Times. He has pieced together that he and the staffer were going to go back to the office to look at cards. Lindy Paull and her husband gave the staffer a ride, and offered to wait for her; she declined. He did not recall how he got back to the office. He stated that once at the office, he and the staffer began going through his card file, and he pointed out the names of some labor leaders. He did not recall kissing the staffer that evening, and has no idea what happened after he left the office.

Senator Packwood testified that about a year later, around October 1991, he and the staffer invited a reporter to come by for a glass of wine. The reporter left about 7:00 or 7:15, and the staffer stayed, and they continued drinking. Later, the Senator got up to change a tape or to go to the bathroom. When he came back, the staffer wrapped her arms around his neck, and gave him a big romantic kiss, telling him that he was "wonderful," "warts and all."[12]

In February or March of 1992, Elaine Franklin told the Senator that she had heard from others that the staffer claimed that the Senator had kissed her after the Irish Times party. Ms. Franklin claimed that she had sat the staffer down and asked her about it; the staffer told her that it was nothing, they were both drunk, that it was a harmless kiss, and that she was flattered. Ms. Franklin also told him that the staffer drank a lot and could not hold her liquor well.

Senator Packwood did not recall that the staffer had talked to him about the incident at any time, or more specifically in the

---

[12] This incident is recounted in Senator Packwood's diary. He also recounted it during the floor debate on enforcement of the Committee's document subpoena. The staffer has indicated, through her attorney, that this incident never occurred.

spring of 1992, when she met with him and Elaine Franklin to tell them about the Vanity Fair article.[13] He assumed that the staffer was trying to help them, but that he and Ms. Franklin just did not trust the staffer, as far as what she said her sources were for the rumors about the story.

The staffer left Senator Packwood's office in 1992. He recalled a brief conversation with her current supervisor, asking if the Senator would mind if they hired the staffer. Senator Packwood told him that he would not mind. He testified that he was happy to have her go.

Senator Packwood was shown a press release from his office, noting that the staffer's new employer was getting an experienced press person in the staffer, and quoting Senator Packwood:

[The staffer] has spent years working on issues related to the [new employer]. She will serve them well. This is really a golden opportunity for her.[14]

Senator Packwood testified that he could not recall when he first saw this press release, or if anyone else in his office saw it before it went out. He did not know if it was customary for his office to issue a press release when a staffer took another job, or whether this was the first time such a press release had been issued.

Senator Packwood testified that the staffer was overtly friendly to him, hung around and drank with him, flirted with him, and sought his attention and approval. He thought that she wanted to be close to him, to be his "number one." But he stated that it

[13] There is an entry in Senator Packwood's diary for April 29, 1992, recording this meeting with the staffer and Ms. Franklin.

[14] This press release was provided to the Committee by the staffer's attorney.

would be too strong a characterization to say that she wanted a romantic or sexual relationship with him. He never had the sense that she wanted to have an affair with him, or to go to bed with him.

Senator Packwood recalled that the staffer wore short skirts and low-cut blouses to work, but he never said anything about it. He learned from Lindy Paull, after the *Post* interview, that she had talked to the staffer about inappropriate and unprofessional dress.

In response to the Committee's document requests, Senator Packwood provided "Ramspeck" application forms that had been filled out for the staffer, dated April 29, 1992, in connection with her application to her new employer. One of these forms was signed by Senator Packwood's office manager, Jackie Wilcox, and one purported to be signed by Senator Packwood. The forms indicated that the staffer's performance as an employee had been "extraordinarily effective and efficient." Senator Packwood testified that the signature was not his. He could not say who in his office had the authority to sign his name to official documents, but only that his office had a sort of "rule of reason" approach to the subject. Senator Packwood's attorneys later provided a statement to the Committee from Ms. Wilcox, stating that the staffer had asked her to fill out the form, and that when she learned that she needed the Senator's signature, she had asked Ms. Wilcox to sign it.

In his appearance before the Committee, Senator Packwood repeated his claim that there had been many problems with this employee. He also emphasized that other witnesses had claimed that this staffer acted in such a way to suggest that she wanted a sexual relationship with him, and that on the evening of the incident, she was all over him. He told the Committee that it was understandable that he might have perceived that she wanted him to kiss her, and that he was only human.

Findings

Senate Ethics Counsel finds that the incident as alleged by the staff member did in fact occur. Counsel notes that the staff member's account of the incident has been corroborated, in whole or part, by numerous persons, including Elaine Franklin, Senator Packwood's chief of staff and several staff members. Senator Packwood himself has not denied that the incident occurred; he has testified that he was too drunk to remember the details of the evening.

Counsel notes that Senator Packwood has gone to great lengths to portray this staff member as untrustworthy. This claim, even if proven, has no relevance to a determination as to whether the incident as alleged actually occurred. The fact that this staff member may have lied on other occasions, or that she may have been untrustworthy because her boyfriend worked for one of Senator Packwood's opponents, sheds absolutely no light on whether she fabricated the incident in question. Moreover, the accounts of the numerous persons whom she told about this incident, including Ms. Franklin, his chief of staff, overwhelmingly confirm that it did in fact happen.

Even if Senator Packwood's claims that this staff member was untrustworthy were relevant to a determination of whether this incident in fact occurred, these claims are belied by the lack of any contemporaneous documentation from Senator Packwood's files indicating that this staff member was indeed the terrible employee that he portrays. In fact, she moved from the Finance Committee staff to his personal staff, and received several salary raises. A glowing press release was issued on her departure. And although Senator Packwood made it a practice to critique his employees frequently in his diary, and did not hesitate to make fairly scathing comments about them, there is not one mention in his diaries while this staff member worked for him that indicates she was a problem employee. To the contrary, there are several complimentary references to her.

Senator Packwood himself has as much as admitted that this incident took place: he told the Committee during his appearance before it that several of his staff members have said that this staff member acted in a way to suggest that she was interested in a sexual relationship with him, that it was understandable why he might conclude that she wanted him to kiss her, and that he only acted in a human fashion. In short, he has suggested that the staffer enticed him into an overture that he perceived as welcome. In fact, however, at his deposition, when asked whether he concluded from anything that the staffer did that she wanted a romantic or sexual relationship with him, Senator Packwood responded that although she wanted a close relationship with him, and her nature was "obviously flirtatious" with him, "romantic" or "sexual" would be too strong a word, and he never had the sense that the staffer was saying "let's have an affair," or "let's go to bed together." In other words, this staff member *never* said or did anything that led *him* to conclude that she was interested in a romantic or sexual relationship with him.

Senator Packwood proffers the fact that this staff member continued to work for him, that she continued to send him warm notes, and that she kissed him about a year later. Of course, these facts, even if true, do not prove that the incident did not take place. They may indicate that the staff member did not take the incident seriously, as some of Senator Packwood's staff members have testified. Or they may indicate that the staff member did not feel that she had the power to do anything about the incident, and chose to maintain a good relationship with the Senator for the sake of her job and her career.

Senate Ethics Counsel finds that Senator Packwood's conduct in this instance fits a pattern of conduct that reflects an abuse of his position of authority, a pattern of conduct that constitutes improper conduct reflecting upon the Senate.

JUDY FOSTER-FILPPI

Testimony of Ms. Foster-Filppi

In the early 1980's, Ms. Foster-Filppi was a Packwood supporter who frequently hosted get-togethers for Senator Packwood and his wife and supporters at her home. She was an important contact for Senator Packwood's campaign in the Lane County and Eugene area, and by 1985 was discussing with a Packwood staffer the possibility of heading up the re-election campaign in Lane County.

On a weekday in early 1985, perhaps March or April, when she had known Senator Packwood for about four years, Ms. Foster-Filppi went to Bend, Oregon, with Senator Packwood and Elaine Franklin, for a campaign appearance at a supporter get-together. Senator Packwood and Ms. Franklin picked Ms. Foster-Filppi up at her home in a motor coach, and they travelled about three hours to reach Bend. The motor coach was driven by another staff member, and they were also accompanied by another woman staff member. That evening, there was dinner and wine and dancing for thirty or forty business supporters at the River House, which is where the group spent the night.

After dinner, when the group had moved into another room for dancing, Senator Packwood asked Ms. Foster-Filppi to dance. While they were dancing, Senator Packwood pulled her close, put his hands on her back, and rubbed her back, buttocks and sides. At least twice, she pushed him away, and tried to distract him with conversation. She specifically remembers discussing briefly whether Senator Packwood was going to run for the presidency. Each time, Senator Packwood pulled her back, and again rubbed her back, buttocks, and sides. He nuzzled her neck several times, and several times pushed his hips and pelvic area into her body as he held his hand on her lower back. When the dance ended, she moved away. She knew that he had been drinking that evening, although she did not think that he was drunk. She kept her distance after that, and left the gathering a short time later to return to her room. The next morning, the Senator and his staff dropped her off in Eugene, and traveled on to Portland in the van.

Later in 1985, possibly in the summer, Ms. Foster-Filppi attended a small dinner party in Eugene, Oregon, along with Senator Packwood and Elaine Franklin. When the party was over, at Ms. Franklin's request, Ms. Foster-Filppi drove her and the Senator back to the New Oregon Motel, where they were staying. Senator Packwood sat in the front passenger bucket seat, and Ms. Franklin sat in the rear behind the campaign worker. When Ms. Foster-Filppi pulled into the motel parking lot, Ms. Franklin gave her a hug, said goodnight, and got out of the van. Senator Packwood told Ms. Franklin that he was just going to say goodnight to Ms. Foster-Filppi and he would be right in. After Ms. Franklin left, Senator Packwood moved towards Ms. Foster-Filppi with his hands out. Ms. Foster-Filppi assumed that he was about to give her a hug, just as Ms. Franklin had done, and she moved towards him with her arms out. He grabbed her face with his hands, pulled her towards him, and kissed her on the mouth, forcing his tongue into her mouth. She put her arms on his shoulders and pushed him away, and said goodnight. The Senator said goodnight and got out, and she drove away.

The next day, Ms. Foster-Filppi called Elaine Franklin and told her what had happened. She told Ms. Franklin that she was upset, that she felt deceived, and she was not sure if she could trust the Senator anymore. She asked Ms. Franklin if this was the kind of behavior that she could expect if she became involved in the Senator's campaign. Ms. Franklin apologized and told Ms. Foster-Filppi not to worry, that she could not imagine what had gotten into Senator Packwood; she said that it would never happen again, and that she would talk to the Senator. Several days later, Senator Packwood called Ms. Foster-Filppi at her home; she judged from the stern and forceful tone of his voice that he was upset. He told her that he knew she was upset with him, and that she had talked with Ms. Franklin about something he had done. He told her that she should never talk to someone else if she had a problem with his behavior, but that she should talk with him and he would handle it. He told her that there was no reason to talk to anybody else about his behavior.

After this incident and the telephone call, Ms. Foster-Filppi felt that she could no longer trust Senator Packwood. She did not want to put herself in a position where she would be physically close to him, and she questioned whether she could even continue to support him for re-election. In October or November of 1985, she told Elaine Franklin that she was too busy to manage the campaign in Lane County. Ms. Franklin was very upset, and told her that they had been counting on her.

Corroborating Witnesses

Ms. Foster-Filppi testified that other than Ms. Franklin, she did not tell anyone about the incidents with Senator Packwood. Ms. Franklin confirmed that the campaign worker, who was being considered to be co-chair of the Lane County campaign, had told her, in 1985, that the Senator had hugged her and kissed her, and that Ms. Foster-Filppi was "surprised" by his actions; she passed this information on to the Senator.

Senator Packwood's Response

Senator Packwood met Ms. Foster-Filppi in 1981, when Eugenia Hutton, another campaign worker, had her arrange a coffee for the Senator at her house. From that time until 1986, she and Ms. Hutton were his two principal contacts in Lane County, and Ms. Foster-Filppi ended up taking over from Ms. Hutton.

Senator Packwood claimed that he had checked his travel records, and that he was not in Bend at all in 1985, when Ms. Foster-Filppi claimed the incident occurred at the River House. He stated that it would be unusual to go over the mountains and back, from Eugene to Bend, over so short a time in the winter. He had no recollection of ever driving from Eugene to Bend with Ms. Foster-Filppi in the motor coach, nor did he recall ever being at the River House with Ms. Foster-Filppi. He did not recall the incident that Ms. Foster-Filppi described, whether it occurred at the River House or elsewhere.

Senator Packwood did not recall a specific dinner party that he attended with Ms. Foster-Filppi in Eugene in 1985, but he did recall that Ms. Foster-Filppi drove him and Elaine Franklin back from a function in Eugene, presumably to their motel. He stated that Ms. Foster-Filppi got out of the van to say good night to them, and gave Ms. Franklin a hug. She then put her arms out toward him, and he gave her a warm kiss on the lips; he did not recall if it was a french kiss. He did not recall kissing Ms. Foster-Filppi at any time before that.

Sometime later, perhaps the next time they were in Eugene, Elaine Franklin told him that she had had drinks with Ms. Foster-Filppi, who had told her that Senator Packwood had kissed her. Ms. Franklin told the Senator that he should not be so enthusiastic with volunteers. Senator Packwood thought that he had called Ms. Foster-Filppi and said something to the effect of, "for gosh sakes, Judy, if you've got any problems, call me directly." He claimed that she continued to work actively in his 1986 campaign, and through the election. They had considered her in 1985 for the county chair position, but she declined. Senator Packwood stated that at this point, the county chair position was being phased out anyway.

Senator Packwood was questioned about an entry in his diary for August 5, 1993:[15]

. . . if they're not going to take hearsay, then they've got to take only complaining witnesses. And if they don't have Judy Foster, and whatever that woman's name is, the intern—I mean, ex-intern, she wasn't an intern—as complaining witnesses, then I think there is nothing in this decade of any consequence to be afraid of.

Senator Packwood testified that they had figured out that Ms. Foster-Filppi was making a claim, based on the descriptions in the media accounts. He testified that "they" in the entry referred to the Ethics Committee, and that they believed that if the Committee were to judge conduct that occurred a long time ago differently than conduct that occurred in the last ten years, the only allegation they knew of other than one other staffer's (C-1) was the claim that Senator Packwood tried to kiss Ms. Foster-Filppi. Senator Packwood would not say whether he thought it would be more damaging if incidents occurred in the past decade, as opposed to earlier.

In his appearance before the Committee, Senator Packwood stated that he had searched his records, and that he had con-

[15] According to Senator Packwood, he deleted this entry from his diary tape, either before he left for recess in August 1993, or if the tape was still in his machine when he left for recess, when he got back in September.

cluded that the incident described by Ms. Foster-Filppi as occurring after a dinner party in Eugene had actually happened in 1981, and not in 1985, as she alleges. He claimed that in reviewing her description of the dinner party, he had deduced where it had taken place, and had talked to the persons he concluded gave the dinner party, who confirmed that the dinner party took place in 1981. Senator Packwood offered this conclusion to bolster his claim that all of the incidents, save the incident alleged to have occurred in 1990, had happened more than ten years earlier.

However, Ms. Foster-Filppi specifically recalls that this incident occurred when she had known Senator Packwood for about four years, and close to the 1986 election, and that when she declined the position of County Chair, Senator Packwood's staffer was upset because they had counted on her. The timing is corroborated by the testimony of Elaine Franklin, who recalls that Ms. Foster-Filppi told her of the incident in 1985, at a time when they were considering her to be a co-County chair.

Senator Packwood also claimed that Ms. Foster-Filppi had maintained friendly relations with him, and that she had returned a postcard indicating that she would be happy to allow her name to be used on a list of persons who supported him for reelection in 1992. Senator Packwood has not provided the Committee with this postcard.

Findings

Senate Ethics Counsel finds that the incidents as alleged by Ms. Foster-Filppi in fact occurred. The first incident described by Ms. Foster-Filppi, which occurred during a function in Bend, Oregon, has not been contested by Senator Packwood, except to offer that his travel and other records did not reflect that he went from Eugene to Bend and back in 1985. Otherwise, he has testified that he does not recall the incident.

Although his recollection of the details differs from that of Ms. Foster-Filppi, Senator Packwood has admitted that he kissed her after she drove him and Ms. Franklin to their hotel after a dinner party in Eugene. He does not deny, but simply does not recall, certain details of the incident, such as whether he gave Ms. Foster-Filppi a french kiss. Ms. Foster-Filppi's claim is corroborated, at least to the extent that Senator Packwood kissed her, and with respect to the timing of the incident, by the testimony of Elaine Franklin, to whom Ms. Foster-Filppi complained after the incident.

Senate Ethics Counsel finds that Senator Packwood's conduct in this instance fits a pattern of conduct that reflects an abuse of his position of authority, a pattern of conduct that constitutes improper conduct reflecting upon the Senate.

MARY HEFFERNAN

Testimony of Mary Heffernan

In 1981 and 1982, Mary Heffernan was employed by the National Abortion Rights Action League (NARAL). As part of her job, she communicated with Senator Packwood, who was a powerful NARAL ally, on issues affecting reproductive choice. In connection with her job, she spoke with Senator Packwood six to twelve times a year, mostly by telephone. Senator Packwood frequently wrote Ms. Heffernan notes that were supportive and encouraging, and also sometimes very flattering, telling her what a good job she was doing for the abortion rights movement. He also wrote to her parents praising her work and abilities. Because of the warm and personal nature of the notes, Ms. Heffernan felt that Senator Packwood was singling her out for special attention, possibly grooming her to work for him in the future.

During that time period, Ms. Heffernan set up an appointment with Senator Packwood's staff to meet him at his office in Washington, D.C. to discuss issues relating to abortion legislation. When she arrived at the office, Ms. Heffernan was escorted into Senator Packwood's private office; the Senator sat behind his desk, and she sat in front of the desk. The door to the outer office was closed. They talked for about thirty minutes about abortion legislation issues. Toward the end of the meeting, when Ms. Heffernan got up from her chair and started to move away, Senator Packwood came around his desk, put his hands on her upper arms and squeezed them, and leaned over and gave her a sensual, sexual kiss on the mouth. She stepped back, got her coat, opened the door, and quickly left the room.

After this incident, Ms. Heffernan was careful to avoid being alone with the Senator. She did not complain to anyone about the incident, out of concern that that might adversely affect the abortion rights cause for which she was working so hard. Her contacts with Senator Packwood were less frequent, and the correspondence from Senator Packwood slowed.

Ms. Heffernan left NARAL in March of 1983. Two or three times after that, she heard from Senator Packwood, who called her to ask what she was doing. Although nothing specific was ever said, her impression was that Senator Packwood might be considering asking her to come work on his staff.

Corroborating Witnesses

Ms. Heffernan testified that she told no one about this incident. Her former husband contacted the Committee, and stated that while he did not think that she would lie about the actual incident that occurred, he would not believe her if she claimed that the incident had a negative effect on her. He indicated that in the fall of 1983, when she was living with him, Senator Packwood had called her; after the call, she told him that she thought the Senator was interested in hiring her. Although she did not tell him so, her ex-husband had the impression that she might be interested in taking the job. He indicated that he and Ms. Heffernan had had an unpleasant divorce.

Senator Packwood's Response

Senator Packwood recalled meeting Ms. Heffernan in 1977, when she visited his office with a friend. She was very active in his 1980 campaign, and he continued to see her in 1981 and 1982 when she was active in NARAL. In February 1984, he talked with her on the phone about working for him. About a month later, he and Elaine Franklin took Ms. Heffernan to lunch in the Senate dining room, and Ms. Heffernan asked if there would be a spot for her in the 1986 campaign.[16] Later, she also asked one of his friends the same thing; he talked with Senator Packwood about it. Senator Packwood did not offer Ms. Heffernan a job, because she wanted a job as a volunteer coordinator, and he did not think that was the job for her: she was a good worker, but not very good at producing volunteers.

Senator Packwood did not recall the incident described by Ms. Heffernan, or that he ever kissed her at any time.

In his appearance before the Committee, Senator Packwood emphasized that Ms. Heffernan had maintained a warm, close relationship with him after the incident, that she had sought a job with him, and that she had in fact kissed him on a subsequent occasion.[17]

---

[16] Senator Packwood's diary for August 21, 1993, indicates that in his review of previous diary entries, Senator Packwood found an entry reflecting that Ms. Heffernan wanted a job with him, that he had a telephone conversation with her in 1984, and that she had had lunch with him and Elaine Franklin to discuss the possibility.

[17] The Committee received information from a woman who said that she saw Ms. Heffernan throw her arms around the Senator and kiss him on the mouth at a social function celebrating a legislative victory in September 1982.

Findings

Senate Ethics Counsel finds that the incident as alleged by Ms. Heffernan in fact occurred. Although there are no corroborating witnesses, Senator Packwood has offered no evidence to refute Ms. Heffernan's testimony about the incident; he has testified only that he does not recall the incident. Senator Packwood has proferred evidence that Ms. Heffernan maintained a warm and close relationship with him after the incident, and even sought a job with him, presumably either to show that the incident did not occur, or that if it did, Ms. Heffernan could not have been offended. However, even if true, the fact that Ms. Heffernan maintained a close relationship with the Senator, and sought a job with him, does not prove that the incident did not happen. It could indicate that Ms. Heffernan did not take offense at the incident, or it could indicate that she recognized the need to maintain a good relationship with a powerful person who was very important to her career.

Senate Ethics Counsel finds that Senator Packwood's conduct in this instance fits a pattern of conduct that reflects an abuse of his position of authority, a pattern of conduct that constitutes improper conduct reflecting upon the Senate.

PAIGE WAGERS

Testimony by Paige Wagers

Paige Wagers worked for Senator Packwood as a mail clerk from the summer of 1975 until the summer of 1976. Sometime in late 1975, she was sitting at her desk in the mail room when her intercom buzzed. When the she picked up her phone, Senator Packwood asked her to come to his office. She was nervous, because she had never been called into the Senator's office before. Up to that point, she had seen Senator Packwood at staff meetings, or in passing in the hall; it was not customary for her to have contact with him. She walked towards the Senator's office, and noticed that there was no one in the reception area outside the Senator's office, where the secretary and appointment secretary usually sat. Senator Packwood was standing just inside the door of his office, waiting for her. He told her to come in, and she went into his office.

Senator Packwood immediately closed the door, and without saying anything to Ms. Wagers, grabbed her and pinned her with her back up against a wall or a small desk. He held her hair with one hand, bending her head backwards. His other hand stroked her hair and arm and chest. He pressed his face against hers so hard that she could not move him away, and kissed her, sticking his tongue in her mouth. Ms. Wagers tried to get her hands up to push Senator Packwood away, and to keep his hand away from her breasts. Senator Packwood's body was pressed so closely against Ms. Wagers' that she could not move. When the kiss was over, Ms. Wagers turned her head and started talking; Senator Packwood tried to kiss her again, but she kept turning her head from side to side. She told Senator Packwood that she wanted their relationship to be professional, that she liked him very much, and liked her job very much, but she did not think this was the right thing to do. She told him that she respected him, that he was married, and that it was not proper for them to be in his office alone, or for him to be kissing her. She told Senator Packwood that she did not want this kind of a relationship with him, that it was not right for her, that she respected him and really wanted to keep on working there. Senator Packwood told her that he liked her hair, he thought she was young and beautiful and innocent and wholesome, and he liked her wholesomeness and everything about her. He told her that he just wanted to touch her, and repeated many times that she was so wholesome. He continued trying to kiss her, with one hand holding her head back by her hair, and the other hand touching her arm and chest. Finally he let her go; she told him she had to go back to work, and left his office.

Ms. Wagers returned to her desk, shaking and crying. She told friends about the incident, and was advised to say nothing. This was her first job, and she had been advised that she should stay in a job for at least a year before moving on to another one. She waited until the summer of 1976, and left Senator Packwood's office.

Ms. Wagers continued to see Senator Packwood occasionally, when she attended staff reunions, or functions with Tim Lee, a Packwood staff member whom she dated for a time after she left Senator Packwood's office.

In the spring of 1981, Ms. Wagers was working as a special assistant for legislative affairs at the Department of Labor. One day, as she got off the elevator on her way down to the basement of the Capitol, she ran into Senator Packwood, who was coming up the escalator from the trolley that runs from the Senate office buildings. There were many people around, and she and Senator Packwood ended up by chance right next to each other, between the escalators from the trolley and the elevator. Senator Packwood said hello to her, very politely touched her lightly on both arms and asked how she was, and said that it was nice to see her. He engaged her in conversation.

Although her initial reaction was to experience a jolt of fear, Senator Packwood's conversation made her feel comfortable and secure that nothing would happen. Indeed, nothing had occurred on the few occasions she had seen him since the previous incident which led her to think anything would happen again. She also thought that she had made it very clear to Senator Packwood how she felt, that he was not supposed to touch her or try to kiss her. By his conversation during this chance meeting, Senator Packwood made her feel that he was interested in her as a person—he asked her about her job, told her that he was proud of her for getting her job, and that if he or his office could help her, she should let him know. As they talked, and she told Senator Packwood about her job, he told her that he had to walk down to his office for a minute; he asked her to come with him and tell him what she was working on. Senator Packwood ushered her down a hallway in the Capitol basement that ran from the Senate side to the House side, toward the barber shop.

As they walked, she talked about her job. She felt very good about herself, that she finally had a job with responsibility, and knew a Senator who was willing to help her if she needed help. She felt that Senator Packwood was taking her seriously, as a business person with legitimate business to conduct. Senator Packwood then opened a door, ushered her into a room, and immediately closed the door. The room was a small cubbyhole with a desk, a couch, and some books, and possibly a chair. Without warning, Senator Packwood grabbed her by putting both hands in her hair, and he pressed his body and face against her, pushing her up against the desk. He ran his hands through her hair, and kissed her, sticking his tongue in her mouth. Ms. Wagers struggled to pull back, and to push him away with her hands. Again, she started talking, saying that she thought she had made it clear that she did not appreciate this type of attention, that she would like to think that he would help her if she needed help in her job, that she liked and respected him very much, but she did not want this kind of relationship. She told him that she thought he understood that, that she knew he was married, and she was now married, and this was not what she wanted. Senator Packwood again told her that he loved her wholesomeness and her hair, that he thought she was young and innocent, that he liked her very much, and was very attracted to her. He told her that he could really help her with her job, he liked her so much, and he did not want her to go. He continued to try to kiss her, but she kept turning her head and pushing him away. She was anxious to make it clear that she did not want to do anything, but at the same time, she did not want to offend Senator Packwood. When Senator Packwood reached toward a pillow on the couch behind her, she was able to get away; she stepped around him and left the office.

This second incident had a devastating effect on her. As she had walked down the Capitol hallway with Senator Packwood, she had felt very good, as if she had finally made something of herself, and shed the blond stereotype. She had gotten a serious job, her first job with responsibility. She was pleased that she had a formal relationship with a Senator, that if she needed help, he would help her, and that she could be taken seriously. When Senator Packwood grabbed her, all of her confidence in herself died. She felt betrayed. She felt that she had not done anything to encourage Senator Packwood, and yet he still touched her without her consent. She did not feel that she would be able to work effectively after that with members of Congress, or that she could be anywhere where she would see Senator Packwood. She eventually resigned from the Department of Labor. She believes that this second assault was a contributing factor to her decision to resign, that part of the reason she stopped working was because she was afraid to be around men, and she was specifically afraid of Senator Packwood. Since then, she has not had any kind of business career; she has done menial work for a few months for an agency that was going out of business, and she has taught dance, which is what she does now.

She believes that she has been hurt in every possible way by the incidents with Senator Packwood—that emotionally, financially, and intellectually she has remained frozen in time. She is now divorced, and needs to go back to work, but since she has not worked since the early 1980's, she does not have the background or credentials she needs to get a good job. Her only experience has been on Capitol Hill, and she cannot get a job there now because of her fear, her lack of working experience, and the media coverage of the incidents.

Corroborating Witnesses

The staff has interviewed two persons who recall that Ms. Wagers told them, in the 1970's, that Senator Packwood called her into his office, where he grabbed her and kissed her, and stuck his tongue in her mouth. One of these witnesses was a co-worker with Ms. Wagers, in whom she confided almost immediately after the incident. He stated that Ms. Wagers asked him to take a walk, and she related the incident. She was shocked, disgusted, and very upset.

Four other former coworkers recalled that Ms. Wagers had told them about the incident in varying degrees of vague detail: one recalls that Ms. Wagers said she had had a "contact" with Senator Packwood, which the witness had the impression was a kiss; one recalls that Ms. Wagers said Senator Packwood had made an unwanted advance; one recalls that Ms. Wagers said that Senator Packwood had "hit on her", which he interpreted as a verbal come-on; one recalls that Ms. Wagers vaguely indicated that "something happened" with Senator Packwood. One additional former coworker recalled hearing from others that Senator Packwood had made a pass at Ms. Wagers, although she had not heard about any aspect of forcefulness.

An additional witness, who worked with Ms. Wagers at the Council on Wage and Price Stability, has a vivid recollection of attending a "welcome home" ceremony for the Iran hostages on the South Lawn of the White House.[18] The whole Council had been invited, and he walked over to the ceremony with Ms. Wagers. When they arrived, he saw Senator Packwood, and pointed him out to Ms. Wagers. According to him, Ms. Wagers had a visible, physical, negative reaction; he believes that she recoiled, and changed the direction that she was walking. She indicated to him that she did not want Senator Packwood to see her. When he inquired what had happened, she told him that she used to work for Senator Packwood, and that he had attacked her. He does not recall that Ms. Wagers gave him any more specific details of the incident. A year or so later, Ms. Wagers told this same witness that she had run into Senator Packwood in the Capitol, and that he had pushed her into a room in the "catacombs" where he pushed her on a couch and tried to have his way with her.

The staff has also interviewed another friend of Ms. Wagers, whom she met in 1988 or 1989. During the course of talking about their job histories and career experiences, she told him that she had worked for Senator Packwood and that he had called her into her office and tried to kiss her on the neck; she tried to resist, and made it clear that she was not interested. Ms. Wagers also told him that a few years later, she ran into Senator Packwood in the basement of the Capitol building; that they engaged in conversation, and Ms. Wagers was pleased that he took an interest in her. He then led her into an unmarked office, closed the door, tried to push her against furniture or a wall, and tried to fondle her. Ms. Wagers told him that she had been extremely upset by the incident.

The staff also took the deposition of another former staffer, a friend of Ms. Wagers, who testified that in 1975 or 1976, Ms.

[18] This would have occurred in January 1981.

Wagers told him that Senator Packwood had called her into his office late in the work day, and had embraced and kissed her. She seemed upset and distressed about the incident. Later, in 1980 or 1981, Ms. Wagers, who was working for the Labor Department at the time, told him that she had seen Senator Packwood on the Hill, and that they had been walking down a hallway when he ushered her into a room off the hall[19], and embraced her and kissed her. She appeared upset and distressed about this incident.

In addition, Tim Lee, a former staffer, testified that she told him when they were dating that Senator Packwood had kissed her. Another former staffer testified that she had also told him, when he worked for Senator Packwood, that Senator Packwood had called her into his office and kissed her, and that she had left in tears.

Senator Packwood's Response

Senator Packwood recalled that Ms. Wagers worked in his office in the mid-1970's. He remembered her as young, blond, and personable; he did not recall her duties in the office. He did not recall ever being alone with her when she worked for him. He did not recall the first incident as described by Ms. Wagers, nor did he recall ever kissing her while she worked for him.

Senator Packwood did not recall the incident that Ms. Wagers claims occurred in 1981 in the basement of the Capitol. He stated that he did have a Capitol office, that he did not recall where it was, but it was not in the basement. He recalled that she came back to an office party after she left his office, with Mr. Lee, a staffer whom she was dating at the time. He recalled that she was friends with people in the office, and that she dated another staffer when she worked in the office.

---

[19] He recalled that she told him the room contained a couch and perhaps a mini-bar.

Senator Packwood testified that Mimi Dawson, his former administrative assistant, told him that Ms. Wagers had come to her and told her that she thought Senator Packwood wanted to have an affair with her, and that she was considering whether she should do so. In fact, Ms. Dawson testified that Ms. Wagers had approached her and told her that she thought the Senator wanted to have an affair with her, and that she got the impression that Ms. Wagers was asking her whether she thought she should have the affair. She testified:

A: I got the impression she was asking me whether I thought she should have the affair or not.

Q: And what was there that gave you that impression?

A: Just I didn't get a sense that she was complaining about, but trying to work through something, what should she do. I kind of had the feeling that it was more like this big, important person wants to have an affair with her. Will I offend him if I don't have this affair with him, or do I want to have this affair with him. I don't think she knew. And I got the impression she was asking me for my counsel.[20]

Senator Packwood's diary for December 14, 1992, contains the following entry, recounting his conversation with Ms. Dawson:

Then there was the Paige Wagers incident. It happened in '76. Mimi was press secretary.[21] Alan was AA. Paige, and Mimi sort of remembers this pretty specifically, Paige came to Mimi and said something like "I think the Senator wants to have an affair with me and what do you think I should do about it."

[20] Ms. Dawson also testified that, aside from that conversation, Ms. Wagers never said or did anything that suggested to her that she was interested in having an affair with the Senator.

[21] The press secretary and the administrative assistant are the same person.

Mimi got the very definite impression that Paige wanted to have the affair with me. Mimi says she remembers telling Paige, "Well, you're both consenting adults. Do what you want but I would suggest you go off and get married."

Senator Packwood did not recall that Ms. Wagers ever said or did anything to suggest to him that she was interested in any type of romantic or sexual relationship with him.

Findings

Senate Ethics Counsel finds that the incidents as alleged by Ms. Wagers in fact occurred. Her account of both incidents has been corroborated by numerous witnesses who recall that she told them about one or both incidents, in varying amounts of detail, shortly after they occurred. Senator Packwood has not denied the incidents, but has stated that he simply does not have any recollection of them.

Senator Packwood has attempted to suggest that Ms. Wagers, after the first incident, was entertaining the possibility of an affair with him, based upon her conversation with Ms. Dawson, possibly indicating that his advances, if they occurred, were not unwelcome. Counsel, however, views this conversation as an attempt by a very junior staff member to discreetly and circumspectly seek the advice of a woman supervisor. Senator Packwood himself has testified that Ms. Wagers never said or did anything that led him to conclude that she was interested in a sexual relationship with him.

Moreover, the tone of Ms. Wagers's comments when she related these incidents to others clearly indicated that she was upset by them, *not* that she was considering whether to have an affair with the Senator.

Senate Ethics Counsel finds that Senator Packwood's conduct in this instance fits a pattern of conduct that reflects an abuse of his position of authority, a pattern of conduct that constitutes improper conduct reflecting upon the Senate.

EUGENIA HUTTON

Testimony of Eugenia Hutton

In November of 1979, Eugenia Hutton responded to a fundraising letter written by Gloria Steinem by contributing money to Senator Packwood's campaign. A few weeks later, Brad Stocks, a Packwood staff member contacted her and asked if she would be willing to be involved in the campaign, clipping newspapers or something of that nature. Ms. Hutton indicated that she would be interested, and Mr. Stocks met with her for coffee when he came to Eugene. Later, Mr. Stocks called her and asked if she would be interested in being the chairperson for Lane County. Ms. Hutton responded that she had no experience in that sort of thing, but Mr. Stocks indicated that they could teach her what she needed to know. She told Mr. Stocks that she was interested in the opportunity. Senator Packwood then called her on the telephone to congratulate her for being on his campaign, to tell her that he knew she could handle the job and would do a great job, and that they could teach her everything she needed to know.

Subsequently, Ms. Hutton hosted coffees and volunteer functions at her house, which were attended by Senator Packwood as well as his wife, Georgie. As the campaign intensified, Ms. Hutton travelled to volunteer functions and appearances with the Senator.

In about March, 1980, Ms. Hutton went to the restaurant at the Red Lion Inn on Coburg Road in Eugene, Oregon, to meet with Senator Packwood and Mimi Dawson, his chief of staff. Senator Packwood was going to Coos Bay the next day, and wanted to prepare for that, and he also wanted Ms. Hutton to meet his chief of staff. Ms. Hutton arrived at the restaurant in the early evening, about 5:30 or 6:00, and sat in a booth with Senator Packwood and two staff members, Mr. Stocks and Bob Witeck. Ms. Dawson arrived and sat down at the booth, where she was introduced to Ms. Hutton. They chatted for a while, and Ms. Dawson left.

After a while, Senator Packwood asked the other staff members at the table to leave. There was teasing from the staff members, who told Senator Packwood that they were going to stay and hang around with him. Ms. Hutton had the impression that the staff members were staying at the table on purpose. Senator Packwood became more firm in his suggestions that the staff members leave. Finally, Senator Packwood made it clear that he wanted himself and Ms. Hutton to be left alone, and everyone left. Ms. Hutton recalls that the Senator may have been drinking, although she does not recall that he had any difficulty in walking. She does not remember if she had anything to drink, although she could have.

As they sat in the booth, the Senator asked her questions about herself. Ms. Hutton, assuming that Senator Packwood wanted to get to know her, as his Lane County chairperson, talked about herself, and showed him photographs of her children and cats; when she showed him the pictures, he moved closer to her in the booth, shoulder to shoulder. Ms. Hutton felt a little uncomfortable, but assumed that he had moved over to look at the pictures. She felt special, because she thought that the Senator was truly interested in getting to know her, as his Lane County chairperson, without everyone else around.

After about twenty minutes to half an hour, it was time to leave, and Senator Packwood offered to walk Ms. Hutton to her car. When they got to her car, Ms. Hutton unlocked it. Senator Packwood pulled her toward him, put his arms around her back and kissed her, putting his tongue in her mouth. Ms. Hutton pushed away from him, and acted as if she were trying to protect him: she told him that it was too dangerous to do that in public, that the press could be anywhere. She told him to get in her car, and she would drive him to his room, which was at the Red Lion Inn. Senator Packwood got in the car.

As Ms. Hutton drove the Senator to his room, which was across the parking lot and around the corner, he asked her to come to his room with him. She remembers that he said things to the effect of, "Come into the room with me; do you have to go home so soon; couldn't you come on in; couldn't you just sit and be with me for a while; it won't hurt anything." She told Senator Packwood that it would look very bad if someone were to see them, that they had a busy day ahead, and that he had been drinking. Senator Packwood tried a few more times to convince her to come in. He told her that it was okay, it would be fine. She told him that she thought he was a wonderful man, but that it was wrong for her to come into his room. Finally, he nodded, said okay, and got out of her car, and she drove away.

Ms. Hutton started to cry as she reached the street. She felt humiliated, confused, and angry. She was angry at Senator Packwood for being offensive and inappropriate, and angry at herself for trying to save his feelings at the expense of her own.

Ms. Hutton saw Senator Packwood the next day, when she went to the campaign trailer in the parking lot. Although no words were spoken about the night before, she and the Senator exchanged a long look when she walked in.

Ms. Hutton continued to work as the Lane County campaign chairperson, and Senator Packwood was friendly and respectful towards her; the incident was never mentioned. Ms. Hutton describes their relationship as being a little more businesslike after that incident.

Ms. Hutton continued to work for Senator Packwood's campaign through November of 1980. In 1981, Ms. Hutton asked Senator Packwood to write a letter of recommendation for her, which he did. When Ms. Hutton was starting a business that did artwork on T-shirts, she sent Senator Packwood a T-shirt, and he wrote her a thank you note.

Corroborating Witnesses

The staff interviewed Ms. Hutton's sister and a close personal friend who related that Ms. Hutton told them about the incident in 1980 and 1989, respectively.

Senator Packwood's Response

Senator Packwood recalled that Ms. Hutton was his Lane County Campaign Chair in 1980, and one of his two principal campaign workers for the next six years. She had made a contribution to his campaign in response to a direct mail piece, and someone on his staff interviewed her to see if she would be interested in working on his campaign. She attended a campaign volunteer kickoff, a two-day seminar, in January, 1980 in Portland, where Senator Packwood first met her.

Senator Packwood also recalled a meeting that took place at the Roadway hotel in Eugene, Oregon in March, 1980.[22] Ms. Hutton, a staffer, his administrative assistant, possibly another staffer, and himself, had drinks and dinner. He did not recall

---

[22] Both this evening, and the events of a following day, appear to be recounted in Senator Packwood's diary, in entries for February 11 and February 13, 1980. They do not include Senator Packwood walking Ms. Hutton to her car. Senator Packwood stated that these entries were reasonably accurate, as far as they concerned Ms. Hutton, but he could not swear to the accuracy of everything in the entry.

what the group discussed during the several hours they were there, or that Ms. Hutton showed him any photographs. He did not recall how the group broke up. He did recall that afterwards, he walked Ms. Hutton to her car and kissed her. He did not recall what time that was, whether he was drunk at the time, how it was that he came to walk her to her car, or what everyone else did when he left.

He did recall that when they got to Ms. Hutton's car, she got her keys out, turned around, and he kissed her goodnight. He did not recall if it was a french kiss, or whether he put his arms around her. Although he did not recall what Ms. Hutton did, he stated that she was "not unreceptive," meaning that she did not push him away and tell him to quit; she did not kiss him back. He recalled that she got in her car and left, and he walked back to his room.

Senator Packwood stated that the next day was very full. Ms. Hutton was very excited and enthusiastic, and had the crew to lunch at her house. About 4:00 or 5:00 that afternoon, when it was time to go on to the next town, they dropped Ms. Hutton off in a parking lot, or somewhere where she had her car. As Ms. Hutton got out of the van, and they all said goodbye, she kissed the Senator on the lips as he stood in the van by the door. It was not a french kiss, or a passionate kiss, or the kind of a kiss you would have if you were dating someone, but not a peck on the cheek kiss either.[23]

Ms. Hutton was very active in Senator Packwood's 1980 campaign. He related a specific instance where Ms. Hutton met the traveling crew one evening in Eugene, and they had wine and

---

[23] Senator Packwood stated that he had talked to two staffers who were in the van at the time, and that one of them, Terry Kay, remembered Ms. Hutton kissing him, while the other did not. Mr. Kay confirmed that he had seen Ms. Hutton kiss the Senator on this occasion. Senator Packwood's diary reflects that on the afternoon that Ms. Hutton was dropped off, she "gave each of us a kiss."

pizza, and played charades until about 11:00 p.m. He recalled that in 1983 or 1984, Ms. Hutton sent him a T-shirt from her new business; she wanted Elaine Franklin to loan or invest some money in the business. They kept up a close relationship for six years, and she was active in his 1986 campaign. Senator Packwood could not recall any other instances where he kissed Ms. Hutton, or she kissed him; he could not recall anything Ms. Hutton ever said or did to lead him to believe that she was interested in a romantic or sexual relationship with him.[24]

Senator Packwood was asked about his statements to the media in January, 1992, where he reportedly acknowledged that he had french kissed Ms. Hutton, and propositioned her or asked her to go to bed. He stated that he had not said that, that he had only said that he would not challenge her word. He stated that he wanted the press to accept her claims as true for the sake of argument, but to also consider Ms. Hutton's conduct toward him after the alleged incident.

Senator Packwood was asked about his reported comments to the Albany Rotary Club, that Ms. Hutton had kissed him many times after the alleged incident. He stated that he only recalled Ms. Hutton kissing him one time, and that he may have overstated this to the Rotary Club.

Findings

Senate Ethics Counsel finds that the incident as alleged by Ms. Hutton in fact occurred. Ms. Hutton's account has been corrob-

[24] Senator Packwood's attorneys have provided statements from two men who knew Ms. Hutton in the late 1970's and early 1980's. One of these men, John Morrison, who told Staff Counsel that he himself was interested in Ms. Hutton, said he had observed in social situations that Ms. Hutton was "coming on" to the Senator. The other man, Dr. Pat Golden, claimed that Ms. Hutton gave him the impression that she was a good friend of Senator Packwood, that she was close to him and enjoyed campaigning for him, and that she was fond of him.

orated by two persons to whom she related the incident, albeit several years later. Senator Packwood has also admitted the incident, although his recollection of some details differs from that of Ms. Hutton, and he cannot recall some details, for example, whether he gave her a french kiss.

Senator Packwood has emphasized to the Committee that Ms. Hutton continued to work for his campaign, and kept up a warm and close relationship with him for many years after the incident. He also claimed that after the incident, as Ms. Hutton prepared to part company with the group, she gave him a kiss. His diary entry for that day also reflects that she hugged and kissed each of the group. As Senator Packwood appears to admit that the incident took place, it appears that he intends to suggest by this information that Ms. Hutton could not have been offended by his behavior. Again, the fact that Ms. Hutton continued to work on Senator Packwood's campaigns, and that she kept up a relationship with him, a fact confirmed by Ms. Hutton herself, does not necessarily indicate that Ms. Hutton was not offended by Senator Packwood's conduct. It just as easily may reflect Ms. Hutton's inability to do anything about the incident, and her recognition of Senator Packwood's position as a United States Senator.

Senator Packwood has also proffered a statement from one John Morrison, indicating that Ms. Hutton acted in such a fashion as to suggest that she was interested in a sexual relationship with the Senator. However, Senator Packwood himself has testified that Ms. Hutton never did or said anything to suggest that she was interested in a sexual relationship with him. Moreover, such information, even if true, does not establish that the incident did not occur, although it would tend to indicate that she was not offended by his earlier conduct.

Senate Ethics Counsel finds that Senator Packwood's conduct in this instance fits a pattern of conduct that reflects an abuse of his position of authority, a pattern of conduct that constitutes improper conduct reflecting upon the Senate.

GILLIAN BUTLER

Testimony of Gillian Butler

In January, 1979, Gillian Butler began working as a desk clerk at the Red Lion Inn at 310 Southwest Lincoln Street, Portland, Oregon. She worked there, either full-time or part-time, until May of 1983. During those years, Senator Packwood stayed at the Red Lion Inn for several days every few months, with more frequent visits in 1980 during his re-election campaign.

In early 1980, Ms. Butler wrote letters to various Congress persons to protest the reinstatement of the registration for the draft. She received a response from Senator Packwood's office, addressed to "Mr. Butler." Not long afterwards, on a Saturday in February, Ms. Butler was working at the front desk when she noticed that Senator Packwood was checking out. She commented to him to the effect that the next time his office sent her a letter, it should not be addressed to Mr. Butler. When Senator Packwood asked what she meant, she explained about the response to her letter. They discussed the draft for about ten minutes, and Senator Packwood left for the airport. Senator Packwood called her from the airport and told her to write another letter, and he gave her the name of a person to whom the letter should be addressed so that it would get to him personally. He told her that they would talk about it the next time he visited Portland.

Ms. Butler wrote a second letter to Senator Packwood regarding her concerns about the draft, and left a copy for him at the Red Lion Inn in case he came to Portland before he got the letter in the mail in Washington. She put her home telephone number in the letter.

About the end of February, 1980, Senator Packwood called Ms. Butler at home about 7:30 a.m. He told her that he was flying into Portland that night, and he asked her to meet him at 10:00 that evening at the Red Lion Inn, so that they could go to a bar called the Prima Donna across the street, to talk about her letter. Ms. Butler agreed, although she felt a bit uncomfortable about going to a bar with the Senator that late at night. She arranged for her boyfriend to show up at the bar about 11:00 so that she would have a ride home.

That evening, Ms. Butler met Senator Packwood as planned, and they went to the Prima Donna. Ms. Butler and Senator Packwood sat and talked about some of the issues set out in her letter, mostly about international affairs and international aggression. She recalls that the Senator asked her to dance, and although she thinks that she refused, she may have danced briefly with him. About 11:00, Ms. Butler's boyfriend showed up, and the three of them talked for another 45 minutes. Ms. Butler's boyfriend and Senator Packwood got into a heated political discussion about international aggression. Senator Packwood then got up and left.

Sometime later in 1980, Senator Packwood came in one day, she believes on a Sunday, when Ms. Butler was working at the Red Lion Inn. The Senator asked Ms. Butler to join him in the hotel lounge after she got off work. She told him that she had plans to meet her boyfriend, but the Senator told her that her boyfriend was also invited. When Ms. Butler got off work at 11:00, she and her boyfriend went to the lounge, where they saw Senator Packwood sitting at a table with a woman; both of them appeared to be drunk. Ms. Butler and her boyfriend stood by the table and talked to the couple for about five minutes, and then left.

Later in 1980 or early in 1981, Ms. Butler was working at the Red Lion Inn one morning when Senator Packwood came to the front desk. She was leaning over some paperwork, checking Senator Packwood out of the hotel. She looked up, and Senator Packwood suddenly leaned across the desk and kissed her on the mouth. She was surprised, uncomfortable, and embarrassed, and backed away.

Later in 1980 or early in 1981, Senator Packwood came to the front desk one morning at the Red Lion Inn when Ms. Butler was working. He was leaving and wanted his luggage, which was stored in the closet behind the desk. Ms. Butler told him that she would get his luggage, and turned around and went to the closet. Senator Packwood walked around the desk and into the closet behind her. When she turned around, he leaned over and kissed her, got his luggage, and left.

After these incidents, Ms. Butler was careful not to be alone behind the desk when the Senator was there; she made sure that there was another clerk behind the desk when she knew the Senator was coming down.

Corroborating Witnesses

The staff interviewed four persons—Ms. Butler's parents, her sister, and her boyfriend at the time—who confirm that Ms. Butler told them about the incidents, in varying degrees of detail, shortly after they occurred. Her boyfriend at the time recalls accompanying Ms. Butler to the hotel bar to meet Senator Packwood, where they found him in a booth, intoxicated, with a woman. They stayed for a few minutes to talk, and left.

Another friend of Ms. Butler's, who ran as a Socialist Workers Party write-in candidate against Senator Packwood in 1980, stated that, shortly after the incidents happened, Ms. Butler told him about two occasions when Senator Packwood kissed her while she was working at the Red Lion Inn. She also told him that Senator Packwood had asked her out for drinks several times. On one occasion, Ms. Butler called him to tell him that she was going to meet Senator Packwood at a bar, and that unbeknownst to Senator Packwood, she was bringing her boyfriend along; he learned from Ms. Butler later that they had talked about military spending and policy.

Senator Packwood's Response

Senator Packwood recalled Ms. Butler as a desk clerk at the Red Lion Inn, where he stayed in Portland. They chatted when he checked in and out; she was anti-war, anti-draft, and anti-military. He recalled discussing a letter with her, in which she said that he should feel free to call her at home, which he did. He suggested that Ms. Butler meet with him to talk about the letter. He recalled that he met with her only once, at the bar in the motel. The Senator was with someone, and Ms. Butler came with her boyfriend. They chatted awhile; he believed that Ms. Butler and her boyfriend remained standing.

Senator Packwood did not recall any other meetings or contacts with Ms. Butler. He stated that it would have been difficult for him to lean over the counter and kiss her, because the counter is about four feet high and three feet wide.

Findings

Senate Ethics Counsel finds that the incidents as alleged by Ms. Butler in fact occurred. Senator Packwood recalled Ms. Butler, but he did not recall the incidents themselves. Senator Packwood has offered no evidence, other than his claim that it would be difficult to lean over the counter as described by Ms. Butler, to refute these allegations, nor has the Committee uncovered any such evidence. The claims are corroborated by the persons to whom Ms. Butler spoke at the time of or shortly after the incidents, and who, in the case of her then-boyfriend, participated in some of the events leading up to the incidents.

Senate Ethics Counsel finds that Senator Packwood's conduct in this instance fits a pattern of conduct that reflects an abuse of his position of authority, a pattern of conduct that constitutes improper conduct reflecting upon the Senate.

PACKWOOD STAFF MEMBER[25]

Testimony of Staff Member

This individual worked on Senator Packwood's personal staff from September of 1978 through August of 1979, when she returned to school. She then worked for the Senate Commerce Committee, where Senator Packwood was the ranking minority member, from June, 1980 through August, 1980.

One day in May of 1979, when the staffer was in Senator Packwood's office with a number of other staffers, he leaned over and told her in effect that he would like to see her playing softball in the dress she was wearing, bending over, or moving in certain positions, so that he could see her figure. He made comments about how the dress fit her, and how she would look playing softball or pitching if she were wearing the dress, and said that he would like to be there to watch her move.

Sometime later, when the staffer was on the Committee staff, one evening six or seven of the staff, and Senator Packwood, went to a restaurant for pizza and beer. While they all sat around

[25] This staff member is designated "C-7" in the Committee's Exhibits.

a table, Senator Packwood put his arm around the staffer, drew her very close, and told her he knew that he could persuade her to be a Republican. He kept his arm around her most of the evening.

These instances with the Senator made the staffer very uncomfortable about being in a position where something similar might happen again. She wanted to avoid Senator Packwood, but at the same time, she wanted to have her work recognized by him.

One evening in the early summer of 1980, the staffer was working in the Senator's office, and she realized she would be the last staff member working in the office.[26] She was apprehensive about what might happen, given the other instances that had occurred, and she wanted an excuse to leave the office. About 7:00 or 7:30, she called a friend and asked him to drive over and come upstairs to the offices to get her. After making the phone call, the staffer walked back into the Senator's office. He came around his desk, and either rubbed her back or put his arm around her. He then grabbed her shoulders, and tried to push her down on the couch. He kissed her on the lips. She tried to get up, and he pushed her down again; this happened three times, maybe more. She tried to push him away, and told him to leave her alone, not to touch her, and that she had a friend coming to pick her up.

As the staffer struggled with Senator Packwood, her friend arrived at the office and began calling her name. The staffer was able to get away from the Senator, and locate her friend, whom

[26] The staff member does not recall why she was working in Senator Packwood's office at the time. She may have been going over Committee work with the Senator, or talking about the recent eruption at Mount St. Helen's. She stated that it was not too uncommon for Committee staffers to be working in Senator Packwood's personal office.

she introduced to the Senator as her boyfriend.[27] The staffer and her friend then left the office. The staffer was upset and crying, and spent some time walking around the Capitol with her friend, whom she told what had happened before he took her home.

Corroborating Witnesses

In his deposition, the friend whom the staffer called the evening of the incident in Senator Packwood's office confirms that she called him to pick her up from work one evening, that she was upset and crying, and that she told him that Senator Packwood had been making advances or passes at her, and that it was not the first time it had happened.[28]

Senator Packwood's Response

Senator Packwood did not recall the staffer, or the incidents that she alleges occurred.

Findings

Senate Ethics Counsel finds that the incident as alleged by the staff member in fact occurred. Senator Packwood has testified that he does not recall the incident. The staff member's allegations have been corroborated by the friend whom she called to pick her up on the evening that the incident occurred. Senator Packwood has offered no evidence, nor has the Committee found any, that would tend to refute the allegation by the staff member.

[27] The staff member had the idea that she might be safe from Senator Packwood if he thought she had a boyfriend.

After that, the staffer avoided the Senator "like the plague." She left the office at the end of August.

[28] There appears to be some confusion about the time period of the incident: the staff member remembers that it happened in the early summer of 1980; her friend seems to recall that it happened during the college Christmas break in late 1980 or early 1981. Nevertheless, her friend clearly recalls the incident.

Senate Ethics Counsel finds that Senator Packwood's conduct in this instance fits a pattern of conduct that reflects an abuse of his position of authority, a pattern of conduct that constitutes improper conduct reflecting upon the Senate.

SENATE STAFF MEMBER[29]

Testimony of Staff Member

In 1979, this individual worked for another Senator, in an office on the first floor of the Dirksen Building, Room 1200. The office was only one room, in which six to seven persons worked. A corner of the room, in the front to the right of the door, was partitioned by a cubicle; the staff member sat at a desk in this cubicle. The office was located around the corner from the Senate elevators, and at the corner of the building, near an outside entrance. It was an interior office with no windows, and the door was customarily kept open. Senators often passed by on their way to the subway or across the street to vote.

Senator Packwood passed by frequently, and at some point got in the habit of stopping in the office to chat with the staff member. She was friendly to Senator Packwood when he dropped in; their conversation was superficial, in the nature of "Hello, how are you, are you having a good day," etc. The staff member cannot remember Senator Packwood talking with anyone else in the office other than her when he came in.

It was not uncommon for the staff member to be in her office alone after the rest of the staff had gone home for the evening. She was often at the office until 6:00 or 7:00 p.m., alone, catching up on the mail. One evening, as best as she can recall,

---

[29] This person is designated "C-8" in the Committee Exhibits.

in 1979, possibly in the spring, the staff member was working late, alone in the office. She was sitting at her desk proofing mail, with mail in her lap and her feet up on the feet of the swivel chair, leaning back comfortably. Senator Packwood came in the office, and stood three or four feet away, chatting. All of a sudden, he lunged down, kissed her on the lips, and turned around and left without saying a word. She stated that the kiss was not a french kiss, but it was a full kiss on the mouth. It was not like a kiss from a grandfather, nor was it a romantic kiss. The staff member described the kiss as unwanted, and stated that she felt violated by Senator Packwood approaching her in that manner.

The staff member did not notice any odor of alcohol about Senator Packwood. She does not have a specific recollection of Senator Packwood placing his hands on her shoulders or on the chair, but she states that he would have had to brace his arms either on her shoulders or on the chair in order to be able to push himself away from her.

After that, the staff member started closing the office door. Senator Packwood did not stop by the office anymore, nor did he speak to her.

Corroborating Witnesses

Two witnesses, the staff member's boyfriend and a friend from the Senate, both recalled that, sometime after the allegations became public, the staff member told them that Senator Packwood had come into her office and kissed her.

Senator Packwood's Response

Senator Packwood could not recall the staff member, or the incident that she alleges occurred.

Findings

Senate Ethics Counsel finds that the incident as alleged by the staff member in fact occurred. Senator Packwood did not recall the incident; he has not offered, nor has the Committee uncovered, any evidence tending to refute the staff member's allegation.

Senate Ethics Counsel finds that Senator Packwood's conduct in this instance fits a pattern of conduct that reflects an abuse of his position of authority, a pattern of conduct that constitutes improper conduct reflecting upon the Senate.

KERRY WHITNEY

Testimony of Kerry Whitney

Ms. Whitney worked for the Senate in Washington, D.C. from approximately September, 1976 through October, 1978, as a part time elevator operator on the Senate side of the Capitol, running the elevators from 8:00 a.m. until 1:00 p.m., unless there were scheduled sessions that started earlier, in which case she started work earlier. The rest of the day, she worked in a Senator's office. Her job as an elevator operator involved standing by her assigned elevator and transporting passengers to their requested floor. For the first nine months, she was assigned to operate one of the elevators available for use by the public; the last two of those months she was assigned to the public elevator that also served as the alternate Senators' only elevator. She was then assigned to the Senators' only elevator, which she operated for eight months, and then to the Senators' only elevator which went to the Senate dining room. She remained there until she left her job.

Ms. Whitney first came to know Senator Packwood when she was assigned to operate the alternate Senators' elevator in approximately April 1977. He was always friendly and attentive, and expressed an interest in her as a person, asking her questions about herself, and remembering her name. Ms. Whitney was flattered by this attention from a U.S. Senator. For about the first few months after she met Senator Packwood, her interaction with him was limited to friendly conversation on the elevator.

Sometime during June or July, 1977, after she had been assigned to operate the Senators' only elevator in the main corridor, Senator Packwood entered the elevator, and greeted her by name. As soon as the doors closed, he suddenly cocked his head to the side, and said "kiss." He grabbed her by the shoulders, pushed her back to the side wall of the elevator, and started kissing her on the lips. He stopped as the elevator came to a halt. After that, Senator Packwood grabbed and kissed her most of the times when he was alone with her on the elevator. Frequently he would precede the kiss by cocking his head and saying "kiss" before he grabbed her.

Some time in late July, 1977, Senator Packwood asked Ms. Whitney where she lived, and for her telephone number, saying he might like to come over some evening. She gave him the information, thinking that if she had the opportunity to talk with him, she could get him to stop the kissing and have just a friendly relationship. One evening in early August, 1977, Senator Packwood called Ms. Whitney at home about 9:30 p.m. and asked if he could come over. Ms. Whitney was surprised, but also flattered. Because her roommate and a Russian friend of hers were also home, she said yes. Senator Packwood arrived a short time later, knocked on the door, and she let him into the vestibule. He appeared to her nervous, and she smelled alcohol on his breath. Senator Packwood heard voices from the living room, asked who it was, and backed away from the entrance into the living room. When Ms. Whitney told him it was her roommate and a Russian student, he said "a Russian" and jumped behind the door to the living room. He then walked into the living room and introduced himself.

Senator Packwood asked Ms. Whitney what she had to drink. She went to the kitchen; he followed her. She gave the Senator a beer. He put his beer on the counter, put his arms around her and began kissing her. She put her hands on his chest, pushed him away, and said, wait a minute, what do you want from me? He stated that he wanted two things from her: to make love to her; and to hear what she heard in her job, as she heard a lot of things. Ms. Whitney was stunned, and asked him if he weren't married. He responded that he was, and he loved his wife very much. Ms. Whitney told him that she was not interested in having sex with him.

Senator Packwood then suggested that they sit down somewhere. They went to the back yard, and sat around a table for about thirty minutes while Senator Packwood drank his beer. Ms. Whitney does not recall much of the conversation, other than the Senator saying that they had a special relationship that they would have forever, and they were obviously attracted to each other. He indicated that he had a campaign coming up, giving Ms. Whitney the impression that he was dangling the opportunity to work in his campaign in front of her.

It began to rain, so they went back into the house. Ms. Whitney's roommate and her friend had left. Ms. Whitney and Senator Packwood went into the living room and sat on the couch, where the Senator again began trying to kiss her, and repeatedly asked to spend the night. Ms. Whitney kept pushing him away, and declining his invitation to have sex, saying that they should just talk. She finally got up from the couch, and told him he had to leave. He continued to beg her to let him spend the night, saying that he had nowhere to go. She suggested that he go home; he told her it was too far away. She then told him to go to his secretary's house, as she understood he sometimes stayed there. He rejected that suggestion. She finally told him he would have to sleep in his office. Eventually, she was able to lead him out the door by his arm.

About five minutes later, she heard a loud banging on the door, which lasted about three minutes. She did not answer the door, as she believed it was the Senator. About ten minutes later, the phone rang. It was Senator Packwood, who asked why she had not answered the door; she told him she was getting ready for bed. He again begged her to please let him spend the night, and she again refused. She saw him again the next morning at 7:00 a.m. by the elevators, and he told her he had slept on the couch in his office.

After the incident at her house, Senator Packwood continued to grab and kiss her when they were alone in the elevator. Sometime in late August or early September, 1977, after a kissing episode, she told Senator Packwood that his touching was getting in the way, and asked if they could go somewhere public and talk about it. He told her that he could not do that because he was married.

In early September, 1977, Senator Packwood called her house again. Ms. Whitney was not home and her roommate answered the phone. Senator Packwood told her roommate that it was too bad Ms. Whitney was not home, that he wanted her to get a hamburger with him. He then asked the roommate if she wanted to go; she declined.

After the second phone call, the grabbing and kissing episodes on the elevator became less frequent, and eventually ceased in late fall. In February, 1978, Ms. Whitney was reassigned to the

Senators' only back elevator which leads to the Senate dining room, and she did not see Senator Packwood very much after that. She does not have any recollection of Senator Packwood grabbing and kissing her during the time she ran the dining room elevator.

Corroborating Witnesses

The staff has interviewed four witnesses who corroborate portions of Ms. Whitney's allegations. Her roommate at the time, who is married to Ms. Whitney's brother, confirms that Ms. Whitney told her that Senator Packwood had kissed her numerous times in the elevator. She also recalls the evening that Senator Packwood came over to their apartment; she recalls that she had a Russian student visiting, and that after Senator Packwood greeted them, he and Ms. Whitney went into the kitchen. She recalls, however, that she and the Russian student were still in the living room when Senator Packwood left about an hour later. She also recalls that some time later, Senator Packwood called one evening for Ms. Whitney, and when he learned that she was not at home, he invited her out for dinner; she declined.

A staffer who worked with Ms. Whitney in the Senator's office at the time also recalls that Ms. Whitney told her that Senator Packwood had made passes at her a number of times when he was alone on the elevator with her, and that he had come over to her house.

Ms. Whitney's brother also recalled that while she worked in the Senate, Ms. Whitney told him that Senator Packwood had tried to kiss her on the elevator more than once, and that he had showed up at her apartment and wanted her to go out.

A roommate of Ms. Whitney's in 1978, after she left the Senate, recalled that Ms. Whitney told her that Senator Packwood had pinned her and kissed her in the elevator, and that he had come to her house and asked her for a date; he jumped on her, and later pounded on her door and called her on the telephone.

Senator Packwood's Response

Senator Packwood did not recall Ms. Whitney or the incidents she alleges occurred. He did not recall ever kissing or propositioning any Senate elevator operator.

Findings

Senate Ethics Counsel finds that the incidents as alleged by Ms. Whitney in fact occurred. Ms. Whitney's allegations have been corroborated by the persons to whom she described the incidents after they occurred, including her roommate at the time, who personally observed Senator Packwood when he came to their apartment, and who talked to him when he called to ask Ms. Whitney to dinner. Senator Packwood has not denied the incidents, except to state that he does not recall ever kissing a Senate elevator operator; he has no recollection of the incidents described by Ms. Whitney. Senator Packwood has offered no evidence, nor has the Committee uncovered any, that tends to refute the allegations of Ms. Whitney.

Senate Ethics Counsel finds that Senator Packwood's conduct in this instance fits a pattern of conduct that reflects an abuse of his position of authority, a pattern of conduct that constitutes improper conduct reflecting upon the Senate.

JEAN MCMAHON

Testimony of Jean McMahon

In 1976 or 1977, Jean McMahon heard that Senator Packwood's staff office in Portland was looking for additional staff members. She was interested in moving to Portland, so she called Senator Packwood's office to see if she could get an appointment to talk about a job. Within several days, Senator Packwood called her, and told her that he would like to meet her and possibly get some writing samples from her. She understood from the conversation that Senator Packwood was looking for a speech writer. They made an appointment for an interview at a motel in Salem. Ms. McMahon thought it odd that the appointment was at a motel, but assumed that the motel was a convenient place for a traveling U.S. senator.

Ms. McMahon met Senator Packwood at the motel as arranged, and spoke with him for about an hour. She was attempting to get acquainted with the Senator, and to get information from which she could prepare a draft of a speech for him, so that he could see what her writing style was like.

Over the next few weeks, Ms. McMahon prepared a draft of a speech, and talked to Senator Packwood by telephone several times about different points in the speech. Eventually, they agreed to meet again at the Dorchester Conference, a well-known event among Republicans in Oregon. Ms. McMahon took her drafts, and drove from Salem to the coast, where the Dorchester Conference was taking place. Senator Packwood had given her the address of a motel, with a room number. Ms. McMahon knocked on the door of the room, and Senator Packwood answered; he was the only person in the room. She and the Senator sat at an oval table in a sitting room area. Ms. McMahon had her draft speech with her, and she brought it out, gave the Senator a copy of it, and began talking about it. Within about five minutes, it became obvious to her that the Senator was not at all interested in her speech. The Senator got up quickly from the table, and moved around toward her. She became alarmed, got up, and started to go around the edge of the table, in order to put distance between herself and the Senator. Senator Packwood started moving faster, grabbed her by the shoulders, and pulled her up to him and kissed her. She pulled away, and quickly left the room.

It took a few days for Ms. McMahon to realize that Senator Packwood was not at all serious about hiring her as a speech writer. She called his office in Portland, to tell them that she had a draft speech for the Senator, thinking that someone on the staff was waiting for it. She told someone at the office that she had the draft speech ready for the Senator, and she needed to know what to do with it. The reaction from the staff at the Portland office was that they had never heard of any speech, and they did not care what happened to the draft she had prepared. Ms. McMahon never spoke to Senator Packwood again.

Corroborating Witnesses

The staff deposed six witnesses who learned about this incident, in varying detail, from Ms. McMahon in the late 1970's. Her husband (they were dating at the time) recalled receiving a phone call from Ms. McMahon after the incident; he knew she had gone to deliver a speech to Senator Packwood. Ms. McMahon told him that Senator Packwood had come on to her, and she had to leave. Four close friends of Ms. McMahon's also confirmed that she told them about the incident, and the fact that she had been led to believe that there was a job opening for a speechwriter. Ms. McMahon's friends indicated that she seemed to be excited about the prospect of the job, and had taken work for Senator Packwood to review. However, Senator Packwood appeared to have no interest in her work, and used the opportunity to make an unwanted physical advance upon her. Three of these witnesses recalled that Ms. McMahon told them that Senator Packwood chased her around a table, or around the room, in his hotel room.

Senator Packwood's Response

Senator Packwood did not recall Ms. McMahon, or the incident that she described. He stated that it would be unusual for him to consider a person for a job as a speech writer, as he has never used one. He writes his own speeches, except for formal floor speeches on subjects with which he is not familiar, which he has written for him by staff members.

There is an entry in Senator Packwood's diary for February 16, 1977, indicating that he met with Ms. McMahon, and that they might want to use her as a writer.[30] After his first deposition, Senator Packwood provided the Committee with a draft of a speech that Ms. McMahon had worked on for the Senator. He testified at his second deposition that he still had no recollection of Ms. McMahon, but the speech appeared to be one that he gave her to edit, probably to see if she would be able to write for him. He stated that looking at the speech, and the edits, Ms. McMahon probably talked to him about the speech, but he had no recollection of that.

Senator Packwood testified that according to news statements, Ms. McMahon had stated that she phoned his office after the incident to see if she had gotten the job.

Findings

Senate Ethics Counsel finds that the incident as alleged by Ms. McMahon in fact occurred. Ms. McMahon's account is corroborated by the persons to whom she described the incident shortly after it occurred. Several details of her testimony are corroborated by Senator Packwood's own records—her first meeting with him is reflected in both his diary and his calendar of events,

---

[30] Senator Packwood's calendar for 1977 indicates that he met with Ms. McMahon at 6:15 on February 17.

and the fact that he was considering her for a position involving speechwriting is confirmed by the speech she critiqued for him.

Senator Packwood has not denied the incident; he has testified that he has no recollection of it. He did emphasize in his deposition that Ms. McMahon was still interested in working for him, as she had apparently called his office after the incident to inquire about the job, as if to suggest either that the incident did not occur, or that she could not have been offended by it if she still wanted to work for him. The fact that Ms. McMahon may have called to inquire about the job after the incident, even if true, does not cast any doubt on Ms. McMahon's allegation. If true, it may just as easily indicate that she was willing to overlook the incident because she needed a job.

Senate Ethics Counsel finds that Senator Packwood's conduct in this instance fits a pattern of conduct that reflects an abuse of his position of authority, a pattern of conduct that constitutes improper conduct reflecting upon the Senate.

PACKWOOD STAFF MEMBER[31]

Staff Member's Testimony

This individual worked for Senator Packwood from March, 1972 through April, 1975 in Washington, D.C., as a staff assistant. One evening, when the staff member was at a bar with her husband and a friend, a staffer for another Senator staff apparently overheard the staff member talking about Senator Packwood, saying that he drank too much, and had to have somebody drive him because of his drinking. The next day, Senator Packwood called her into his office and confronted her with this

---

[31] This staff member is designated "C-12" in the Committee's Exhibits.

information. The staff member, worried about losing her job, denied that she had been talking about Senator Packwood, and claimed that she had been talking instead about her former boss. Senator Packwood told her that he did not think that she would say anything about him, got up from behind his desk, and came around and kissed her on the cheek. The staff member described the kiss as inappropriate, but without sexual overtones. She was relieved that she had not lost her job.

Sometime after this incident, during the spring of 1975, the staff member began riding to work with her husband, whose job required him to be in his office early. Consequently, the staff member would arrive at the office at about 7:00 or 7:30 a.m.; she usually was the first one in to work. At some point, Senator Packwood started coming in to the office early as well, and he and the staff member would chat in the mornings in the office she shared with another staff member. One morning in April, 1975, as the staff member stood in her office, engaging in small talk with Senator Packwood, he grabbed her firmly with both arms around her shoulders, held her tightly, pressing his body into hers, and kissed her on the mouth. She describes the kiss as that of somebody who wanted to be involved or passionate. She pushed him away, and told him to get off of her, that she was a happily married woman. Senator Packwood appeared bewildered, told her that he was sorry, and left the room.

The staff member quit her job, because she felt that after the incident involving the kiss in her office, every time she was around the Senator, he was looking at her, and it made her uncomfortable.

Corroborating Witnesses

The staff has interviewed one witness, the staff member's aunt, who worked on the Hill at the time, who confirmed that the staff member told her that she had to leave Senator Packwood's employment, because she was afraid to be alone in the office with him. The staff member told this witness that Senator Packwood had kissed her.

The staff member's husband recalled that she told him, eighteen or nineteen years ago, while she worked for Senator Packwood, that someone had overheard a conversation among himself, his wife, and a friend about Senator Packwood's womanizing which they had reported to Senator Packwood. Senator Packwood questioned the staff member about it, and she denied having said anything. Senator Packwood seemed satisfied, and gave her a "wet" kiss on the lips. Sometime later, Senator Packwood and the staff member were in the office early, and he grabbed her and kissed her. At the time, her husband was an officer with the Metropolitan Police Department. He was upset when his wife told him about these incidents, but he was worried that it could cause trouble for him or his wife if he mentioned anything about the incidents. Had it been anyone but a Senator, he would have confronted the person about the incidents.

Senator Packwood's Response

Senator Packwood did not recall the staff member or the incident that she alleges occurred.

Findings

Senate Ethics Counsel finds that the incident as alleged by the staff member in fact occurred. Two witnesses have confirmed that the staff member told them about the incident shortly after it occurred. Senator Packwood has not denied the incident; he has testified that he did not recall it. Senator Packwood has not offered, nor has the Committee uncovered, any evidence tending to refute the staff member's allegations.

Senate Ethics Counsel finds that Senator Packwood's conduct in this instance fits a pattern of conduct that reflects an abuse of his position of authority, a pattern of conduct that constitutes improper conduct reflecting upon the Senate.

PACKWOOD STAFF MEMBER[32]

Testimony of Staff Member

This individual worked for Senator Packwood in the early 1970's as a caseworker in his Senate office in Portland. Sometime in the early 1970's, she was at work alone in one of the office rooms late one night. She testified that she had been drinking, and it was possible that she had gone out after work with some of the other staff and come back to the office. She was just finishing a telephone call when Senator Packwood came in, and chased her around the desk several times. She does not remember Senator Packwood saying anything to her, and she does not think that he actually touched her. She thinks that she was already standing when Senator Packwood came into the room, but she cannot remember what he did that made her suspicious and made her try to get away from him; she believes that he must have said something to her, although she does not remember that. At the time, she thought that all he was going to do was to kiss her. She remembers that he chased her, and that she went around the desk several times. She was so upset that she left the office without her purse and coat. The staff member continued to work in Senator Packwood's office for a short time after that incident.

[32] This staff member is designated "C-13" in the Committee's Exhibits.

Corroborating Witnesses

The staff member provided the names of two persons whom she told about the incident. The staff was not able to contact either person.

Senator Packwood's Response

Senator Packwood did not recall either the staff member, or the incident that she alleges occurred.

Findings

Senate Ethics Counsel finds that the incident as alleged by the staff member in fact occurred. Although no witnesses were found who could corroborate the staff member's account, Senator Packwood did not deny the incident, nor did he offer any evidence that would tend to refute her allegation.

Senate Ethics Counsel finds that Senator Packwood's conduct in this instance fits a pattern of conduct that reflects an abuse of his position of authority, a pattern of conduct that constitutes improper conduct reflecting upon the Senate.

GAIL BYLER

Testimony of Gail Byler

In 1970, Gail Byler worked as the dining room hostess at the Ramada Inn, which had opened in February, 1970 at 4th and Lincoln in Portland, Oregon. It is now a Red Lion Inn. One evening in March, April, or May of 1970, she was sitting at the hostess desk working on paperwork after the dining room had closed for the evening. The dining room was dark except for a light that was on over the area where she was working. The dining room itself was open to the lobby area, and was separated from the lounge by a screen.

Ms. Byler got up from her station to get a glass of ice water from the waitress station, which was in a hallway off the dining room, fairly close to the entrance to the dining room from the lobby. She had her back to the dining room. All of a sudden, she felt a hand go from her ankle, up the inside of her leg, to her crotch. She turned around quickly, and saw Senator Packwood behind her, leaning against a doorway. She stepped back, and told him to stay away from her, and not to touch her. He said, "Do you know who I am?" Ms. Byler told him that she knew who he was, she didn't care, and for him to stay away from her. He told her that she had not heard the end of it, and walked out of the dining room.

Corroborating Witnesses

Ms. Byler's minister provided an affidavit to the Committee. Ms. Byler has been a parishioner and a friend of his for a number of years.

The minister stated that shortly before the death of Ms. Byler's husband about three years ago, he was at their home, and he and her husband were teasing Ms. Byler about all of the men who would be chasing after her when her husband died. Ms. Byler told them, in effect, that she had been pursued by loftier men than the two of them. She then told them that years earlier, when she was working as the dining room manager at the Ramada Inn, she had been going over the waitress slips in the dining room after it had closed down. She stepped into a waitress station for a glass of water, and Senator Packwood came up behind her, and ran his hands from her legs to her waist. He appeared to her to have been drinking. She told him in no uncertain terms to get away from her, and to leave her alone.

After stories appeared in the newspapers about allegations of misconduct by Senator Packwood, the minister reminded Ms.

Byler of their conversation several years earlier. Ms. Byler was reluctant to go forward or make any kind of statement about what had happened to her. Although the minister felt that Senator Packwood had done good things as a Senator, he also felt that it was important for this information to become public. He encouraged Ms. Byler to go forward, and to make a statement about the incident.

Senator Packwood's Response

Senator Packwood did not recall Ms. Byler, or the incident that she alleges occurred.

Findings

Senate Ethics Counsel finds that this incident as alleged by Ms. Byler in fact occurred. Senator Packwood does not recall this incident. No evidence has been offered by Senator Packwood or obtained by the Committee to refute Ms. Byler's claim, and it is corroborated by her minister, to whom she recounted the incident after it occurred.

Senate Ethics Counsel finds that Senator Packwood's conduct in this instance fits a pattern of conduct that reflects an abuse of his position of authority, a pattern of conduct that constitutes improper conduct reflecting upon the Senate.

PACKWOOD STAFF MEMBER[33]

Testimony of Staff Member

This individual worked for Senator Packwood for about six months from April to October, 1970. She worked at a desk in the front office. One afternoon, after 5:00, she was sitting at her

---

[33] This staff member is designated "C-15" in the Committee Exhibits.

desk when Senator Packwood walked over, grabbed her by the shoulders, and kissed her on the mouth. It was not a french kiss, but it was a sexual kiss, the type that a boyfriend would give to a girlfriend. She believes that she pushed Senator Packwood away, and tried to make a joke out of it. He walked away, and the incident did not happen again.

Corroborating Witnesses

The staff member could not recall telling anyone about this incident.

Senator Packwood's Response

Senator Packwood could not recall either the staff member, or the incident that she alleges occurred.

Findings

Senate Ethics Counsel finds that the incident as alleged by the staff member in fact occurred. Although no witnesses were found who could corroborate the staff member's account, Senator Packwood did not deny the incident, nor did he offer any evidence that would tend to refute her allegation.

Senate Ethics Counsel finds that Senator Packwood's conduct in this instance fits a pattern of conduct that reflects an abuse of his position of authority, a pattern of conduct that constitutes improper conduct reflecting upon the Senate.

SHARON GRANT

Testimony of Sharon Grant

In early 1969, sometime in the spring, Sharon Grant met Senator Packwood at a reception on Capitol Hill, and she talked with him about the possibility of working for his office or one of his committees. Senator Packwood told her to come by and see him to discuss this possibility further.

Within a week or two, Ms. Grant called someone in Senator Packwood's office to set up an appointment to talk to him. She went to Senator Packwood's office toward the end of a working day, and met with the Senator in his office for about 45 minutes. Ms. Grant talked with the Senator about herself, her work experience and interests, and job possibilities. Senator Packwood indicated to her that she should consider filling out an application with his staff people. Toward the end of the meeting, Senator Packwood suggested to Ms. Grant that they go and have a drink, and asked her, how about spending the evening with me? Ms. Grant picked up a tone of voice, or a loaded quality to the Senator's comments, that caused her to interpret his request as a proposition for her to spend the night with him. She told him that she did not think that was appropriate, that it was time for her to go, and she left. She did not pursue a job possibility any further.

Corroborating Witnesses

There were no witnesses located who could corroborate Ms. Grant's testimony.

Senator Packwood's Response

Senator Packwood could not recall Ms. Grant, or the incident that she alleges occurred.

Findings

Senate Ethics Counsel finds that the incident as alleged by Ms. Grant in fact occurred. Although no witnesses were found who could corroborate Ms. Grant's account, Senator Packwood did not deny the incident, nor did he offer any evidence that would tend to refute her allegation.

Senate Ethics Counsel finds that Senator Packwood's conduct in this instance fits a pattern of conduct that reflects an abuse of his position of authority, a pattern of conduct that constitutes improper conduct reflecting upon the Senate.

GAYLE ROTHROCK

Testimony of Gayle Rothrock

Gayle Rothrock worked for another Senator from December, 1968 until September of 1970. During that time, she became acquainted with Senator Packwood by virtue of her visits to his office on business, or to say hello to acquaintances who worked there.

In early spring of 1969, probably early April, Ms. Rothrock was visiting friends in Senator Packwood's office. Mrs. Packwood was there, and Ms. Rothrock heard her say that she needed a babysitter for one of the next few evenings for their two preschool children. Ms. Rothrock volunteered to babysit, and on the evening in question, the Packwoods picked her up after work and took her to their home. She took care of the children for the evening while the Packwoods attended an event. When the Senator and his wife returned about 11:00 p.m., they paid her for babysitting, and Mrs. Packwood told her that the Senator would run her home.

As Ms. Rothrock was reaching for her coat from an area close to the front door, Senator Packwood grabbed her shoulders and back with both of his hands, rubbed and massaged her shoulders and back, and gave her a sloppy, forceful, wet and insistent kiss on the mouth. Ms. Rothrock pushed him away with her hands, retrieved her coat, and started talking about Northwest issues, what a nice family he had and how attractive the children were, how she hoped that his days in Washington were going to be good ones, and that he was off to a good start.

Although Ms. Rothrock detected a slight odor of alcohol about Senator Packwood, and the Packwoods had told her they had been to a party where there were drinks and hors d'oeuvres, neither of the Packwoods displayed signs of drunkenness.

Ms. Rothrock sat in the front seat during the ride to her apartment. As he started the car engine, and before he pulled away from the curb, Senator Packwood reached over and put his right arm around Ms. Rothrock's shoulders. He then touched her left leg just above the knee. Ms. Rothrock pushed back against the right side of the car, and continued to talk about issues and family. The Senator drove her to her apartment, where he dropped her off.

After this incident, Ms. Rothrock did not babysit again for the Packwoods, and she took care not to place herself in a position where she would be alone with Senator Packwood.

Corroborating Witnesses

The staff has obtained affidavits from two witnesses, Ms. Rothrock's mother, and her roommate at the time, who stated that Ms. Rothrock told them that Senator Packwood had kissed her, or made an advance, while she was babysitting for the Senator's children. Ms. Rothrock's mother recalls that her daughter told her that she had babysat for the Packwoods, and that he had given her a kiss on the porch; she was upset by the incident. Her roommate recalls that she told her either that evening or the next day that the Senator had made passes involving inappropriate touching or kissing, either at his house, or in the car on the way home. Another witness recalled that in the spring or summer of 1992, but before the allegations became public, Ms. Rothrock told her that Senator Packwood had grabbed her and made an advance to her after she babysat for him. Georgie Packwood recalled that Ms. Rothrock babysat for them at least once, but that at the time, they had only one child. She could not recall any details, but believed that at the time that Ms. Rothrock babysat for them, the Senator's eyesight was still good enough that he would drive their babysitters home.

Senator Packwood's Response

Senator Packwood remembered Ms. Rothrock as a friend of persons in his office; she was in his office frequently to visit. He vaguely recalled that she might have applied for a job in his office.

Senator Packwood recalled that Ms. Rothrock babysat at least once for him and his wife, although because she made reference to babysitting for two children, it would have had to happen after 1971, when they adopted their second child. He could not recall if she babysat for them more than once. With respect to the one instance that he recalled, the Senator did not remember the event that he and his wife attended, how Ms. Rothrock got to their house, or when he and his wife returned home. He did recall that while his wife waited in the car to take Ms. Rothrock home, he went inside the house. Ms. Rothrock had her shoes off, and she could not find them. He helped her look for them; he did not remember where they found them. He stated that he then put his arms around Ms. Rothrock and gave her a kiss, and she put her arms around his neck and kissed him very "ful-somely." He did not recall where in his house that this took place. He described the kiss as romantic, although he could not recall if it was a french kiss; he said that she responded in kind—she put her arms around him, held her lips to his, and made no effort to get away. He did not recall if they had any conversa-tion. Nor did he recall if this was the first time he had kissed Ms. Rothrock in this fashion. He could not recall that Ms. Rothrock had ever given him any indication that she would be interested in this sort of a kiss, or what prompted him to kiss her that evening, nor did he recall speaking to her afterwards about the kiss. Senator Packwood saw Ms. Rothrock at a wedding in 1982. In the mid-1970's, they also arranged to have dinner together in Seattle or Tacoma as he passed through on his way to Portland, but they had to cancel.

Findings

Senate Ethics Counsel finds that the incident as alleged by Ms. Rothrock in fact occurred. Although her recollection of the number of children she babysat may be inaccurate, her account is corroborated by three witnesses to whom she related the incident, two of whom she told shortly after it occurred. Senator Packwood testified that he recalled kissing Ms. Rothrock after she babysat for him and his wife, although he portrays Ms. Rothrock as a willing participant; he also testified that he did not drive her home. However, both Ms. Rothrock's mother and her roommate at the time recall her distress at the incident, and her description of the advances as unwanted. Senate Ethics Counsel finds this corroborating evidence persuasive, and finds that the incident occurred as described by Ms. Rothrock.

Senate Ethics Counsel finds that Senator Packwood's conduct in this instance fits a pattern of conduct that reflects an abuse of his position of authority, a pattern of conduct that constitutes improper conduct reflecting upon the Senate.

JULIE WILLIAMSON

Testimony of Julie Williamson

In late 1967 or early 1968, Julie Williamson worked as Senator Packwood's Clatsop County campaign chairperson. In September,

1968, after her husband was transferred to Portland, she began working on Senator Packwood's general election campaign, running a phone bank. In January, 1969, she was hired as a member of his Senate staff. About six or eight weeks after she started, she was asked to staff a dinner the Senator was hosting for the Portland press corps at a local restaurant called Burt Lee's. Not knowing that staff spouses were generally not invited to such events, she invited her husband to attend. When her husband arrived at the dinner, Senator Packwood appeared displeased, and seated him at the far end of the table. He seated Ms. Williamson next to him at the head of the table, and two or three times during dinner he reached over and patted her on the leg. After dinner, Ms. Williamson, her husband, and Senator Packwood sat in a booth in the bar and talked. When Ms. Williamson's husband got up to go to the bathroom, Senator Packwood fell over Ms. Williamson, and gave her a big kiss on the side of the face. She pushed him off.

On a Thursday afternoon about 2:00 p.m. later that spring in 1969, shortly before the annual Dorchester conference, an annual Oregon Republican event founded by the Senator, Ms. Williamson was working alone in the office. As she talked on the phone in the front office, Senator Packwood came in, walked around the desk and behind Ms. Williamson, and kissed her on the back of the neck. She finished her call, turned to him, and told him never to do that again. She walked into the back office, and Senator Packwood followed her. Ms. Williamson became worried, and tried to get around the Senator to get out of the office; he tried to grab her, and she moved around the office to try to get away from him. Finally, he grabbed her; when she tried to kick him in the shins, he stood on her feet. He grabbed her ponytail with his left hand, pulled her head back forcefully, and gave her a big wet kiss, with his tongue in her mouth. She did not smell or taste any alcohol. With his right hand, he reached up under her skirt and grabbed the edge of her panty girdle and tried to pull it down. She struggled, got away from him, and ran into the front office. He stalked out past her, paused at the threshold to the hallway, and told her, "If not today, someday," and left.

Ms. Williamson called a friend, Ann Elias, and asked if she could come over to her apartment, because something terrible had just happened. At the time, Ms. Elias was the office manager for Senator Packwood's 1968 campaign committee, and her husband was the campaign manager. Ms. Williamson locked up the office and went to Ms. Elias's apartment; they talked for some time, with Ms. Williamson telling Ms. Elias what had happened, and Ms. Williamson then went home.

The next weekend, Ms. Williamson and her husband attended the Dorchester conference. Ms. Williamson spoke to Senator Packwood only once, as she sat in a bar next to his wife, Georgie. He slid up on the bar stool next to Ms. Williamson, and whispered in her ear, "Don't tell your husband, and don't quit your job," and then walked off.

The following Monday, Ms. Williamson told Roy Sampsel, Senator Packwood's driver about what had happened. Mr. Sampsel told her, in effect, "Don't take it personally, the Senator's just like that." She also told Senator Packwood's administrative assistant about the incident.[34]

---

[34] In a letter to Senator Packwood dated November 19, 1992, which Senator Packwood forwarded to the *Post*, the administrative assistant states that he does not recall the staff member telling him about the incident; he also confirmed this in an interview with the staff. A diary entry and a memo provided to the Committee by Senator Packwood indicate that this individual did tell Senator Packwood that he had heard from others that Senator Packwood had tried to "screw" the staff member. Senator Packwood testified that the individual had used that term not in a sexual sense, but in the sense that he had made a pass at her.

About two weeks later, Ms. Williamson picked the Senator up at the Multnomah Athletic Club, to drive him to the Civic Auditorium for an appearance. When Senator Packwood got in the car, she angrily confronted him about the incident, and asked him what it was that he had thought was going to happen the other day. She asked, in effect, whether he thought they were just going to have at it on the office floor. He responded, "I suppose you're one of the ones who want a motel." Senator Packwood appeared to be angry that Ms. Williamson had confronted him. He got out of the car at the Auditorium, delivered a speech for the Girl Scout cookie drive, and got back in the car. She drove him back to the Multnomah Athletic Club, and he got out, slammed the front door, retrieved his package of Girl Scout cookies from the back seat, and left. That was the last time she spoke with the Senator. She quit her job shortly thereafter, although she did not have another job at the time. With her typing and secretarial skills, she was able to get a job fairly quickly with a Portland law firm, although she had to take a cut in pay.

Corroborating Witnesses

The staff interviewed eight witnesses who recall that Ms. Williamson told them in the late 1960's or early 1970's about an incident that had occurred involving Senator Packwood. Their recollections of their conversations with Ms. Williamson vary as to the details they recall; five, including her husband at the time, recall that Ms. Williamson told him or her that Senator Packwood had "attacked" her, or tried to take her clothes off; four of these witnesses recall that Ms. Williamson was very upset by the incident. A sixth witness recalls that Ms. Williamson told him that she had left Senator Packwood's office because of an incident involving sexual harassment,[35] and the other two witnesses recall that Ms. Williamson told them that Senator Packwood had made a "pass" at her.[36]

A ninth witness recalls that Ms. Williamson told him in 1992, shortly before the allegations became public, that Senator Packwood had grabbed her and kissed her, and tried to pull her girdle off.

The staff also deposed Ann Elias, the friend to whom Ms. Williamson spoke immediately after the incident. Ms. Elias is a long-time friend of Senator Packwood's. Shortly before the *Washington Post* story was published, Ms. Elias wrote a statement at Senator Packwood's request, in which she opined that Ms. Williamson was interested in a "romantic" relationship with Senator Packwood. At her deposition, Ms. Elias testified that Ms. Williamson had come to her apartment one afternoon in early 1969, and told her that Senator Packwood had kissed her. She testified that Ms. Williamson had not told her anything about Senator Packwood standing on her toes, pulling at her clothes, or pulling her ponytail.[37] She testified that Ms. Williamson was "titillated" by the incident, although she could not point to anything to support that opinion. She testified that Ms. Williamson discussed with her the possibility of a relationship with the Senator, and wondered if she should tell her husband about the incident.

[35] This witness's spouse recalls that when asked why she left Senator Packwood's office, Ms. Williamson made vague comments indicating that "something" had happened.

[36] One witness did not believe Ms. Williamson when she told her about the "pass." The other witness recalled that Ms. Williamson told her that Senator Packwood had made a "pass" at her, and had chased her, but she did not recall the incident as being as serious as Ms. Williamson now alleges, and she did not think that Ms. Williamson seemed agitated or upset at the time.

[37] Ms. Elias claimed that Ms. Williamson did not wear her hair in a ponytail at the time, and that her hair was not even long enough to tie back.

According to Ms. Elias, Ms. Williamson has been telling this story on the "cocktail circuit" for years; she suggested that the story has gotten better with each telling.[38]

Senator Packwood's Response

Senator Packwood recalled that he first met Ms. Williamson in late 1959 or 1960 when he worked as an attorney in private practice; Ms. Williamson was a legal secretary at a different firm in the same building. She worked as a volunteer on his campaign in 1962. During his 1968 campaign, she acted as his Clatsop County campaign chair. After her husband was transferred back to Portland, she worked in his campaign headquarters until the fall of 1968, when he hired her onto his Senate staff. He did not recall her position or duties, the size of his staff, or the size or layout of his office at the time. He did recall that part of Ms. Williamson's duties would have been to answer phones, type, and act as a receptionist, although he did not recall where she sat in the office.

Senator Packwood described Ms. Williamson as having short, close blond hair. He recalled that she was a very good county chair, and a good headquarters worker, but he did not recall what type of employee she was while she was on his Senate staff.

---

[38] Although Ms. Elias, Elaine Franklin, and Senator Packwood himself all testified that Ms. Williamson had been telling her story on the "cocktail circuit," the staff was unable to find anyone, other than Ms. Elias who claimed to have actually heard Ms. Williamson telling her story" in social settings over the years, or who could verify that it had "grown" with the retelling. In addition, Senator Packwood's diary entries indicate that Ms. Elias was uncomfortable with the statement she prepared for Senator Packwood, specifically that she was torn between her loyalty to Senator Packwood and her desire to tell the truth. The entries indicate that she was "buoyed up" by Jack Faust, a friend of Senator Packwood's, who convinced her that Ms. Williamson had been telling her story on the "cocktail circuit" over the years, and that it had grown as it was retold.

Senator Packwood did not recall the dinner at Burt Lee's that Ms. Williamson referred to, or any other dinner that she staffed for him, or that she and her husband attended. He did not recall anything about this incident described by Ms. Williamson.[39]

Senator Packwood had no recollection of the incident described by Ms. Williamson as taking place shortly before the Dorchester conference in 1969, in which Ms. Williamson claims that Senator Packwood grabbed her, pulled her ponytail, kissed her, and tried to take off her girdle. Senator Packwood stated that Ms. Williamson had very short hair at the time, and that she did not have a pony tail. He provided photographs of Ms. Williamson taken at his campaign headquarters in the fall of 1968, before the election.[40]

Senator Packwood recalled nothing about the incident described by Ms. Williamson as taking place at the Dorchester conference.

Senator Packwood did recall that on a weekend day, Ms. Williamson had driven him to a Girl Scout function, possibly the cookie drive kickoff. He did not recall why she was driving him that day, but he believed that she was driving her car. He recalled that the two of them talked about the possibility of having an affair, and that Ms. Williamson asked where they would do that. He told her they could do it in the office, and she responded that she could not possibly do that. He jokingly responded that he supposed they could use a motel. Senator

---

[39] Senator Packwood's diary indicates that on February 10 1969, he hosted a dinner at Burt Lee's for the media.

[40] These pictures show Ms. Williamson from the front, with short, wispy hair. One witness has stated that at the time of the incident in the spring of 1969, or shortly thereafter, Ms. Williamson did indeed wear her hair in a ponytail. She describes her as having fine hair that she was trying to grow long, which she pulled back in a short ponytail. Another witness stated that as of late 1968 and early 1969, Ms. Williamson had short stringy hair that she pulled back from her face with bobbypins; as it grew longer, she pulled it back in a ponytail.

Packwood could not recall if this was the first time they had discussed the possibility of having an affair, nor could he recall who brought up the subject. He did not recall ever discussing this subject with Ms. Williamson again. He could not recall any physical contact between the two of them before this conversation. He did not recall what they were doing at the time the conversation took place, if anyone else was in the car at the time, whether the conversation took place as they drove to the Girl Scout event or afterwards, or where Ms. Williamson took him after the Girl Scout event.[41]

Senator Packwood recalled that Ms. Williamson left his employ in late spring of 1969. He did not recall why she quit, or whether she had another job at the time.

Senator Packwood stated that he had heard from others in the past, he did not know when or from whom, that Ms. Williamson had made a passing comment to the effect that he had made a pass at her. It was possible that Ann Elias had told him about the incident sometime before he talked to her about it in May, 1992.

Senator Packwood testified that he had called his former driver, Roy Sampsel, because he had read a story in the paper wherein Ms. Williamson claimed to have told her coworkers about the incident in his office. He stated that Mr. Sampsel told him that Ms. Williamson used to talk to him about her terribly unhappy marriage, and specifically that she wanted to have an affair with Senator Packwood. She asked Mr. Sampsel if she should do so. Several weeks before the Dorchester conference, she told Mr. Sampsel that Senator Packwood had hugged her, and asked Mr. Sampsel if she should go to the conference. Mr. Sampsel told the Senator that Ms. Williamson was in a "dither."

[41] Senator Packwood's diaries have an entry dated Saturday, April 5, 1969, which reflects that he attended a Girl Scout event. It does not reflect that Ms. Williamson drove him, or any conversation about an affair.

He told the Senator that he advised Ms. Williamson against having an affair with the Senator.

Mr. Sampsel was contacted by the staff shortly after Senator Packwood gave this testimony. He provided a sworn affidavit stating that in 1969, shortly before the Dorchester conference, Ms. Williamson told him that Senator Packwood had hugged her and made a pass at her in the office. Mr. Sampsel believed that Ms. Williamson told him about this the same day it happened, or the next day. They talked about this incident more than once. Mr. Sampsel told Ms. Williamson that the situation could not be allowed to get out of hand, because of the political implications for Senator Packwood. He did not tell Senator Packwood what Ms. Williamson had said. He described Senator Packwood as a flirter, and stated that he had had general conversations with him about his tendency to be overly flirtatious.

Mr. Sampsel stated that Ms. Williamson liked Senator Packwood a lot. At the time, she was not getting along with her husband. But she never told him that she wanted to have an affair with Senator Packwood, nor did he ever tell Senator Packwood that Ms. Williamson wanted to have an affair with him. Senator Packwood never indicated that he was interested in having an affair with Ms. Williamson. Although Ms. Williamson was outgoing, perky, and a flirt herself, he saw no indication that she was interested in a sexual relationship with the Senator.

Mr. Sampsel stated that about three months before he was contacted by Committee staff, Senator Packwood called him, and said that he was under a little heat, and needed to see what Mr. Sampsel knew. He asked if Mr. Sampsel recalled Ms. Williamson telling him about the version of the incident that appeared in the paper. Mr. Sampsel told the Senator that he did not recall Ms. Williamson describing the incident as graphically or in as much detail as the version that appeared in the newspaper.

In his appearance before the Committee, Senator Packwood stated that he did not recall the incident, but that he denied that it happened as described by Ms. Williamson. He based this denial on the fact that several persons claim that Ms. Williamson told them of the incident at the time, but she did not tell them about details such as him standing on her toes, pulling her hair, or attempting to pull down her undergarments.

Findings

Senate Ethics Counsel finds that the incident as alleged by Ms. Williamson in fact occurred. Although it occurred many years ago, Ms. Williamson has a vivid recollection of the incident. Additionally, several witnesses clearly recall that Ms. Williamson told them about the incident, including her distress at the incident, in some detail, shortly after it happened.

Senator Packwood has testified that he does not recall the incident described by Ms. Williamson. At the same time, however, he has denied that the incident occurred *as she now describes it*. His basis for this denial is his conclusion that Ms. Williamson has embellished upon the incident, because several persons have stated that she told them of the incident at the time, but that she did not provide the details that she has now given to the Committee. Leaving aside the fact that Senator Packwood seems to be conceding that *something* happened, the fact that Ms. Williamson did not share all of the details of the incident with some of these witnesses does not mean that they did not occur. In addition, there are several indications in Senator Packwood's diary, and from testimony from one of Senator Packwood's closest friends, that one of these witnesses may have lied about her recollection of conversations with the staff member about the incident.

Senator Packwood has also suggested that even if he did make advances to Ms. Williamson, they were welcomed, because she wanted to have an affair with him. He testified that they talked after the incident about having an affair (although he could not recall the details of the conversation), and that she told his driver that she wanted to have an affair with the Senator. Senator Packwood's driver has specifically denied that Ms. Williamson ever told him that she wanted to have an affair with the Senator. Senator Packwood's recollection of the conversation with Ms. Williamson after the incident is not inconsistent with Ms. Williamson's recollection, and is not persuasive evidence that the incident as alleged by Ms. Williamson was welcomed.

Senate Ethics Counsel finds that Senator Packwood's conduct in this instance fits a pattern of conduct that reflects an abuse of his position of authority, a pattern of conduct that constitutes improper conduct reflecting upon the Senate.

ADDITIONAL FINDINGS

Senator Packwood has testified that until he entered a treatment program in late 1992, he had significant problems with alcohol: he drank often and heavily, and he suffered blackouts. He considers himself to be an alcoholic. Senator Packwood has offered this testimony not as an excuse for his actions, but perhaps as an explanation.

Counsel notes that several of the incidents occurred in the morning, and that Senator Packwood testified he did not drink in the morning. Several occurred in the afternoon during office hours. In only a few instances was there any indication that Senator Packwood could have been intoxicated at the time of the incident. Senate Ethics Counsel finds that in each of the incidents alleged, regardless of his state of sobriety at the time of any given incident, Senator Packwood is responsible for his actions.

Senate Ethics Counsel finds that these incidents, taken collectively, reflect a pattern of abuse by Senator Packwood of his position of power over women who were in a subordinate position, either as his employees, as Senate employees, prospective employees, campaign workers, or persons whose livelihood prevented them from effectively protesting or seeking redress for his actions. These women were not on an equal footing with Senator Packwood, and he took advantage of that disparity to visit upon them uninvited and unwelcome sexual advances, some of which constituted serious assaultive behavior, but all of which constituted an abuse of his position of power and authority as a United States Senator.

Senate Ethics Counsel does not accept the notion that this type of conduct at one time was not viewed as improper, and that Senator Packwood is being punished for actions that were acceptable at the time. It has never been acceptable conduct to force unwanted physical attentions on another. Moreover, Senator Packwood's conduct is exacerbated by the fact that the incidents occurred with persons who were effectively powerless to protest in the face of his position as a United States Senator.

Senate Ethics Counsel finds that Senator Packwood's conduct, spanning a period of more than twenty years, constitutes a pattern of abuse of his position of power and authority, and is improper conduct reflecting upon the United States Senate.

During his appearance before the Committee in June 1995, Senator Packwood was asked to assess whether his conduct would reflect upon the Senate, if the alleged conduct actually happened, in only those cases which he had testified he did not recall.

Q: (by Senator Dorgan) . . . I guess my question was: If it happened, is it, in your judgment, behavior that brings discredit upon the Senate?

A: If it happened—and of course this is always—if it happened and it became public, it brings discredit on the Senate. If it happened and it doesn't become public, does that not bring discredit on the Senate? It doesn't make the incident any better or worse, but is the discredit the publicity of it?

Senate Ethics Counsel rejects any suggestion that such conduct may not reflect discredit upon the Senate, if it remains undiscovered or unpublicized. It is the behavior which is discrediting, and it is no less so if only its victims know of it.

Senate Ethics Counsel notes that there are no time limitations on the Senate's authority to discipline Members. Some of the incidents occurred twenty-five years ago. But these incidents cannot be considered in isolation. Counsel finds that all of the incidents, taken collectively, constitute a pattern of abuse by Senator Packwood, and improper conduct. Counsel notes that the age of any particular incident is appropriately considered, not in a determination of whether the incident was part of a pattern, but in a determination of the appropriate sanction to be imposed upon Senator Packwood with respect to the pattern of improper conduct.

5

Evidence Regarding the Allegations
of Altering Evidence

SUMMARY AND OVERVIEW OF THE EVIDENCE

SENATOR PACKWOOD'S DIARIES comprise over 8,000 pages of single-spaced entries for virtually every day since 1969, including weekends and vacations. They set out minute details of his life since 1969, from security briefings by the White House, to meetings with constituents, lobbyists and other senators, to detailed descriptions of meals and social occasions.

Senator Packwood dictated his diaries, first on dictation belts, and later on audiotapes, which were transcribed by Cathy Cormack, who was his personal secretary from 1969 to 1981, when she went to work for the Republican Senatorial Campaign Committee. While Ms. Cormack worked for the Republican Senatorial Campaign Committee, she continued to type the diaries, and received a modest reimbursement from Senate funds. When she left the Committee in 1983, she continued to type Senator Packwood's diaries, for which services she was paid by Senator Packwood's campaign committee.

NOTE: (For a detailed explanation of events leading up to the Committee's review of the Senator's diaries, see discussion in the Procedural Background section.)

Results of Comparison of Tape to Transcript

In view of Ms. Cormack's testimony in December, 1993 about changes made by Senator Packwood to tapes which she was transcribing, it was necessary to compare the transcripts which she typed from tapes altered by Senator Packwood with transcripts prepared from the original unchanged tapes to determine if there were any differences. The staff compared the transcripts prepared from the original unchanged audiotapes to the "Cormack" transcripts for 1989 through 1993, in order to determine if there were entries on the audiotape that had been left out of the Cormack transcripts, if there were entries on the audiotape that had been changed in the Cormack transcripts, or if there were passages on the Cormack transcripts that that were not on the audiotape.

As the staff compared the transcripts prepared from the original unchanged audiotapes to the Cormack transcripts for 1992 and 1993, it discovered numerous differences between them. These differences fell into three broad categories:[1]

a. Large portions of the audiotape that were completely missing from the Cormack transcripts;
b. Numerous instances, especially in the last half of 1993, where entries from the audiotape appeared on the Cormack transcripts, but were heavily reworded;
c. Many instances where entries related to the Committee's inquiry or arguably incriminating or embarassing entries on the audiotapes were missing from the Cormack transcripts, and different entries were substituted in their place.

The staff found no differences, other than minor differences that could be laid to transcriber error, between the audiotapes for 1989, 1990, and 1991, and the corresponding Cormack transcripts.

---

[1] Not included in these three categories are differences that are minor, and appear to be the result of transcriber error or editing, such as cleaning up grammar and taking out repetitions.

The Focus on Certain Changed Entries

Differences in these first two categories could arguably be attributed to the transcriber, particularly since Ms. Cormack had testified that she had been under intense time pressure to transcribe the audiotapes for 1992 and 1993, and that she had condensed many entries. Senate Ethics Counsel focused on the third category, and isolated entries related to the Committee's inquiry or where potentially incriminating or embarassing portions of the audiotapes were missing from the Cormack transcripts, and neutral or arguably exculpatory entries were substituted in the Cormack transcripts.

The entries in this third category fall into several groups:

a. Entries dealing with the Committee's inquiry into alleged sexual misconduct and witness intimidation;

b. Entries indicating Senator Packwood's knowledge of, and possible involvement with, independent expenditures made on his behalf during his 1992 campaign;

c. Entries discussing Senator Packwood's possible use of office staff or facilities for campaign purposes;

d. Entries dealing with the Oregon Citizens Alliance (OCA), which had accused Senator Packwood of making a "deal" during the 1992 senatorial campaign, that the OCA would not run a candidate against him in return for promises by him;

e. Entries referring to contributions to Senator Packwood's legal defense fund.

Once these entries were isolated, the staff questioned both Cathy Cormack and Senator Packwood to determine who was responsible for making the changes.

Brief Summary of Senator Packwood's Response

For the most part, Senator Packwood took responsibility for the deletions from the audiotape where there were corresponding substitutions in the Cormack transcripts. He testified that he began making changes to his untranscribed diary tapes in January 1993, and through the spring of 1993, after his attorneys requested that he provide them with excerpts from his 1992 diaries that might deal with the issue of witness intimidation.[2] He stated that he was fearful that his diaries would be leaked to the press from his attorneys' offices, and he knew that there were entries in the diaries that he did not want to appear in public. As the Senator listened to the audiotapes to find the portions relating to possible witness intimidation to provide to his lawyers, he believes that he made notes about the location of passages he might later want to delete. After a January 1993 trip to Oregon and the intense media attention that was focused on him, his fear of leaks intensified.

Through the spring of 1993, while he reviewed his diary tapes for 1992 looking for the excerpts requested by his attorneys, and for other entries that might be helpful to his attorneys, Senator Packwood also deleted certain potentially embarassing passages from the audiotapes, and in many cases, substituted different passages, more from a compulsion to fill up the space on the tape than anything else.

Senator Packwood was not concerned about leaks from his 1993 diary audiotapes at this time, as his attorneys had not

---

[2] James Fitzpatrick, one of Senator Packwood's attorneys at Arnold & Porter, testified that he could not recall making any request for copies of Senator Packwood's diary pages, per se. Rather, Senator Packwood was requested to and did provide his lawyers with a broad range of information to assist them in representing him, including his recollection, memoranda, clippings, and summaries of or excerpts from his diaries.

requested them. Thus, during the spring of 1993, as he reviewed his diaries for previous years (including his 1992 audiotapes) for information that would be helpful to his attorneys, and at the same time many changes to his 1992 audiotapes to delete embarassing references, Senator Packwood continued to dictate contemporaneous entries with no effort to monitor his dictation to exclude embarassing or damaging entries.

Sometime later that summer, in late July or early August, 1993, Senator Packwood's attorneys asked that he get the rest of his audiotapes transcribed.[3] Fearing that the 1993 diaries would now be leaked to the press through his attorneys' offices, Senator Packwood went through these tapes and again deleted entries that might prove embarassing to himself or others if they got to the press. In many cases, he also substituted different entries on the tape, again, more out of a compulsion to fill the space on the tape than for any other reason.[4]

After dropping off all of the outstanding audiotapes to his transcriber, Cathy Cormack, in early August 1993, Senator Packwood took all of his previously transcribed diaries, from 1991 going back to 1969, home with him during the August 1993 recess, where he reviewed them for information that might be helpful to his attorneys. However, despite the fact that he was fearful that the press would obtain all of his diaries, he made no

---

[3] Mr. Fitzpatrick testified that he could not specifically recall asking Senator Packwood to get the rest of his diaries transcribed. Steven Sacks, another attorney at Arnold & Porter, after consulting with Senator Packwood's current attorneys, represented that no one who worked on Senator Packwood's matter at Arnold & Porter could recall when this request was made, but that July or August 1993 sounded "about right."

[4] In one instance, Senator Packwood deleted an entry that would be very embarassing to him and one of his staff members if it became public, but substituted in its place an entry that also would have been very embarassing to a different staff member if it became public.

changes to any of these transcripts to delete entries that would prove embarassing to himself or others if obtained by the press. Senator Packwood testified that he felt no need to excise embarassing entries from his 1969–1991 diaries, because he was selecting pages from these years to give to his attorneys.

After he returned from the recess, Senator Packwood asked Ms. Cormack to give him the audiotapes back, as he had neglected to make a copy for himself of the changed 1993 audiotapes that he had given to her before the recess.[5] Ms. Cormack recalled that Senator Packwood told her he wanted the audiotapes back because of the possibility that there might be a subpoena; Senator Packwood did not recall that conversation, although he thought it was possible he might have mentioned the word "subpoena" to her in a different conversation. Both now recall that event taking place sometime in September 1993. Senator Packwood returned the tapes to Ms. Cormack within about a week.

Again, during this time when he was changing prior tapes to remove embarassing entries, Senator Packwood continued to dictate contemporaneous entries with no effort to monitor the content of those entries. He made changes to one of those tapes, covering August and possibly part of September 1993, as soon as he was finished dictating it, and before he gave it to Ms. Cormack to type.

Senator Packwood delivered all of his diaries that had been transcribed to date to his attorneys on October 7, 1993, shortly after his first deposition was interrupted so that the Committee could review the diaries.[6] Ms. Cormack continued to work on

---

[5] Senator Packwood testified that when he changed the 1992 and 1993 tapes, he made a duplicate of the original tape, and made the changes on the duplicate. He then made a copy of this changed tape, which he gave to Ms. Cormack to type. When she completed typing the tape, she destroyed hers, and he destroyed his.

[6] These diaries cover 1969 through January of 1992.

the untranscribed audiotapes for 1992 and 1993, and Senator Packwood provided his attorneys with transcripts as they were finished.[7] Because she was in a rush to complete the diaries, Ms. Cormack skipped over, with Senator Packwood's approval, passages that she deemed to be unimportant, dealing with things such as squash games with fellow Senators, food, stereo equipment, music, and movies.

Senator Packwood made some changes to his diary tape covering August 1993. He testified that he made no changes to September entries, but he did change some October entries after Ms. Cormack had typed them, marking up the pages and giving Ms. Cormack instructions on what changes he wanted made. Although some of these changes were made after his deposition was interrupted, he testified that he felt free to edit entries which were made after the deposition was interrupted. With respect to any entries he changed after he received the Committee's subpoena, he testified that he did not feel that the subpoena prevented him from editing his diaries as they were typed and he saw them for the first time. Senator Packwood also testified that it was possible he may have made changes to transcript pages for dates prior to his deposition, after his deposition was interrupted and after he received the Committee's subpoena. Senator Packwood also testified that as Ms. Cormack completed the transcription of tapes after his October 1993 deposition was interrupted, and after he received the Committee's subpoena, he continued to destroy the corresponding tapes.[8]

---

[7] Senator Packwood did not inform his attorneys that the transcripts he was delivering to them for 1992 and 1993 had been typed by Ms. Cormack from the altered tape, and not from the original, contemporaneous tape.

[8] A letter from Senator Packwood's attorneys to the Committee, dated October 20, 1993, indicates that approximately half of 1992 was typed after that date. This is consistent with Ms. Cormack's testimony in which she indicated that during mid to late October, she was really pushing to get the diaries transcribed.

Senator Packwood's attorneys were not aware that he kept original, backup tapes for his diaries.[9] They learned of the existence of these tapes on the evening of November 21, 1993, and the tapes were delivered to them by Senator Packwood on November 22. That same day, Arnold & Porter terminated their representation of Senator Packwood.

TESTIMONY AND EVIDENCE

Testimony by Cathy Cormack

Ms. Cormack's deposition was taken a total of three times. It was taken in November 1993 to determine how she was paid for her transcription of the diaries. After she provided an affidavit to the Committee on December 10, 1993 (after having reviewed her deposition), indicating that some of the tapes she typed had been changed, her deposition was taken again in December 1993. Once the staff had had the chance to compare the transcripts she typed for Senator Packwood with the original unchanged tapes, her deposition was taken again in December 1994.

Historical Transcription of the Diaries

Ms. Cormack testified that she had transcribed the diaries while she was a member of Senator Packwood's personal Senate office staff, from 1969 to 1981. She was not paid any additional compensation, over and above her Senate salary, for transcribing the diaries. She then moved to the Republican Senatorial Campaign Committee, where she was paid a small sum from the Sen-

---

[9] For the years 1989, 1990, and 1991, these backup tapes would correspond with the written transcript. For 1992 and 1993, however, they would not, because they were typed from a duplicate of the original, on which Senator Packwood had made the changes. This duplicate was destroyed after it was transcribed.

ate Disbursing Office to transcribe Senator Packwood's diaries. Shortly after she left the Campaign Committee, she began to be paid to transcribe the diaries from Senator Packwood's campaign fund. She has never been paid for transcribing the diaries from the personal funds of Senator Packwood. Senator Packwood also provided her with an IBM Selectric typewriter, which she used to type the diaries, and dictation equipment.

Ms. Cormack testified that over the last 23 years or so, Senator Packwood has dictated his diaries on audiotapes, which he periodically provided to her, either delivering them to her, or having her pick them up from his office. For a short time, she lived with her husband in California and later Japan, and received tapes from Senator Packwood by mail. Once she returned the typed transcripts to Senator Packwood, she would erase the audiotape, and either return it to Senator Packwood, or throw it away. A single tape, both sides, covered, on the average, about three weeks to one month of entries, and took about eight to ten hours to type. Ms. Cormack usually received six to eight tapes at a time from Senator Packwood and typically was about a year or so behind in her transcription. Except for the time period when she lived in California and Japan, when she knew that she received copies of the tapes, Ms. Cormack assumed that she was working from the original diary tapes. As she completed typing a tape, she would erase it and throw it away. Sometime after her first deposition in December 1993, she had occasion to see Senator Packwood, and he commented to her that he had the original diary tapes, and she had received copies to transcribe.

Early 1993 Request to Transcribe Excerpts

Ms. Cormack testified that in January 1993, Senator Packwood asked her to transcribe diary entries surrounding the 1992 general election out of sequence, as he had been asked for these entries by his attorneys. At that point, she was about a year and half behind in her transcription, and although she may have been working on the backlog for earlier in 1992, she had not yet reached the time period surrounding the 1992 election. She had some tapes from early 1992 in her possession, but she did not know specifically which ones; in any event, she did not have the tape or tapes that covered the general election in the fall. She believed that at this time, she had a backlog of 1991 and 1992 tapes going up to, but not including, the period around the general election of 1992. Senator Packwood provided her with the tape or tapes for this time period, along with a separate tape that contained instructions on which entries she should type. She typed the entries as instructed within a few days, and provided them to Senator Packwood. Because these entries were being typed out of sequence, she did not number the pages.[10] Because she knew she would have to come back eventually and type the entire tape, she did not erase it, but she did not recall if she kept the tape or gave it back to Senator Packwood. Ms. Cormack then resumed her normal transcription of the diaries.

August 1993 Delivery of Tapes

Ms. Cormack may have done a small amount of transcribing between January 1993, when she finished the 1992 election entries out of sequence, and August of 1993, for tapes for late 1991 and early 1992. In August 1993, about the time of the August recess, she received six to eight tapes for transcription from Senator Packwood, covering the first half of 1993, up to

[10] Indeed, the Cormack transcripts received by the Committee are not numbered after January 1992.

the August recess. She also had a backlog of tapes going back to the first part of 1992, which she had not yet transcribed. Altogether, including the tapes that Senator Packwood brought to her in August, she had about 20 tapes to be transcribed.

Request to Bring Transcription Up To Date

Ms. Cormack did not begin working on the backlog right away, as she left for vacation in August. She did some work on the tapes when she returned from vacation. Sometime in early September, around Labor Day, or possibly later in September or October, Senator Packwood asked her to get caught up to date in typing the transcripts. Ms. Cormack described this as the "crunch time," when she was working hard to get the diaries up to date.

In the past, Ms. Cormack had typed the transcripts virtually verbatim, correcting a name if she knew it was incorrect, cleaning up grammar, leaving out repetitions, but never intentionally deleting, paraphrasing, or adding material as she typed. In contrast, during this "crunch time," Ms. Cormack asked Senator Packwood if she could "boil down" passages having to do with things such as stereo equipment, squash games, and meals; Senator Packwood assented. However, she *never* added information to the transcript that was not on the tape (with one exception relating to Senator Packwood's purchase of a condominium where she acted as his real estate agent).

During this time period, that is, early September 1993, Senator Packwood telephoned her and asked her to type three or four months in 1992 out of sequence. She did so, and got the transcripts to him right away, as she assumed that he was meeting with his attorneys. She then returned to typing the backlog of tapes.

Senator Packwood Asks For The Return of the Tapes

Sometime in early September, but before mid-October, Senator Packwood called her, and asked her to give all of the tapes back.[11] He said something to her about "the possibility of a subpoena," and that "he didn't want me to have anything in my possession if that were to occur." She believed that he was trying to protect her. Within the week, however, Senator Packwood returned the tapes to her for transcription, bringing them back in two batches.

Discovery of Changes to Tapes

Because Senator Packwood had requested that she bring the transcription up to date, Ms. Cormack spent the next several weeks working feverishly to transcribe all of the tapes. In transcribing those tapes, Ms. Cormack sensed that there may have been some alterations: there were differences in the sound on the tape, differences in background noises, differences in volume, breaks in the dialogue. She could not recall how many tapes sounded "irregular," but she recalled that it was more than one. At one point, Ms. Cormack asked Senator Packwood if he was making changes in the tapes, and he confirmed that he was, either verbally or by his body language.

In addition, Ms. Cormack testified that during mid to late October, when she was really "crunching" to catch up on the backlog of tapes, Senator Packwood occasionally asked her to

[11] In her second deposition, taken in December 1993, Ms. Cormack could not place the time of this conversation any more precisely than sometime between early September and mid to late October, although she was asked several times, and in several different ways, to do so. When her deposition was taken again a year later, in December 1994, Ms. Cormack recalled that this conversation took place in early September.

make changes in the text of diary entries she had recently typed. More specifically, Ms. Cormack testified as follows:

Q: You mentioned that he would ask you to make changes in text. Were these changes made after you had typed the transcript?

A: In some cases.

Q: Tell us how that happened.

A: Some times he would mark up a piece of paper and I would redo it. And on a few occasions, he would dictate, on a separate tape, a few changes, and give me the pages.

Q: What time period did this occur in, that he was asking you to make—

A: All within the same—I'm sorry, go ahead.

Q: What time period did that occur in where Senator Packwood was asking you to make changes in the text?

A: This would be mostly, as best I can recall, within the fifteen—mid-to-late October period, when I was crunching to get this done.

Q: Of 1993?

A: Yes.

Ms. Cormack does not recall Senator Packwood asking her to do this often, but it happened more than once. She recalled that the changes mostly covered the backlogged months, that is, a good part of 1992 and 1993. Ms. Cormack testified that historically, there were less than five occasions when Senator Packwood had asked her to make changes on diary pages that had already been typed.

Ms. Cormack did not recall the precise dates that were affected by Senator Packwood's alterations, but she did know that the general time period would have included a large portion of 1992, and a large portion of 1993, as those were the tapes that she had backlogged at the time. She could not remember if any of the changes to the typed pages were for years earlier than 1992.

Completion of the Tapes

Ms. Cormack finished transcribing a good portion of the backlogged tapes by mid to late October 1993. Once every other day during this September–October 1993 time period or as she completed a fair amount of transcript, Ms. Cormack would deliver it to Senator Packwood. In addition to her backlog of tapes, and the six or eight tapes that Senator Packwood gave her around the time of the August recess, she also received one or two tapes during the "crunch time" covering August, September, October, and early November 1993, which she completed transcribing in early November.[12] Ms. Cormack recalled that all told, she completed the backlog in a time frame of about six weeks.

Comparison of Tape to Transcript

For those entries where material had been added to the Cormack transcript that did not appear on the audiotape, Ms. Cormack was asked to compare the transcript that the Committee had prepared from the audiotape to the corresponding Cormack transcript. In general, she testified that although in a few of these instances, she may have skipped over some of the material that was on the tape, in no instance did she add any of the information that was on the Cormack transcript, but not on the corresponding audiotape (with the one exception about the Senator's condominium that was mentioned earlier).

[12] Ms. Cormack did not complete her transcription until at least November 9, 1993, which was the last date she transcribed.

Testimony by Senator Packwood
Mechanics of Diary Keeping

Senator Packwood testified that he began keeping his diaries in 1969, first dictating entries on dictabelts or disks, and later switching to audiotapes. Cathy Cormack, who had been his legislative and legal secretary in Oregon, and his secretary in the Senate, and was his longstanding friend and confidant, transcribed his diaries for him from the beginning, up until the fall of 1993.[13] This task was not part of her official duties, and she was not paid anything over her Senate salary for typing his diaries while she was on his Senate staff. When she left his staff and went to work for the National Republican Senatorial Committee, she continued to transcribe the diaries, and she remained on the Senate payroll, not for transcribing the diaries, but because she still did some official Senate work for Senator Packwood.[14] After Ms. Cormack left the Campaign Committee, she continued to transcribe the diaries, and she was paid from Senator Packwood's campaign funds. No one but Ms. Cormack transcribed the diaries, and she is the only person, other than the Senator, who ever saw the diaries up until the Committee's inquiry.

Senator Packwood testified that he used tapes that were sixty minutes on each side, and on average, one tape would hold about a half month's worth of diary entries. He typically made a duplicate of the tape for Ms. Cormack, which she erased when she was finished typing.[15] Ms. Cormack was traditionally about a year and

---

[13] The diaries themselves strongly suggest that Senator Packwood and Ms. Cormack had a very close personal relationship.

[14] Senator Packwood testified that Ms. Cormack did "modest" work for him, although he could not recall what it was. In contrast, Ms. Cormack testified that after she left Senator Packwood's staff, she performed *no* work for him other than transcribing his diaries.

[15] Senator Packwood testified that he sometimes made another duplicate, if for some reason he thought the original tape might be of poor quality.

a half behind in her transcription. Periodically, either she picked up tapes from him, or he dropped them off to her. Ms. Cormack would not necessarily run out of tapes, but if she were down to, say, her last two tapes, she would ask him for more tapes. Upon receiving the typed transcripts from Ms. Cormack, Senator Packwood organized them in binders, and kept them in his safe. He and Cathy Cormack are the only persons who have the combination to this safe. He seldom reviewed the typed transcripts or made changes to them; occasionally, maybe ten or twenty times over the course of over twenty years, he edited them.[16]

Accuracy and Reliability of the Diaries

Senator Packwood was questioned at length at his January 1995 deposition about the accuracy and reliability of the entries in his diaries. Senator Packwood stated that he did not always dictate his diaries daily, and he often went two or three days before dictating entries. He stated that he usually dictated entries the next morning, but very seldom on the same day, using his daily calendar of events as a reference guide.[17]

> Q: And from that schedule, and your memory, you would dictate the diary entries?
> A: Yeah, memory, I suppose real or imagined.

Senator Packwood stated that one purpose of keeping the diary was as therapy—that while some people talked to psychologists, he talked to his diary. He described it as a potpourri of everything, with perhaps no single purpose. He stated that there

[16] Ms. Cormack testified that historically, Senator Packwood asked her to make changes in the typed transcript no more than five times.

[17] This was a calendar in which Senator Packwood recorded his activities for the day after the fact, as opposed to a calendar which listed his appointments.

was no overwhelming reason he kept his diary, and that perhaps it was just the result of compulsion.

Senator Packwood stated that it was sometimes his intent to create an accurate record of events, and sometimes he simply gave voice to thoughts that he would put in narrative form, even though a conversation may not have happened in that fashion. During his 1995 deposition, Senator Packwood stated that he would attribute statements to someone if he thought that was what the person felt, even if that person had not said it at the time. He might record a detailed conversation that never took place.

Q: Was it your intention to create an accurate record of events?

A: Well, sometimes yes. Sometimes I say I would give voice to conversations or thoughts and I would put them in narrative form, even though they may not have happened in that fashion.

Q: Let me ask the question this way: Was it your intent in recording diary material to create a nonfictional account?

A: No, not necessarily. I don't mean to say I was writing a novel with it, and I don't mean to say I was lying to it, but to the extent—have you ever seen this situation? In fact, I've seen memos to this effect. You have a meeting with somebody, some lobbyist comes in. And then the memo later—you get a memo later that's given to you of the lobbyist's report of the meeting. And it doesn't comport with what you remember at all. And you may say to your staff, God, did I say that? And they'll say well, no, or maybe, Senator, unfortunately you did, and the lobbyist thought totally different than you remembered it. So I may put things in there that others would totally remember as different.

Q: But the point that I'm trying to get to is you would, would you not, attempt to honestly record what you saw and heard and your impressions of what took place at a meeting? You weren't trying to record something that didn't happen, were you?

A: No—I don't mean no as the answer. As I said, I would put things into narrative form, conversations, between Jones and Smith or Packwood and Green that I would picture I would have thought or they might have thought that might not have been said.

Senator Packwood was asked about his intent in making entries in his diary:

Q: But it was your intent, was it not, to capture the essence of what happened and to express that accurately?

A: Again, I don't think I can answer the question any better than I have.

Q: I'm not sure that the question has been answered here quite yet. And that is a very simple question. Were you, in dictating the diary entries, making an effort, or was it your intent to record events or your impression of events accurately, truthfully and honestly?

A: Well, again, I'll try to answer it once more. I could put into it conversations, because I dictate in a conversational narrative form that may not have taken place.

Q: But were you trying accurately and truthfully to capture the substance of what took place?

A: I'm saying the conversation may not have taken place.

Q: But as you dictated the conversation, which didn't take place, were you—was it your intent to have that conversation reflect the substance of what happened?

[Witness conferred with counsel.]

MR. MUSE: Ask that question again, because you combine a whole lot with those questions.

Q: Was it your intention in dictating entries to the diary and relating an event or a meeting to capture and express accurately the substance of what took place at that meeting or event?

A: Well, it would depend on my mood, the day, the thoughts, the pressure. But I'll say once more, I might relate a conversation that did not take place on a subject that did not take place.

Although he indicated that his diary was generally an accurate record of time and place and events, Senator Packwood recollected numerous times that the substance of the entries in his diaries may not be accurate, and that conversations reflected therein may or may not have occurred, or if they did, they may or may not have been recounted accurately. Nor could he provide the Committee with any way to determine which entries were accurate and which were not.

Senator Packwood was referred to an entry from his diary for July 21, 1989, which reads as follows:

Had an interview with somebody doing a book on Tom McCall. I did both of these at   's request. This guy is well documented in his facts and the one embarassing thing he had was that allegation that I met with Tom at his beach place in 1972 to try to talk Tom into running against   .
I don't know what my diary may show on this. I don't recall. I denied that the conversation had ever taken place and now in my life I don't recall if it took place or not. My diary would be a better testimony to that, dictated at the time.

Senator Packwood was questioned as follows:

Q: You appeared to recognize as early as 1989 that your diary was a reliable reference or resource document, did you not, Senator?

A: Mr. Baird, sometimes it's accurate. Sometimes it's inaccurate. Sometimes it's fact. Sometimes it's fiction. It is not a reliable document. I didn't prepare it for anybody to rely upon it. I never reviewed it. I never edited it. I never saw it again. It is no—I didn't draft it. It's not like doing a letter or a memo. It cannot be regarded as accurate.

Q: How does one tell which parts of it are accurate and which parts are not?

A: I have no idea how you tell. I have no idea how a historian tells. As a matter of fact, I think this particular meeting with Tom McCall is recounted in his book, too. Whether he sees it the same way I saw it or not, I don't know.

Q: Why would you have thought it was a reliable source to look to here to find out whether or not you had had a conversation?

A: I've already indicated that if somebody else has a different view of something that appears in here, I'd be inclined to defer to how they heard it rather than I heard it. Am I going to say this diary is always accurate? It clearly is not always accurate. Am I going to say it's always inaccurate? It is clearly not always inaccurate. It clearly was not always inaccurate. If I were to look up something and find it would I say boy, that's it, that must be exactly it, no. Nor could anybody say that about anything they put in a diary that they've never seen before, never cleaned up, never edited.

Q: But you think it is better evidence of whether or not something happened than your current recollection, do you not?

A: I'm not even going to say that.

Q: Isn't that what you said in July 1989?

A: Mr. Baird, I am not going to say that this diary is exactly accurate or can be an accurate recollection. We can read Tom McCall's book as to what he said about it.

Q: You wouldn't say today what you said in 1989, that it might be a better testimony as to what happened than your current memory?

A: All I'm going to say is that—this statement was never intended to be relied upon by anybody for anything, and I'm not going to say—I'm not going to have you say and attempt to put in this record that everything in this diary is accurate.

Q: That's not what I'm attempting to say. I'm asking you the question: Would you say today what you said at the time of this diary entry, and that is that the diary is better testimony than your present recollection?

A: Not necessarily.

Finally, Senator Packwood testified in January 1995 that it was not necessarily his intent to create a nonfictional account, but he was not lying to his diary. He stated that he may have put things in that others would recall as totally different.

In contrast, Senator Packwood testified at his earlier deposition in October 1993 that he would frequently refer back to his diary as a "resource document," that he would use it as a "memory tool," that he had a "strong sense of history," and that he might use it to write a book. When he was asked about this earlier testimony at his deposition in January 1995, Senator Packwood testified that he did not find his diary nearly as accurate a reference tool as staff memos. He stated that in the past, he would look back at it from time to time, but that he finally quit, because it did not give him the answer to his questions. He stated that the diaries were not a reliable reference tool, and to call them a resource tool, as he had in his previous deposition, would be overstated. He stated that information was missing from the diary, and that there were inaccurate entries, including just about any conversation that was recounted. Senator Packwood stated that on occasion, he would put things in his diary that just did not happen.

Senator Packwood confirmed that he has left his diaries in trust to the Oregon Historical Society, although he could not recall the purpose of the trust. He stated that the diary has some historical value, although the Historical Society will not be able to determine which parts of it have value, and which do not.

Senator Packwood appeared to have used his diaries to refresh his recollection about matters to which he testified during his deposition.[18] For example, his testimony at his first deposition in 1993 about the incident with Ms. Hutton in 1980, and about a subsequent occasion when Ms. Hutton joined the road crew in Oregon for pizza and charades, both of which occurred in 1980, very closely tracks diary entries for these occasions.[19] Senator Packwood also testified at his first deposition in 1993 about a conversation with Ms. Williamson in 1969 when she drove him to a Girl Scout function; the Girl Scout function itself is reflected

---

[18] Senator Packwood confirmed, as do his diary entries, that he reviewed his diaries before his 1993 deposition.

[19] Senator Packwood testified that he had an independent recollection of these occasions.

in his diary.[20] Senator Packwood testified at his first (1993) and second (1995) depositions about the details of the evening of the alleged incident with Complainant 1 in 1990, in which Complainant 1 claims that Senator Packwood kissed her when they returned to his office after an informal staff party at the Irish Times. Senator Packwood stated that he "pieced together" the details of that evening by talking to others who were present at the Irish Times, as he had had too much to drink to remember anything about the evening. Yet the diary entry for this evening sets out in some detail the events that took place at the Irish Times and the substance of his conversations with Complainant 1, details that would be known only to Complainant 1 and Senator Packwood. Senator Packwood would not say how he obtained the information that appeared in that entry, whether it was accurate, or whether he intended it to be accurate at the time he recorded it.

In his earlier 1993 deposition, Senator Packwood recounted an evening in October 1991 when Complainant 1 was in his office, and the two of them were drinking wine. He described how he got up from his desk, and Complainant 1 gave him a big hug, a kiss on the lips, and told him "You are wonderful," to which he responded "Warts and all." This incident, and the conversation, are recounted in his diary word for word as he testified before the Committee at his 1993 deposition. When asked at his second (1995) deposition if this entry was an accurate recounting of what happened that evening, Senator Packwood testified that he could not say if it was accurate, and that he could not guarantee if the conversation occurred as set out in the diary. When it was

[20] Senator Packwood testified that he had an independent recollection of this 1969 event and conversation.

149

pointed out to him that his testimony at his previous deposition matched exactly the conversation as set out in the diary entry, he stated that he could not guarantee that his previous testimony before the Committee was accurate.[21] Finally, he stated that his testimony during his earlier deposition was accurate, and conceded that the diary entry itself was also accurate.

As a general matter, Senator Packwood emphasized that the diaries are different in kind from things such as memos and letters, which may go through many revisions to achieve accuracy. His diaries, in contrast, were dictated, sometimes "on the fly," and transcribed and thereafter almost never reviewed, and were not intended to be relied upon for any specific purpose.

Alteration of Diary Tapes

REVIEW OF DIARIES IN LATE 1992, EARLY 1993

Senator Packwood testified that in December 1992 or early January 1993, his attorneys asked him to review his diaries for relevant passages having to do with the issue of intimidation of witnesses. He testified that as of early January 1993, he had all of the 1992 diary tapes in his possession, as Ms. Cormack had not caught up to that point in her transcription.[22] Senator Packwood listened to tapes covering from March to early June, and after Labor Day in 1992, and identified a period from October 20 to

---

[21] Senator Packwood also recounted this incident, and the conversation, word for word, in early November 1993 during debate on the Senate floor over the subpoena for his diaries.

[22] Ms. Cormack testified that at the time Senator Packwood asked her to type entries out of sequence, she had "some" tapes for 1992, possibly tapes going up to, but not covering the period surrounding the general election. Ms. Cormack also testified that when she typed the entries out of sequence for Senator Packwood in early January 1993, she did not number the pages. The Cormack transcripts are numbered up through the end of January 1992.

November 10 for Ms. Cormack to transcribe out of sequence. He recalled that he directed Ms. Cormack to type certain entries from this time period, although he did not recall exactly how he did so—that is, whether his instructions to her were written or on a separate tape, or were incorporated on the tape itself.

FEAR OF LEAKS TO THE PRESS

At the same time, as he listened in December 1992 to the audiotapes of the 1992 diary entries, Senator Packwood found entries that he did not want to get out of his hands. He started to become apprehensive at the prospect of turning any portions of his diaries over to his attorneys. While it was no secret that he kept diaries, and indeed news accounts had previously referred to his diaries, no one but he and Ms. Cormack had ever actually seen them. He feared that once they went to his attorneys and were out of his hands, they would almost certainly be leaked to the press. This fear was heightened when he returned to Oregon in January 1993, and he was met with protesters everywhere he went, at times fearing for his personal safety or the safety of his supporters. He believed that if the press obtained even a few paragraphs of his diary, they would be embarassing and harmful both to himself and to others who were mentioned in the diaries. Thus, in early 1993 as he searched for entries in 1992 to provide to his attorneys, he started making changes to the untranscribed tapes for 1992.

CHANGES MADE TO THE 1992 TAPES

Senator Packwood testified that starting in January 1993, he began to change his untranscribed 1992 tapes, to delete entries that could potentially be embarassing if obtained by the press. These entries included references to the Oregon Citizens Alliance (OCA), conversations with Committee Members about the Committee inquiry that he thought would suggest a "Republican conspiracy" to the press,[23] comments about his chief of staff, comments about women whose names had not been reported by the press in connection with the allegations of sexual misconduct, and anything that might have caused personal harm or adverse publicity to others. He also changed embarassing references to others, including some very descriptive sexual references. According to Senator Packwood, he changed anything that could get to the press and embarass his friends or other persons. He testified that this was a "catch as catch can" effort and he did not get everything.[24]

At his January 1995 deposition, Senator Packwood was asked about approximately forty (40) altered diary entries, most of which involved the deletion of information from the original tape and the substitution of new information.

Senator Packwood testified that he sometimes simply deleted entries, and sometimes deleted entries and substituted entries in their place. He stated that he had no particular reason for sometimes substituting entries in the place of entries he deleted other than his compulsion to fill up the space. These substitutions might be on the same subject matter as the deleted material, or they might be totally different. When shown one such entry where material was substituted, the Senator testified as follows:

Q: Why, Senator, did you feel that all these spaces on the tape that you were creating by eliminating passages had to be filled?

A: I can't answer that.

[23] About fifteen (15) entries concerning communications with Committee Members, mostly Senator McConnell, appeared to have been changed, some by deletion, others by deletion and substitution of new language.

[24] In fact, a review of the transcripts prepared from the 1992 and 1993 tapes shows that many entries which would have been highly embarassing were not changed.

MR. MUSE: You said "all." It wasn't all.

A: There's great gaps that are missing.

Q: Why did you feel that some of them had to be filled?

A: I don't know. Maybe it's just compulsive dictation. I have no answer to that.

Senator Packwood testified that his sole motivation in making these changes was to prevent the leak of potentially embarassing or politically damaging information to the press by way of his attorneys' office.[25]

Senator Packwood first stated that he finished making the changes to the 1992 tapes by the end of February 1993.[26] Although he stated that he could have changed his 1993 tapes during this same time, he testified that he did not know if it was going to be necessary, as his attorneys had not asked him to provide any transcripts for 1993. Indeed, after he provided his attorneys with the transcribed excerpts for October and November 1992, they did not ask him for any more transcripts, per se.[27]

At the same time that he was revising his diary tapes, up through May of 1993, Senator Packwood continued to pinpoint

[25] There is no evidence to suggest that any diary material was ever leaked by Senator Packwood's attorneys or their office.

[26] Later in his deposition, Senator Packwood stated that he finished making the changes to the 1992 tapes by the end of February or March, or in early April, 1993.

[27] Although Senator Packwood forwarded excerpts that he selected from his diaries to his attorneys through the spring of 1993, his attorneys did not ask him to turn over any portion of his diaries *in toto* until after the Committee specifically requested them in October 1993. The exception to this was the diaries for the October–November 1992 period which the Senator provided to his lawyers sometime in January 1993. The Senator testified that after he provided these diaries, his attorneys told him to stop transcribing his 1992–93 tapes.

relevant portions of his diaries for his attorneys, some of them referring to the women who had made allegations against him. If these entries were in portions that had already been transcribed (i.e., 1969–1991) he would provide a copy of the entry to his attorneys. If the entries had not yet been transcribed, he would send a memo to his attorneys, describing the nature of the entry. Senator Packwood testified that he sent these excerpts in the form of memoranda, which might quote from a diary entry, or might refer to or summarize a diary entry.[28]

During the same time that he was revising his diary tapes for 1992 to delete potentially embarassing or damaging information, Senator Packwood continued to dictate contemporaneous daily diary entries. Despite the fact that he was simultaneously deleting potentially embarassing or politically damaging entries from his 1992 tapes, Senator Packwood continued to dictate entries of the same character, entries he would then delete only months later. At his 1995 deposition, Senator Packwood testified that he did so out of compulsion, and that he could not change his long-standing style of dictation.

After you've dictated for twenty five years, you don't consciously think of that as you dictate. You don't say oh, better not do this, better not do this. It becomes sort of a stream of consciousness thinking.

During his June 1995 appearance before the Committee, the Senator added that since his attorneys had not requested any 1993 entries so he did not feel those entries would ever be requested by them.

---

[28] These memoranda were withheld from the Committee on the grounds of attorney-client and work-product privilege.

CHANGES TO THE 1993 TAPES

Senator Packwood assumed that he gave Ms. Cormack a fair amount of tapes to transcribe during the spring and summer of 1993, and thinks that she gave him more typed transcript during that same time period. Sometime in mid-summer, or early August of 1993, his attorneys told him that they wanted all of the 1992–1993 diaries transcribed. Realizing then that the transcripts made from the 1993 tapes could be going to his attorneys, Senator Packwood made changes to them along the same lines as he had changed his 1992 tapes.[29] Senator Packwood made these changes shortly before he left for the August recess in 1993. He then gave all of the tapes he had, including 1993 up-to-date, to Ms. Cormack to type.[30] He asked her if she could hurry up and get these tapes transcribed.

Again, at the same time, Senator Packwood continued to dictate contemporaneous diary entries of the same character that he was deleting from his previous tapes, out of compulsion and in keeping with his long-standing style of dictation, entries that he would go back and delete only weeks later. At his June 1995 appearance before the Committee, Senator Packwood testified as follows:

BY SENATOR MCCONNELL:

Q: So some time in the first quarter then of 1993, you were doing some deletions for what you viewed to be embarassing material?

A: Yes. I think I'd probably finished listening to the '92 tapes by late April, mid-April, early May, something like that.

---

[29] Senator Packwood also testified that he deleted entries in which he recorded unflattering comments about his attorneys, a friend, and his marriage counselor.

[30] Senator Packwood thought that Ms. Cormack had the 1992 tapes by this time.

Q: And then contemporaneously, you were continuing your practice of dictating?

A: Yes.

Q: And the continued practice of the dictating also included some embarassing material, did it not?

A: Yes.

Q: So you were dictating embarassing material contemporaneously while you were also deleting embarassing material retroactively?

A: Yes. So long as you understand my dictation habits. I'd been dictating this for 25 years and it's a stream of consciousness, pour everything into it, pour my heart into it, and I was not consciously, when I was dictating, think now should this be in there, should this be out. That thought wasn't in my mind. It's only in listening to it, and I was finding things, did I find things that I wanted to take out. Bear in mind, I was kind of hoping, by the time I'd gotten a few months into '93, that they weren't going to ask for anything more, they'd gotten what they wanted, and I was sending them along these memos from '69, '80, or wherever I'd find some reference to a complainant, a copy of the diary page that related to that complainant. And they weren't asking for anything more what I'd call en masse, so when I finished the '92, I kind of crossed my fingers and hoped they wouldn't ask for anything more, wouldn't ask for all of '92 or '93.

Senator Packwood testified that in order to make the changes to his diary tapes for 1992 and 1993, he made a duplicate copy of the tape, and then made the changes to the duplicate. He then copied the duplicate, giving one copy of the changed tape to Ms. Cormack, and keeping one for himself. When Ms. Cormack finished typing any given tape, he destroyed his corresponding copy. He retained the original, unchanged tape.

SENATOR PACKWOOD RETURNS TO OREGON OVER RECESS

After giving Ms. Cormack his up-to-date diary tapes to transcribe shortly after the start of the August recess, Senator Packwood then returned to Oregon for the recess, taking with him all of his transcribed diaries from 1969 through 1991. Senator Packwood testified at his deposition that he was concerned that the press would obtain his diaries, and he took all of his diary transcripts with him to Oregon. A review of the transcripts prior to February 1992 (as far back as 1989) shows that although there are many entries that would seem to be embarassing or potentially damaging if leaked to the press, and which fall within the same categories as the changes that Senator Packwood made to the 1992 and 1993 tapes, *no* changes were made to these (1989–1991) transcripts.

In his appearance before the Committee, Senator Packwood testified that he felt no need to delete embarassing information from his previously transcribed diaries (pre-1992) because he was providing to his attorneys only selected excerpts from these pre-1992 transcripts, and there was no fear that other pre-1992 transcripts would be requested by his attorneys.

Although Senator Packwood testified that his goal was to remove entries that would be embarassing to himself or others, in substituting one entry in place of an embarassing entry he had deleted, Senator Packwood discussed details of the sex life of one of his long-time staffers. When he was asked why he added an entry that was of the same character as those he was deleting, and how he thought the press might have reacted to that information, Senator Packwood stated that he should not have done it, the entry was factually incorrect, and that in any event it was obviously in jest.[31] In fact, an entry in Senator Packwood's diary dated June 11, 1992 describes an occasion when he had dinner with this long-time staffer, and she related to him the information that appears in this later, substituted entry.

SENATOR PACKWOOD ASKS MS. CORMACK TO RETURN THE 1992 AND 1993 TAPES

Very shortly after the end of the 1993 August recess, within a day or two of when he came back to town, Senator Packwood asked Ms. Cormack to give him back the untranscribed tapes. He testified that he only wanted the 1993 tapes, but Ms. Cormack gave him all of the tapes, including the 1992 tapes, in a bag. Senator Packwood stated that in his rush to make the changes to the 1993 tapes, he had not made a copy of the changed tapes for himself, and he wanted the 1993 tapes back so he could make a copy in case something happened to Ms. Cormack's copy before she had a chance to transcribe it. He copied the 1993 tapes, and returned all of the tapes to Ms. Cormack within days, in two separate batches.

Senator Packwood testified that he did not use the word "subpoena" during whatever conversation he had with Ms. Cormack about returning the tapes. He stated that it was possible that he may have used that word during other conversations with her, although he had no reason to use that word, because he was not thinking of the possibility of a subpoena for his diaries.

During August and September, Senator Packwood continued to dictate his diaries, making at least one entry in August that he deleted after the tape was transcribed.

---

[31] At his appearance before the Committee, Senator Packwood repeated that he had made up this entry about his long-time staffer, and that she had never told him about her private life as reflected in the substituted entry.

At the time he asked Ms. Cormack to return the tapes, Senator Packwood was somewhat perturbed that Ms. Cormack had done so little on transcribing the diaries. He again asked her to hurry up, and she typed transcripts during September and October 1993, giving him back pages she had transcribed from the tapes every few days during that time. Senator Packwood delivered these diary pages to his attorneys as Ms. Cormack finished them.[32] As to the status of her efforts at this time, Senator Packwood testified as follows at his January 1995 deposition:

Q: Over what period of time did she complete her typing of the '92 and '93 tapes?
A: September and October.
Q: Both months, both full months?
A: Yeah. You know, she's got a full-time job, so she can't type all day long. There are a lot of tapes, but she finally got at it. . . .

Senator Packwood was aware that as she typed the diaries during September and October 1993, Ms. Cormack left out a lot of material. She had told him that in order to finish quickly, she needed to consolidate entries, and leave certain things out—for example, entries dealing with his stereo equipment, and his squash games with another Senator. Senator Packwood indicated to her that she could do so, and he left it to her judgment as to what should be left out of the transcript.

Senator Packwood testified that in response to requests from his attorneys, during the fall of 1993, as Ms. Cormack sought to

---

[32] According to Senator Packwood's attorneys, they received the first set of transcripts from Senator Packwood on October 7, 1993. These transcripts, which were numbered, covered 1969 through January 1992.

get the transcripts up to date, he asked her to type certain entries out of sequence.

Senator Packwood testified that as Ms. Cormack finished typing portions of the diary, he erased the corresponding tape in his possession, which was a duplicate of the changed tape used by Ms. Cormack. Ms. Cormack also erased her copy of the changed tape. Senator Packwood kept the original tape, even though it did not correspond to the diary transcript, because he had historically kept the "original."

Sometime during the fall of 1993, Ms. Cormack asked Senator Packwood, in an offhand sort of way, if he had made changes to the diary tapes. He confirmed to her, either with words or a smile, that he had done so.

CHANGES TO OCTOBER AND EARLY NOVEMBER 1993 TAPES

Senator Packwood testified that he made no changes to his diary tapes for September, October, or November 1993.[33] However, Senator Packwood testified that during late October and possibly early November, as the pages of the diary covering late October and early November were typed by Ms. Cormack, he would make changes to them and have Ms. Cormack retype the pages. He believes, but cannot be sure, that all of these types of changes were made only to entries for October 1993.[34] Senator Packwood stated that he may have given Ms. Cormack instructions on how

[33] It appears that the tapes that Senator Packwood gave Ms. Cormack in early August prior to departure on recess would have brought him up to August 5, since there is a tape which ends August 5, 1993 and a new tape which begins on August 5, 1993 and extends well into the August recess. The tape that covers the August time period after August 5, which was not included in the group given to Ms. Cormack because it was still in use by Senator Packwood, had several entries that were changed. Senator Packwood testified that he made these changes when he was finished with that tape, after he came back from recess.

[34] There are only two entries in September, October, and November 1993 where a passage appearing on the tape does not appear on the Cormack transcript, and a different passage is substituted. These entries appear on October 9 and 10, 1993.

to retype these pages on a separate tape, with the entries under-
lined in yellow on the pages; he did not recall actually redictating
the tapes. Senator Packwood continued to make changes to diary
entries dictated after his receipt of the Committee's subpoena, as
he did not feel that the subpoena affected his right to edit his
post-subpoena diaries as they rolled off the press.

Senator Packwood also continued to erase his copy of the
changed diary tape, even after receipt of the Committee's subpoena. In this regard, he testified at his 1995 deposition as follows:

Q: So the tapes—when she transcribed during October after
   delivery of the subpoena, any tapes that she transcribed
   during that period, you would have erased the duplicate
   of them?

A: Yes, I think so. I'm quite sure I probably did. To the
   extent the transcript is different than the tape, you can
   tell the original tape from the transcript. The transcript
   would be the changed one that she typed from which she
   erased and I erased and the original would be whatever is
   in the transcript you have now is [sic].

The Senator went on to testify as follows:

Q: Now, as she was completing tapes after your deposition
   and your awareness that the Committee was reviewing
   them, after she was completing those, and bringing the
   transcripts to you, were you then continuing to destroy
   your copy of the tape which she had transcribed?

A: Yes.

Q: And you presume she was destroying her copy also?

A: That's what she had done for 15 years. I didn't think
   about it. It's just what she had been doing over the years.
   The thought didn't enter my mind, let's put it that way.

Q: And just so I'm clear on this, there was never any instruction, either after the deposition when you understood that the Committee staff was going to be reviewing transcripts being prepared by Cathy Cormack or even later after there had been a subpoena, there was never any instruction from you to Cathy Cormack to say Cathy, don't destroy the tapes as as you make the transcripts?

A: I don't recall discussing with her at all.

Q: And, in fact, as you have said, you yourself destroyed those tapes during that time period as she returned the transcripts to you?

MR. MUSE: I think he followed the same practice with them. And also, there are some copies that are still with Judge Starr that are to be delivered to you that cover this category.

Q: Other than the copies that are with Judge Starr [Note: which turned out to be duplicate unchanged originals], all the other tapes that matched the changed tapes which you had given Cathy Cormack, you destroyed those?

A: That's correct.

As Senator McConnell pointed out at Senator Packwood's June 1995 appearance before the Committee, the destruction of the altered tape by Senator Packwood makes it difficult to determine which changes were made by whom:

BY SENATOR MCCONNELL:

Q: You noted that Ms. Cormack made 99 percent of the changes to the diary material in the '92–'93 period?

A: Yes, I think 99 percent would be it, I might be off a percent but I think that would be a fair—by changes, I mean including deletions. . . .

Q: I guess my question is, without a copy of the altered diary tapes, how can we tell who is responsible for which deletions or alterations? In other words, how do we—these particular altered tapes, we don't have, is that correct?

A: That's correct.

At his January 1995 deposition, Senator Packwood testified as follows:

Q: And at the time now, once you had received the subpoena and Arnold & Porter had, Cathy Cormack was still processing some of these tapes, was she not?

MR. MUSE: Typing transcripts.

BY MR. BAIRD:

Q: Yes typing transcripts from tapes which you had previously given her.

A: Yes, . . . certainly she was typing what had come out in October and November. She was typing things after the subpoena. I don't know at what stage she finished the backlog.

Q: But she continued typing throughout the rest of October and on into November?

A: Into early November, yeah.

Q: Once you got the subpoena, did you go to Cathy Cormack and suggest any changes in her handling of the tapes which she had had?

A: No, I didn't.

Q: Because I think you have told us earlier that it's possible that during this time, she was still typing on 1992 or 1993 tapes, that that's possible?

A: She could have been because I remember there was a portion of '92 tapes. I think it's early on, February and March where I never found anything, and it wasn't of consequence to them. We'd get to it, but it wasn't as important to the lawyers I guess as some other period. She could have been into the first three or four months of '93 and not have done the first three or four months of '92 or something like that.

Q: But in any event, your process, that is Cathy Cormack typing the tape, sending the transcript to you and your then destroying the tape that related to that transcript—

A: My copy of that tape.

Q: —copy of that tape did not change after you received the Committee's subpoena; is that correct?

A: To the best of my knowledge, it did not because I would not have destroyed the tape until I got the transcript from Cathy in case something went wrong with her tape.

Q: So if, in fact, Cathy Cormack transcribed tapes covering the period of 1992 and returned that transcript to you after October 21 of '93, you would have destroyed the corresponding tape?

A: I think so. The reason I say I think so, there was some extra tapes left over that I may not have gotten—I think they're September, October and November and they appear to be around. And whether I just didn't get to it or not, by this time we're into a totally different issue of the law and whether you have a legal right to the diaries and that whole battle had started, but it was my normal practice, I think to get rid of them.

Senator Packwood testified that sometime shortly after his deposition was interrupted in early October 1993, he delivered the entire typed transcript to his attorneys. Thereafter, as Ms. Cormack finished typing entries, he provided them to his attorneys. He did not, however, tell his attorneys that these transcripts had been typed from altered tapes. At his June 1995 appearance before the Committee he testified as follows on this point:

BY SENATOR BRYAN

Q. Did you at any time provide any diary information to your attorneys that had been changed—and I'm defining "change" as either a deletion, a substitution, or addition—without telling them that, look, I did change this from the original.

A. Yes. I'm sure that must have happened because they were getting these jumping-about portions of 92 and 93, many of which, or some of which had changes on them.

The testimony goes on to clarify that his attorneys were not told about any changes until after the Department of Justice subpoena of November 19, 1993.

In his appearance before the Committee, Senator Packwood testified that if the Committee had gotten up to 1992 in its review of his diaries, he would not have let the Committee review the altered transcripts, and he would have notified his attorneys that he had changed the tapes. However, even as the Committee staff was reviewing his already transcribed diaries during the second week of October, Ms. Cormack was typing the 1992 and 1993 transcripts *from the altered tapes,* as evidenced by the testimony below from the Senator's January 1995 deposition.

Q: Sometime that week after your deposition, you would have understood, though, that we were, in fact, after your attorneys had masked certain materials, that the Ethics Committee staff was reviewing your diaries beginning in 1969 and working our way back to the present, meanwhile Cathy Cormack is continuing to produce transcript for you; correct?

A: Yes.

Q: Did you understand that the Ethics Committee staff would also be reviewing the transcripts which Cathy Cormack was then preparing once those had been masked by your attorneys?

A: Assuming you had gotten to those, yes.

Q: In any event, you did not consider, I take it, once you knew that the Committee would be reviewing the transcript which was being produced by Cathy Cormack, you did not consider having her transcribe from the original as opposed to the changed?

A: No.

Q: When she was in this period after your deposition, she was typing from changed tapes?

A: Yes.

On October 20, 1993, Senator Packwood's attorneys informed the Committee that about half of the 1992 tapes had been typed, and would be available for review shortly, and that the rest of the tapes for 1992 were in the process of being typed and reviewed. Thus, it appears that at least some of the changed tapes covering 1992 and 1993 were typed after the Senator received the Committee's subpoena on October 21, 1993 and that those tapes were destroyed after that date.

SENATOR PACKWOOD REVIEWS TRANSCRIPTS FOR PASSAGES
REFLECTING CRIMINAL CONDUCT

Shortly after the floor debate over the subpoena for his diaries, when Senator Packwood became aware that the Committee was earmarking passages in his diaries dealing with potentially criminal conduct,[35] he retrieved his diary transcripts from his attorneys,[36] to look for any entries that might possibly relate to criminal conduct that would be within the Committee's jurisdiction. He returned the diaries to his attorneys within about a week.

Senator Packwood testified that his attorneys were not aware that he kept backup tapes for his diaries. In his appearance before the Committee, Senator Packwood testified that he told his attorneys about the backup tapes only *after* he received a subpoena from the Department of Justice on November 19, 1993. He stated that because the Department of Justice subpoena could concern criminal matters, he thought the Department of Justice would want the original tapes.[37]

WHY SENATOR PACKWOOD FELT FREE TO CHANGE HIS DIARIES

Senator Packwood testified at his January 1995 deposition that he provided his attorneys with relevant excerpts from his diaries, but that they never turned any of them over to the Committee in response to the document requests. Senator Packwood therefore concluded that the Committee did not have any right to them. He also testified that even after he received the Committee's subpoena, he never imagined that he could not go back and

[35] On the evening of November 1, 1993, after the first day of floor debate, the Senator, his attorneys, the Chairman and Vice Chairman, and staff counsel met to discuss a proposal by Senator Packwood for production of his diaries. Senator Packwood testified that this meeting was the first time he became aware of the nature of the potential criminal activity that the Committee was interested in. This precise information had been provided to Senator Packwood's attorneys by staff on October 18, 1993.

[36] Senator Packwood's diary indicates that he retrieved his diaries from his attorneys on October 31, 1993, which he confirmed at his deposition. He stated that at that time he took the volumes for 1989, 1990, and 1991.

[37] The Committee's subpoena, which Senator Packwood received almost a month earlier, specifically asked for *all* diaries, both tapes and transcripts for the period from November 1, 1989 to October 20, 1993.

edit his diaries as they were being transcribed by Ms. Cormack. In this regard, Senator Packwood testified as follows:

Q: We had talked just briefly about editing you might have done to transcripts which you are getting back during this period, and I think your lawyer, Mr. Stein, suggested that perhaps we should parse the time periods from before your deposition and after your deposition in terms of editing, and I want to focus on that just for a moment. You had said . . . that with respect to diary entries after the deposition, after you were aware that the Committee was reviewing the tape [sic], the transcripts being prepared by Cathy Cormack, I believe you had testified, had you not, that you still felt free to edit entries which were made after the deposition?

A: Yes. It never occurred to me that something that I dictate is forever frozen in time, and I can never edit it or make a change in it.

Q: How about for entries which occurred before the date of the deposition—

MR. MUSE: What's the question?

MR. BAIRD: I haven't asked it yet.

Q: For the time period of tapes which predated your deposition, when those were processed by Ms. Cormack and returned to you after the deposition, did you feel free to edit those transcripts?

MR. MUSE: Victor, you're asking him did he feel free, did he have consciousness of doing one thing or another or not doing one thing or another? The problem I have is you're asking him what was his mental state about those.

MR. BAIRD: Yes.

A: I didn't have a mental state one way or the other. They didn't come back, and I didn't consciously think to myself I can't change these or I can change these. It all kind of fluxes together so there was no thought.

Q: But I believe you told us it is possible you may have edited—

A: Yes, I may have.

Q: —some of those after you knew that the transcripts were going to be reviewed by the Ethics Committee staff?

A: I may have. Could I have? Yes. I'm sitting there with diary entries on my desk and my desk piled up and these transcripts are coming back from Cath and am I looking through them. Could I have looked at some, taken it back to her? I could have. I don't know if I did, but I could have.

Q: And let's go up to the point of the subpoena. Does the situation change any once you have the subpoena, or was that still—did the process remain the same, that is you could have changed the transcript that she had given you—had she given you any transcript, say, from 1992 that she had done after the subpoena had been served, that you might possibly have changed that and given it back to her to make further changes?

A: Again, I have no recollection. I could have, but I'm just trying—this is such a confusing period for me in addition to buying my townhouse at the same time or moving in. Yes, I could have.

At other times during his January 1995 deposition, Senator Packwood testified that while it was possible that he changed transcripts for entries which predated his October 1993 deposition after the deposition and after receiving the Committee's subpoena, he did not think that this had occurred.

Senator Packwood went on to testify at his January 1995 deposition that he did not intend to prevent the Committee from reviewing any information in either the original tapes or the previously transcribed transcripts. He reiterated that he was concerned about leaks to the press. He also testified that the Committee eventually received the original audiotapes.[38]

In his appearance before the Committee in June 1995, Senator Packwood testified, in response to questioning, that he relied on the advice of his attorneys in making changes to his diaries: because his attorneys had determined that the Committee was not entitled to his diaries, he felt free to do with them whatever he wished. However, Senator Packwood could not articulate precisely what his attorneys had told him on this issue. He repeatedly stated that he and his attorneys discussed and argued over what he *was* required to turn over to the Committee, but that there was little discussion about what he was not required to turn over. He did state, however, that the earliest that such discussions occurred—that is, about whether the Committee was entitled to his diaries—was after the Committee's document request of March 29, 1993, at least a full two months after he had been making changes to his diaries.

Also in his appearance before the Committee, Senator Packwood testified that at some stage he had gotten a letter from the Committee saying that the subpoena would only run to July 18, 1993, and to the extent he made any changes after he received that letter, he would have assumed that he could make

---

[38] Of course, the Committee did not have access to the original audiotapes until after the matter was litigated to the Supreme Court and Senator Packwood was ordered to produce them.

any changes that he wanted to entries dated after that date. In fact, the Committee did send Senator Packwood a letter, informing him that although the subpoena called for all diaries up to the date of the subpoena (October 20, 1993), if he wanted to voluntarily produce his diaries pursuant to a procedure similar to the original agreement, the cutoff date of the subpoena would be pushed back to July 18, 1993. However, this letter was not delivered until November 9, 1993, and so could not have been a factor in any changes made before that. And, according to the Senator, the only things he would have changed at that time would have been diary entries made after October 20, 1993.

Testimony of James Fitzpatrick

In order to confirm information provided by Senator Packwood at his deposition about requests that his attorneys had made for his diaries, and Senator Packwood's transmittal of diaries to his attorneys, the staff took the deposition of James Fitzpatrick of Arnold & Porter. Arnold & Porter represented Senator Packwood from late 1992 up until shortly before the hearing before Judge Jackson in December 1993; they terminated their representation on November 22, 1993. Also present at the deposition were Jacob Stein and Robert Muse, Senator Packwood's current attorneys, who were in attendance solely to raise objections, if necessary, to questions that implicated the attorney-client privilege. Mr. Fitzpatrick was represented by Stephen Sacks, an attorney at Arnold & Porter.

Mr. Fitzpatrick testified that Arnold & Porter began providing legal representation to Senator Packwood in the late fall of 1992, after the general election. This representation continued to November 22, 1993.

Requests for Information from Senator Packwood

Mr. Fitzpatrick testified that from the beginning, they were asking Senator Packwood to provide information and facts that might help them to prepare his defense. He does not specifically recall asking Senator Packwood to provide diary entries relating to allegations then under consideration, either sexual misconduct or intimidation of witnesses. Rather, they made requests for information from a broad variety of sources, and they received information from Senator Packwood from a broad variety of sources, including diary material, clippings, memoranda, and recollections.

The attorneys at Arnold & Porter were aware that Senator Packwood kept diaries. Along the way, they received material from him that either referred to or summarized the diaries, and in some instances contained specific excerpts from the diaries. Mr. Fitzpatrick did not know the precise date when they first received any memoranda containing excerpts or entries from the diaries, although it would have been sometime in 1993. Although he did not have an independent recollection of the particular date that any document was received from Senator Packwood, he stated that the privilege log provided to the Committee on August 3, 1993, would reflect any documents that they received from Senator Packwood, but which were withheld from the Committee on the grounds of privilege.[39]

Mr. Fitzpatrick did not recall any specific conversation directing the Senator to review his diaries to look for entries that might relate to the intimidation issue. As they tried to master the facts, they did ask the Senator for any information that might be relevant to the charges, instructing him broadly to provide infor-

---

[39] This privilege log identified memoranda, but it did not indicate in any way that the memoranda included diary excerpts or pages.

mation that would be helpful. There may have been a conversation dealing with diaries.

Among the materials that they received from Senator Packwood during the course of 1993, there were some references to the October to November 1992 time period, although he did not know when the particular memo discussing this time period was provided to them.

After some discussion among Senator Packwood's former and current attorneys, it was represented by Mr. Sacks that the first memorandum that was provided to Arnold & Porter, attaching diary entries or excerpts, was dated January 7, 1993, and that the entries covered the period of October to November 1992.

Mr. Fitzpatrick testified that some of the diary entries excerpted or discussed in the memoranda provided to them by Senator Packwood might have included the names of women who were making allegations of sexual misconduct against Senator Packwood, although he recalled that there was no reference in the diaries to any incident that had been alleged.

Failure to Provide Relevant Diary Entries to the Committee

Mr. Fitzpatrick was asked whether Arnold & Porter had provided any diary entries to the Committee in responding to the Committee's two document requests on behalf of Senator Packwood. He stated that they responded in good faith to the requests, supplying material that was responsive to the requests, and that any material that was called for that they did not produce was identified on the privilege log.[40] At different times in

---

[40] It is very clear, however, that the privilege log contains absolutely no reference to or mention of diaries.

his deposition, he stated that the diary entries that contained references to women who had made claims of sexual misconduct were both outside the scope of the Committee's request, and within the scope of the Committee's request, but subject to a privilege. He testified that to the extent that the material might have been responsive to the request, but protected by a privilege, it was noted on the privilege log. He would not concede that the fact that the privilege log sets out memoranda that incorporated diary entries means that Arnold & Porter made a judgment that the diary entries were within the scope of the Committee's request.

Mr. Fitzpatrick testified that not all of the 112 items identified on the privilege log related to diary excerpts, but they were a wide range of memoranda, some having nothing to do with the diaries.

Receipt of Diary Transcripts from Senator Packwood

On October 7, 1993, Arnold & Porter received from Senator Packwood a series of volumes in black notebooks, purporting to be the diaries from 1969 through part of 1992. They were kept locked in Arnold & Porter's offices. They reviewed the diaries, masked them for review by Committee staff, and provided them for review in the presence of an Arnold & Porter representative until the reviewing agreement broke down.

Mr. Fitzpatrick testified that Arnold & Porter continued to receive additional transcripts after October 7, 1993. Mr. Fitzpatrick believes that they then asked Senator Packwood to bring his diaries up to date for the Committee's review. After a discussion between Mr. Fitzpatrick, Mr. Sacks, Mr. Muse, and Mr. Stein, Mr. Sacks represented that Arnold & Porter requested that Senator Packwood transcribe his diaries some time in July or

August of 1993, as best as they could ascertain. However, Mr. Fitzpatrick himself could not recall asking Senator Packwood to have the remainder of his diaries transcribed at that time. Mr. Sacks represented that that was the recollection of one of the attorneys in the group who was in communication with the Senator's office: Dan Rezneck, Mike Korens, Leigh McAfee, and possibly others. He had no idea who specifically made such a request on any given date, but it "sounds right" to all of them that the request to have the 1992 and 1993 diaries transcribed was made in the July–August time period.[41]

Later in his deposition, Mr. Fitzpatrick testified that they received transcribed diary pages in addition to the material in the binders that they received on October 7, including entries from 1992, but he does not recall when they received those pages, or even whether they were received before or after Senator Packwood's deposition, or before or after the delivery of the binders on October 7. He does know that some time during the period after October 7, they received additional pages dealing with 1992 and 1993, although he could not give a precise date. But he could not recall if they got this material before or after they received the binders.

Mr. Sacks stated that the first diary information Arnold & Porter received was on October 7, which covered 1969 through part of 1992. Thereafter, additional information from the diaries was provided for the remainder of 1992 and portions of 1993.

---

[41] Senator Packwood had previously testified at his deposition that his attorneys asked him in late July or early August to have the rest of his diaries, i.e., the entries for 1992 and 1993, transcribed, and that it was this request that caused him to go back and change his 1993 diary tapes, out of fear that the transcribed diaries would be leaked from his attorneys' office if they should ever be provided to them.

Mr. Fitzpatrick recalled that all of the diary pages they received on October 7 were numbered, but he did not recall whether the pages received after that date were.[42]

On October 31, 1993, Senator Packwood took back the volumes for 1989 and 1990. On November 5, he returned these volumes, and took the volumes from 1991. On November 6, he returned the 1991 volumes, and took the 1992 volumes, which he returned on November 9.

Receipt of Diary Tapes from Senator Packwood

Arnold & Porter received the original tapes of the previously transcribed diaries on November 22, 1993. These tapes covered a time period starting in 1969, and going forward, although Mr. Fitzpatrick does not recall the end date of the tapes. It had been their understanding that the tapes of the transcribed diaries were destroyed; they first learned that such tapes existed on the evening of November 21. They received the tapes the next day, November 22, 1993, and terminated their representation of Senator Packwood.

Specific Entries From the Diary

For the most part, with some exceptions, the focus has been on those entries in the diaries where material that was on the audiotape did not appear on the Cormack transcript, and different entries were substituted in their place. This is the case for several reasons. First, there were a great number of entries on the audiotape that did not appear in the Cormack transcript that

---

[42] This indicates that Arnold & Porter received on this date the transcribed diaries up through the end of January 1992, as that is when the pages cease to be numbered. It also indicates that entries after January 1992 (other than the entries for November and December 1992 previously provided to them in January 1993) were *not* completed until after that date.

dealt with subjects which were not related to the Committee's inquiry, or did not involve conduct that would be subject to the Committee's jurisdiction.[43]

Additionally, it was just as likely that these entries had been left out by Cathy Cormack as she hurried to finish transcribing the diaries. Indeed, she testified that she did leave out a large number of entries that she considered unimportant.

Most importantly, with respect to those entries where material was *added* to the Cormack transcript in the place of material that had been on the audiotape, those changes had been made not by the transcriber, Ms. Cormack, but by Senator Packwood. There is a limited number of such entries, and many of them deal with information on the audiotape that relates to the Committee's inquiry, or that could possibly implicate Senator Packwood in misconduct within the Committee's jurisdiction.

Diary entries in the following categories are set out below, with the original audiotape version on the left, and the corresponding version from the transcript typed by Ms. Cormack from tapes altered by Senator Packwood on the right. The portions that are on the audiotape but were left out of the Cormack transcript are in italics, while the portions that are not on the audiotape, but were added to the transcript, are in bold letters.

- Entries dealing with the Committee's inquiry into allegations of sexual misconduct and intimidation;
- Entries dealing with campaign activity and use of Senator Packwood's Senate office for campaign purposes.

---

[43] Examples include lengthy discourses on food, music, movies, and Senator Packwood's relationships with and observations about various women.

Following these entries is also a summary of other entries that were changed by Senator Packwood, referring to his negotiations with the Oregon Citizens Alliance during his 1992 campaign; contacts with Committee members by Senator Packwood in regard to the inquiry; and entries relating to Senator Packwood's acceptance or solicitation of contributions by lobbyists to his legal defense fund.

Entries Dealing with the Committee's Inquiry into Allegations of Sexual Misconduct and Intimidation

AUDIOTAPE	CORMACK TRANSCRIPT

February 5, 1993

Elaine called, had a sad message. Channel 2 has said that five more women are willing to come forward to say they've been sexually abused by me or sexually harassed or something, including one in the early '90s. I said to Elaine, can't be employees if they are—these are five Oregon women. She said one of them could be [Complainant 1]. *I said well, I hope so, but we're going to take her hard.* She said you and I know it cannot be employees in the Oregon office in the '80s. *It could be [former staff member] from the '70s. I didn't say this to her, but it could.*

Elaine called with a sad message. Channel 2 has said that five more women are willing to come forward to say they have been sexually abused by me or harassed or something, including one in the early '80s. These are five women. I said, "It can't be employees." She said, "One could be [Complainant 1]." I said, **"Well, yes, but she's a habitual liar. We know that. We can prove that. That will surely blow down her testimony."** I said, "You and I know it cannot be employees in the office in the '80s.

At his deposition, Senator Packwood testified that Complainant 1 was a chronic troublemaker, who lied and fantasized, and could not be trusted, although he could not identify anyone on his staff who had made complaints about her, nor could he produce any records reflecting such complaints. Nor do his diaries reflect any such problems with Complainant 1, even though the Senator routinely and often harshly critiqued the performance of members of his staff.

The former staff member referred to in the audiotape, whose name does not appear in the Cormack transcript, appears to be someone the Senator thought could be a potential complainant. However, the Senator testified that it never would have occurred to him that this person could be a complainant.

The information substituted in the Cormack transcript serves to document the Senator's claims that Complainant 1 was a "habitual liar." It also leaves out any mention of a former staff member who it appears that Senator Packwood thought might be a potential complainant.

Senator Packwood guessed that he had deleted the information about the former staff member, because her name had never appeared in the press and he did not want to give the press another lead to chase down. He testified that this change had nothing to do with the Committee. While he was changing that, he thought that he would put in the truth about Complainant 1.

At his appearance before the Committee in June 1995, Senator Packwood was questioned about this alteration by Senator Bryan as follows:

BY SENATOR BRYAN
Q: But, Senator, my point is you knew that in February of
   1993. I mean, by your own statement you knew by

February 5th of 1993, that at least in your opinion she was, you know, not to be trusted and was a liar, but you didn't say that in the dictated portion of the audiotape. Sometime between February 5th 1993, and the later part of 1993—and you may be able to tell us when—you went back and changed that.

A: I am confused now.

Q: Well, February 5th 1993, you dictated the statement about her. Then, the Cormack transcript—

A: Okay. Cathy's is the one that said, "Well, yes, but she's an habitual liar. We know that." Is that—

Q: Yes. And that is the alteration. My point being, that doesn't seem to have anything to do with embarassment or protecting somebody from any sense of awkwardness. And the fact that it was made, Senator, just a few months after the original entry was dictated, at least raises a question as to what the motive was. You knew in February of 1993 that this was not a good and trusted employee. You have indicated that you found that out. And one would think that you would characterize that in your February 5th 1993 original audiotape. When you go back to make the change, you put this negative characterization in— which may be accurate; we don't know—but I mean that is a change that doesn't seem to fit in with the general rubric of embarassment, or trying to avoid hurt or harm to someone.

A: Well, first, as I indicated, when I took that one, one of my reasons was [Complainant 1] name being mentioned there who had never been in the press, and who for other reasons she would not want her name out. And at the time, I am simply dictating that, and—you give a preciseness to this that is not precise. I think you almost think that—again, I am not looking at something. I am listening to something—that with strict attention you hear every bit and you think to yourself every change you're going to make. Whether I not put in in the original transcript she's a liar, I didn't. I knew she was at the time. I'm not sure the fact that I failed to put it in is indicative of anything.

AUDIOTAPE	CORMACK TRANSCRIPT

February 12, 1993

This was the bad day. First, we discovered that Gina is going to have a press conference in Eugene. This is Gina Hutton, my 1980 campaign chair, who appeared in a story this week that I tried to kiss her. Then Lindy Paull called and said she wants to put out a statement to the Oregonian—that a statement she submitted said nothing about women's past sexual history, and she was quite adamant she doesn't want to be associated with that kind of attack, as she regards. She was pissed. She was so pissed, I think she may resign, and of course, she's a hot property and she'll do well. *Then I called Tim Lee, just to remind him not to talk to the press, and he said well, had called*	This was the bad day. First we discovered that Gina is going to have a press conference in Eugene. This is Gina Hutton, my 1980 campaign chair, who appeared in a story this week and said I tried to kiss her. Then Lindy Paull called and said she wants to put out a statement to the Oregonian that the statement she submitted said nothing about anyone's past sexual history and she was quite adamant. She doesn't want to be associated with that kind of attack, as she regards it. She was pissed, so pissed she may resign. She's a hot property. She'll do well. **Lindy really is deceptive. She is sweet on appearance. She is tough of mind but God, is she brilliant with tax law. She can**

again, and   *always*
shuts off the calls and
says he doesn't want to talk to any
paper that's got a vendetta against
Senator Packwood, and
says it's not a vendetta against Sen-
ator Packwood. It's against Elaine.

stand toe to toe with anybody
on the Joint Committee, she can
buffalo any of the minority staff,
she is popular with the women,
she is popular with the tax
lawyers. She'll have no difficulty
getting a very good job.

Now we've got further problems.
Lindy Paull—with the story the Ore-
gonian is going to do listing the peo-
ple who gave names of The
Washington Post, Lindy Paull's name,
of course, is going to be mentioned.
She gave a perfectly harmless state-
ment about the lack of Complainant
1's professionalism, but she wants to
call the Oregonian and make it very
specific, have them make it very spe-
cific that her statement did not relate
in any way to sexual misconduct or
past history. Then Josie wants to call
the Oregonian to find out what their
story is going to be about. Elaine and
Julie called her back from the road
and she was very curt, very short
when Elaine says to what end do you
want to find out? She said I don't
have to tell you. Elaine called and
                says let's face it,
some of those that play in the big
leagues—don't play in the big
leagues are going to bail out. You
might as well assume that the nonpo-

liticals will bail out. And I says yeah,
but—I said later to Elaine, Josie is a
political.   *says you*
don't know who may bail out.

The Committee's original inquiry included allegations that Senator Packwood had attempted to intimidate potential witnesses, and that he had used staff members in an attempt to do so. These allegations were ultimately found by the Ethics Committee not to be supported by substantial credible evidence, but at the time the diary changes were made it was a matter under inquiry by the Ethics Committee. Ms. Paull, who worked for Senator Packwood on the Finance Committee, provided Senator Packwood with a statement about Complainant 1, which he forwarded to the *Washington Post*. This entry indicates that Ms. Paull, along with other staffers, may have had concerns about the use of their statements by the *Post*. It also indicates that Senator Packwood did not want Tim Lee, who had provided a statement about another complainant, to talk to the press about it.

The material that was added to the Cormack transcript is entirely different, deleting any indication that Lindy Paull was uncomfortable with her statement, and painting a flattering picture of Ms. Paull, who gave the statement about the Complainant 1, whose allegation involved a 1990 incident that occurred after the staff party at the Irish Times.

Senator Packwood testified that he did not recall making the changes to the first entry on this date, but looking at it, he was sure that he must have done it. He stated that he wanted to take out the reference to him telling Tim Lee not to talk to the press. He added the flattering material about Lindy Paull out of compulsion, because he had a space left on the tape. He stated that sometimes he filled in these spaces, and sometimes he did not.

He could not say whether he or Ms. Cormack was responsible for leaving out the second entry on this date.

AUDIOTAPE	**CORMACK TRANSCRIPT**

March 20, 1993

My normal morning errands, then into the office about 9:00 for a few hours, worked, *played a couple hands of cards. I really didn't do a lot of work.* Did some thank you letters to people that are giving money to the trust— legal trust fund.

Looked through the diary to see when the famous night with [Staffer 1] was. I don't know why I have a feeling that she might say something—I don't know why. It's probably good she's leaving.

Into the office, after my normal morning errands, where I worked for a few hours. Some thank-you letters to some people who've given to the legal defense fund. **We're not doing as well as I'd hoped and I doubt we'll be able to raise anywhere near the amount of money I need until after this matter is resolved. Gosh, I hope it can be resolved soon. Who knows.**

The deleted entry indicates that Senator Packwood was worried that Staffer 1 (who left his office shortly after this entry) could possibly "say something," in other words, that she might become a complainant against him.

Senator Packwood testified that he guessed he deleted the references to Staffer 1 from the audiotape, as there was no point in involving her in anything. He stated that there were a number of times where he caught her name throughout the diaries, and he took it out. He was trying to protect her from hounding by the press. He did not think that Ms. Cormack would have left out this entry.[44]

---

[44] In fact, Ms. Cormack testified that she could conceive of no circumstances under which she would have typed the entry as it appears in the transcript, had she heard the entry on the audiotape.

AUDIOTAPE

March 29, 1993

Got home about 6:30. Cooked some soup. Got a phone call from Jill that we were still in session, could have a vote, but I doubted it. And I got the phone call, the bomb from Elaine. She had just received, because they didn't know who to deliver it to in the office, a motion to produce documents, voluminous documents, memos, correspondence, phone calls, personal papers. I wonder if that includes diaries. Everything. I was scared to death.

At this stage, there was a vote call, so I came back to the office. And I see Dan Resnick [Senator Packwood's attorney] had called. So I called him. Elaine had already talked with him. He said, well, let's not panic yet. Let me review this document they've sent us. But I said, my God, some of the early memos before you were retained will be very—some of them would be very incriminating. Stayed for a couple hours and went through the entire series of books that I had, as best I could, the binders. There is some damaging stuff. Actually, least of all damaging is probably the diaries, because in it there would be nothing

CORMACK TRANSCRIPT

Got home, had some soup, got a phone call from Jill that we were still in session and could have a vote but it was doubtful. Then I got the phone call with the bomb from Elaine. She had just received, because they didn't know who else to deliver it to in the office, a motion to produce documents, memos, correspondence, personal papers, phone calls—I wonder if that includes diaries. I was scared to death. **I told Elaine I thought as far as the diaries were concerned they would probably be more helpful than hurtful as far as the incidents with the women were concerned. I didn't know because I hadn't reread them but my hunch is that it they would show I'd spent a lot of time with Gena Hutton and time with others after the alleged incidents. I also told her I would take care of everything, that I would protect her, we would represent her, we were entitled to, we'd raise the money, and that I was very concerned for her well-being. She was most comforted. This was one of those situations where I**

about being a rejected suitor only my
successful exploits.

Dictated through midnight,
March 29.

**had to be the strong person and
she had to rely on me.**
Went to bed.

This entry was made on the date that Senator Packwood received the Committee's first request for documents. It indicates that Senator Packwood was concerned that he had incriminating documents that could be subject to the Committee's request, and his fear that his diaries might be included in the request.

Senator Packwood testified that he thought that he deleted the information from the audiotape, and substituted the information that appears on the Cormack transcript. He took the information out of the audiotape because he did not want the press to see an entry indicating that he told his attorney that some of his memos would be very incriminating. He added the information that appears in the Cormack transcript just to fill a gap.

In his appearance before the Committee, Senator Packwood stated that at the time he changed this passage, in the summer of 1993, the Committee already had his memos, implying that there would be no reason for him to want to hide this entry from the Committee. However, Senator Packwood withheld 112 documents, many of them memoranda, from the Committee on the grounds of attorney-client privilege. The privilege log indicates that six of the memoranda were dated before the time when Senator Packwood's attorneys were retained. Thus, it is impossible to determine whether in fact the Committee received the memos referred to in this entry. Moreover, regardless of whether the Ethics Committee had the memos when Senator Packwood changed the tape, this entry evidences Senator Packwood's state of mind when he received the Committee's document request on

March 29, 1993. Senator Packwood's state of mind was discussed at length at his June 1995 appearance before the Committee:

BY SENATOR DORGAN

Q: This is in March in 1993, and you were provided with a motion by the Committee to produce documents, and so on. At that point you say: I wonder if that includes diaries? Everything? I was scared to death. And then you said: 'But, I said, my God, some of the early memos before you were retained will be very—some of them are very incriminating,' and so on. Then you look at the transcript from Cormack, and when you look at this sort of thing you wonder to yourself, gee, isn't this a circumstance where somebody just, first of all, was alerted that they have information that probably is the subject of the motion and probably should be produced at some point, or there may be a question whether it should be produced, and then you go in and you make some alterations that would lead those who eventually got the transcript to a conclusion substantially different. So I'm just wondering. You know, when you look at this, if you put one face on it it looks like just flat-out alteration of diaries in order to prevent the Committee from seeing what it wanted to see. And you've described it in another way, but with respect to this particular instance it looks like in March of 1993 you at least were alerted, yourself, to the possibility that these diaries might have to go to the Committee.

A: Yes. Although, if I read this correctly, the reference to "diaries" is not taken out in either one, is it?

Q: No, no. My point isn't that you took out the reference to diaries.

A: Oh, I see.

Q: I make two points with this. One is, in March of 1993 you at that point were alarmed in your own mind that you might have to produce diaries, but you wondered whether you had to produce diaries to the Committee that early on. The point is, later you were altering a lot of transcripts, including this one, apparently, on the tape, and you did alter this one in a manner that took out the reference to some incriminating—some memos that could be incriminating and so on. So that material that you altered here would obviously be altered if one would look at it that way, and it would obviously be altered to take information out which would be harmful to yourself.

A: Well, . . . I should say I knew exactly what I was talking about here—but in talking to Resnick, they have—in fact, they gave you the memos, as a matter of fact. These are some of the ones I argued with them about that I didn't want to go to you, and they gave them to you. But . . . If I was changing this to fool the Committee, you already had the documents that I didn't want to go to you. But would you want out in the press a statement, God there's incriminating documents—I mean, I don't use the word "incriminating" in the sense of criminal, but I can picture a press saying criminal or Packwood has criminal documents. So indeed I changed this, obviously, sometime— this is March of '93—sometime in July of '93, but it's the kind of thing I wouldn't want out.

But if the argument is that I was changing these in October, apparently, or after the subpoena, to fool the Committee you already had the documents. If I was changing it to fool the Committee, you asked me yesterday about [person], if I was changing it in October, you'd already deposed me about her. I wouldn't have been taking it out to keep it from you, you had it . . . you cannot sense . . . fear of the press and what they were doing to me . . . But do you understand what I mean? That if I took this out when I think someone would say I was taking it out, it was an irrelevancy. . . .

BY SENATOR MCCONNELL

Q: But wasn't the other question, wholly aside from the issue of alteration, was not the other question whether the dictation indicated that at the time it crossed your mind that the diaries might be something the Committee—

A: Well, and it may have been at this stage that they said, no. I'm not quite sure. . . .

BY SENATOR BRYAN

Q: . . . as I understand what [Senator Dorgan's] point is is that you were somewhat concerned or alarmed in March that you might have to turn over the diaries, and so the question at least in our mind is: If that is so, why would you not then have informed your attorney that indeed there was an original audiotape? At least it gives rise to express some concern as to any changes made thereafter, that you had at least in your thought, I might have to produce these diaries. . . .

A: Counsel just called to my attention that March 29th was the date of the document request. Maybe this was when the lawyer said, well, we don't have to turn the diaries over. I don't know. I can't remember. . . .

Q: I think the point that Senator Dorgan, . . . is it's not a question of what you may have legally been required to turn over, it was what was your state of mind. And if this entry is accurate, it would suggest that your state of mind was one of considerale concern that the diary materials

contained incriminating information. And then, apparently . . . the changed part changes the thrust of the
meaning entirely. . . .

A: Well, again, and I'm saying if you're suggesting that I
changed this—well, as a matter of fact, when I changed
this the Committee had the documents. If this is 1993,
this change was made in late July or the first of August
and you already had the documents. I don't take out any
reference to the diaries. I take out references to the
incriminating documents, and you had them.

AUDIOTAPE	CORMACK TRANSCRIPT

May 28, 1993

And I said of course I'd help him [former staffer]. *Then he asked if he could talk to me personally for a moment. I excused staff, and he simply said Lee McAfee [attorney for Senator Packwood] had called him and he said he was happy not only to talk to Leo [sic], although he didn't have much to say other than [former staffer/complainant] claim, shit [sic], she threw him out of her apartment, which is absolutely untrue. He says that she made moves on him* and he said he'd love to be a character witness for me, that he perhaps is on the road 120 days with me and never saw any of the untoward conduct, any of the force, any of the aggres-siveness that's alleged. I thought it was very sweet of him.

I said of course I would try to help him. He also said he would be happy to be a character wit-ness for me if I wished—that he perhaps was on the road 120 days with me and never saw any of the untoward conduct or aggressiveness that's being alleged. I thought that was very sweet of him.

The former staffer referred to in this entry provided Senator Packwood with a very derogatory statement about another former staffer/complainant, claiming that on a certain occasion, she acted sexually aggressively toward the former staffer, which Senator Packwood forwarded to the *Washington Post*. The deleted passage indicates that the former staffer/complainant may have had a different version of the incident with the former staffer.[45]

Senator Packwood testified that the portion of the audiotape that was left out of the Cormack transcript was the kind of deletion that he would have made, although there were parts of it that he would rather have left in, as far as they concerned the former staffer/complainant. But if this entry were to come out, that the former staffer had offered to say something about the former staffer/complainant, the press would be all over the former staffer. He agreed that he had already given the *Washington Post* a statement by the former staffer about the former staffer/complainant, but he did not believe that his name had appeared in public at the time of this diary entry.

Senator Packwood stated that he would have made these changes in late July or early August 1993, very close to the recess time.

AUDIOTAPE	CORMACK TRANSCRIPT
June 29, 1993	
Fundraiser was fine. On the way home, *I discovered something that was disturbing, however. S-1 had told S-2 about our evening in the*	The fundraiser was fine and on the way home **we again kidded about S-2's relationship with that fellow she'd been sleeping with**

---

[45] The deleted entry corroborates information from another witness, who told the staff that the former staffer/complainant told him one day at work that the former staffer had gotten drunk at her apartment and spent the night on her couch, and that she was telling the witness about this because she was worried that the former staffer might tell others that he had spent the night with her.

office, only she told S-2, the way she told it to me, and she's straight out lying. She says we were drinking. She admitted she was drunk, and that I came out of the bathroom nude. And then I didn't ask S-2, did she say we had a sexual relationship where I forced myself on her or what? I should have thought to pursue it. I did not tell S-2 the specifics of what I remember from my diary because I didn't want S-2 to know it was in the diary, but goddamn, S-1 used the same expression, a statistic—she felt like a stat—a statistic. And then S-2 said that S-3 used the word statistic. I'll bet anything S-1 has told this to S-3.

Now, interestingly, she told S-2 just a few days before she left here, this is about the same time she told me, in exactly the same story as if she's trying to build a case, and she tells everybody three years—well, it is three years after the event. Came here in '89—I think she came in '89, and she's not telling them about the time she came into my office and another time when she practically put it to me. She's not telling them about the time she took me home from the Crawfords after swimming, lay on my bed, took off her blouse, took off her bra and asked me to rub some aloe on her very badly burned

or nooning with, I guess, three times a week for seven years. And S-2 goes, "Oh for heaven's sake. I shouldn't have ever told you that." And she acted put out much like the way would act, with a slight difference in emphasis.

*skin from the sunburn at Crawfords. I
won't describe in full detail here
what happened while we were doing
that, but it was a lot more than rub-
bing aloe on her bare back.*

*I had also forgot to say I called Lee
McAfee after S-2 dropped me off and
told her what S-2 had told me, and
Lee said this is very important
because S-1 had never told Lee about
the consensual situation. She had
alleged some other groping or grasp-
ing when I was drunk and admits
that I was drunk, is what she said to
me. She wasn't really mad about it
even. But she's never said anything
about our consensual relations. Lee
says it's quite helpful. S-2 also said
that S-1 confronted her and then
said well, there must be——I think
this is what she said——now, I may
get it confused——I think S-1 said to
S-2 well, of course, you've had a
relationship with the senator. S-2
said she has looked at her and said
no. Now, I may have had that confused with what S-2 said as follows:
S-1 apparently said to S-3 and S-3
said to S-2 that S-1 on one occasion
said to S-3, you know, the senator
and S-2 must be having a relationship, and S-3 said no, I don't think
so. Well, I don't know what to make
of all this.*

And I thought to myself—would
I have to courage to do that. I'm
trying to think of what would
be the federal equivalent in Oregon and there is none because
we don't have a big federal presence. But let's say they were
going to move a thousand people from the Corps of Engineers
headquarters or five hundred
people from the Forest Service
regional headquarters. There
may be that many. Would I have
the courage that   did?
I don't know.

The deleted passages discuss Senator Packwood's concerns that the staffer, S-1, who is also referred to in the March 20, 1993 entry above, might "build a case." These entries, as well as an entry for November 29, 1989, indicate that Senator Packwood had a consensual sexual relationship with this staff member while she worked for him.[46] It also suggests that there could have been non-consensual aspects to Senator Packwood's relationship with that staffer, which created his concern that this staffer might talk to the Committee.[47]

Senator Packwood testified that he thought he was responsible for the deletions in the first entry for this date, and the corresponding substitutions to the Cormack transcript. He was asked by Counsel why he made the changes, and he testified that he took this passage out of the audiotape because he did not want the press to have it. However, despite his testimony that he was worried that the press would obtain his diaries, and he was reviewing them during the first half of 1993 and over the August 1993 recess, Senator Packwood did not delete the November 29, 1989 entry, which recounts the "famous night" and is at least as explosive as the deleted June 29, 1993 entry.

Senator Packwood was asked why he had substituted embarassing details in the Cormack transcript about another staffer's (S-2's) personal life. He stated that it was "kind of facetious," and not entirely true. He stated that he should not have put this entry in, because there was no point in his talking to the press—which is what he would be doing if his diaries came out—about that kind of a conversation.

---

[46] The diary entry for November 29, 1989 contains a graphic description of Senator Packwood and the staffer making love in his Senate office. [See Publisher's Appendix for diary entry.]

[47] The staffer was interviewed by the staff, but would not answer questions about whether she was ever the subject of any unwanted sexual advances by Senator Packwood.

Q: How do you think the press might have reacted to that kind of information about [S-2]?

A: I think, as you'd read it, there's almost a lilt, a kidding to it, and it is kidding. And I meant it as that way when I put it in. This three times a week for seven years, I mean, you ever talk about things not being true? She never told me that she had been going with some guy making love to him three times—what did I say—three times a week for seven years.

Q: It would appear that the kind of information you have added here about [S-2] is of a similar kind to the information about others which you might have deleted.

A: It was just dumb on my part. I shouldn't have put it in. I meant it in a kidding fashion. I did not mean it here in a— I think you can tell from the way it's phrased. I didn't mean it in a serious sense, but I still shouldn't have put it in.

Although Senator Packwood testified at his deposition and later in his appearance before the Ethics Committee that S-2 never told him "that she had been going with some guy making love to him three times . . . a week for seven years," there is in fact a lengthy entry in Senator Packwood's diary for June 11, 1992, in which he recounts an evening when he and S-2 went out for dinner, and after S-2 had quite a bit to drink, she told him about a man she had been seeing for seven years, and making love with two or three times a week, unbeknownst to Senator Packwood and the others in his office. Senator Packwood then kidded S-2 that he and S-2 had made love six or seven times, because he felt sorry for her, and out of a sense of Christian duty, and it turned out that she had been "banging" another man three times a week for seven years.

With respect to the second set of entries for this date, Senator Packwood stated that in general, although 99 percent of the "bulk" changes were done by Ms. Cormack, in this particular case, he thought that he was responsible for the deletion of the entry that appears on the audiotape, because it involved S-1, who had been one of his favorite employees. He thought that he probably substituted the material that appears on the Cormack transcript, out of a compulsion to fill in a big blank spot on the tape.

AUDIOTAPE	**CORMACK TRANSCRIPT**

July 26, 1993

Talked with   . God, was she pissy. She's mad about having to go through 300 pages of phone calls on the campaign credit card to see who was called, and this is in response to the request to a demand for all of the phone calls that might have been made to any of the women involved or to attempt to intimidate any of the women. God, I've not seen her so pissed, not at me, just pissed generally. *And she made the statement, I don't know why we're giving them everything. My lawyer's not going to be as easy as yours. Senator, you just be assured that I'm going to cover— I'm going to protect my interest in this. I said, that's fine. God, as much as I love her, now that I know I'm not going to be expelled or lose my seniority, I'd just as soon get this over with. She really has nothing she can say. In this particular case, she*

Talked with   and she was really pissy. She's made [sic] about having to go through 300 pages of phone calls on the campaign credit card to see who was called. This is in response to the request from the Ethics Committee. She's not pissed at me. Just pissed generally. **And she really has nothing to add. I think I've said this before. She knows almost nothing about any of the incidents. I made the alleged phone calls trying to get information about the women. I don't recall that** made any. **She really has nothing to fear.**

sure could, on politics in the office,
but she was up to her neck in that
also. But in this, there's nothing she
can say, and if she were to try to
rat on me, it would probably end
our relationship. And if she did try
to rat, it would end our relationship,
and perhaps that would be just as
well. This is exacting a tremendous
toll.

The deleted passage suggests that the person referred to did not know a lot about the allegations of sexual misconduct, but that if pressed, she would protect herself (i.e., give up whatever information she did have) rather than protect the Senator. It also indicates that she knew a lot about "politics in the office," that she herself was "up to her neck," or heavily involved in using Senator Packwood's office for political purposes, and that Senator Packwood had some concern that she would try to "rat" on him. Instead, a passage has been substituted indicating that she knew nothing that could implicate Senator Packwood in either the issue of sexual misconduct, or the issue of witness intimidation.

Senator Packwood testified that the information that was added to the Cormack transcript would have been done by him, and not by Ms. Cormack. He stated that the person referred to in fact knew next to nothing, but he did not want the press to see the part indicating that if she were to "rat," it would be the end of their relationship, and to speculate about what it was that she knew. He testified that he substituted in its place a statement that was accurate.

Senator Packwood was asked what he meant when he said in the audiotape that the person referred to was up to her neck in politics in the office. He stated that he assumed that it referred to research that his office did for his 1992 campaign, and that he might have had one or two people who were doing a fair amount of research. He did not recall who those people were.

Senator Packwood guessed that he changed this entry for July 26, 1993 in early August of 1993, before he left for recess.

AUDIOTAPE	CORMACK TRANSCRIPT

August 5, 1993

. . . if they're not going to take hearsay, then they've got to take only complaining witnesses. And if they don't have Judy Foster, and whatever that woman's name is, the intern——I mean, ex-intern, she wasn't an intern——as complaining witnesses, then I think there is nothing in this decade of any consequence to be afraid of.

There is no woman and never will be any woman for me like   . We argue, we bitch but the sheer wit, love, humor, bonding I've never had with any man or woman like I do with her. All I really want, if I can, is to spend the rest of my life taking care of her and loving her very much.

The deleted passage indicates that Senator Packwood was aware that there were two women who were possible complaining witnesses, whose complaints would have occurred in the last ten years. At this point, the Committee had not notified Senator Packwood that Ms. Foster-Filppi was a complainant, nor had her name appeared in the press. This entry indicates that Senator Packwood may have been concerned that the Committee would uncover allegations by Ms. Foster-Filppi and the "ex-intern," and that if the Committee did not find them the only conduct he would have to worry about would be conduct occurring more than ten years ago. The substituted passage in the Cormack transcript discusses an entirely different subject——it sets out his reassurance of support to the woman referred to in the entry.

Senator Packwood testified that he assumed that he substituted the information that appears on the Cormack transcript, but not on the audiotape. He stated that he took out the entry about Ms. Foster-Filippi because the press did not have her name, and obviously, he just filled in the blank space on the tape.

AUDIOTAPE	CORMACK TRANSCRIPT

August 7, 1993

Met Cath at Sutton Place to take a look at a unit that had become available. It's an end unit. They're asking 230,000. The end unit, unfortunately, has an extra window upstairs in what I will use as the study, which cuts down my space a bit, but it's clean, it's ready to go. I can use it the way it is. It has the large patio, and it has the large patio with some sun on it, so I'm prepared to make an offer.

I then asked Cath if I were to pay her a little extra, would she be willing to take a week off and she and I would simply go through the diary? She said yes. In a week, with Cathy typing, I think she could bring everything up to date, and I could be going through it, the diary. It will actually be helpful.

Came to the office. Dictated through Saturday, August 7 at 10:30.

Met Cathy at Sutton Place to look at a place that had become available. It's an end unit. It's clean, ready to go, has the large patio with some sun on it, and I think I'm going to make an offer. **I really am kind of looking forward to settling in for these last five years and working hard in the Senate and voting for what's good for America and leaving a legacy that everyone can be proud of if I can get this ethics matter behind me.**

Well, the only main difficulty we will have is I think the diary's going to be very helpful, *is any diary entries related to the gathering of the information about the women and did Ann Elias lie. Did I attempt to unjustifiably gather information, et cetera.*	Well, the only main difficulty we will have is I think the diary is going to be helpful. **The only slight downside will be a mixed bag on intimidation. We never intended to intimidate anyone. We never intended to make any information public. They'd already talked to the Post. How could we intimidate them?**
Dictated through 6:45, Saturday, August 7, just prior to—arrived about on time.	Dictated through 6:45, Saturday, August 7, just before getting together with . arrived on time.

The first deleted passage indicates that in early August 1993, shortly after receiving the Committee's second request for documents (July 16, 1993), Senator Packwood was reviewing his diary, and he concluded it would be helpful in his defense. In its place, a self-serving passage has been added reflecting that Senator Packwood wants to work hard for what is good for America.

Senator Packwood testified that it appeared that he had deleted the highlighted information in the first passage from the audiotape, and substituted the information that appears on the Cormack transcript. He stated that Ms. Cormack had told him that she could bring the diaries up to date, but she did not have any of it done when he got back from recess around Labor Day 1993. He took these entries out so that she would not see them and think that he was mad at her.

Senator Packwood recalled asking Ms. Cormack on this date if she could hurry up with the transcribing. It was probably at this time that he gave her six to eight additional tapes, covering 1993 up to date, and including a tape that ended immediately before the recess. He could not remember if he gave her these tapes on Saturday August 7, or on Sunday; he had worked all night on them. According to the dates on the tapes themselves, the Senator would have given her a tape covering up through August 5, 1993 before leaving on August recess.

The second deleted passage suggests that there are diary entries relevant to the allegations of witness intimidation, which was a subject of the Committee's inquiry, and also suggests that there may have been some concern that Ann Elias, who provided a statement about Julie Williamson which Senator Packwood forwarded to the *Washington Post,* and who had by this time testified before the Committee, had lied. Ms. Elias stated in her deposition that Ms. Williamson came to her house after Senator Packwood kissed her in his office, and that she concluded that Ms. Williamson was interested in having an affair with the Senator. She also told the Committee that Ms. Williamson did not tell her the details about the Senator pulling her hair and grabbing her girdle. Her statement that went to the *Washington Post* claimed that Ms. Williamson was interested in having an affair with Senator Packwood, but did *not* include the fact that Ms. Williamson had told her about the incident almost immediately after it happened.

There are in fact other diary entries that suggest that Ms. Elias had misgivings about her statement—that she felt torn between her loyalty to the Senator and her desire to tell the truth—and that she was "buoyed up" by Jack Faust, a friend of the Senator's, who convinced her that Ms. Williamson had been telling her story on the "cocktail circuit" for years, and that it had changed over the years with the retelling.

Senator Packwood testified that this was the kind of deletion and addition he would have made as he was changing his diary tapes, although he did not find much difference between the two entries. He was not sure that he deleted the reference to Ms. Elias, and he stated that Ms. Cormack may have taken out her name, as they were old friends, but he thought that he had made the other changes. He added the information that appears in the Cormack transcript because it was accurate information, and he thought that he would put it in.

Senator Packwood was asked if he had some concern in August of 1993 about whether Ann Elias had lied. He stated that somebody in the press had claimed that Ms. Elias had lied, but in fact, she had not. He did not know what he meant by this entry, but he knew that when he made the original entry on the audiotape, he did not in fact think that some of his diary entries might raise an issue as to whether Ms. Elias had lied.

This entry is for Saturday, August 7, 1993, the same day that recess began. Senator Packwood stated that it appeared from his diary that he went to Oregon on the following Monday. He did not know when he dictated this entry, but stated that it would have been after 1:30 p.m. on the Saturday before he left, which is the time of this entry. Senator Packwood was unsure about when he changed this entry, but he testified that he did not make changes to the tape that was in his machine when he left for recess until he returned in September. Given the fact that the tape that covers this entry begins on August 6, 1993, it appears that this entry was changed in September.

At his June 1995 appearance before the Committee, Senator Packwood was again asked about this entry:

BY SENATOR SMITH:

Q: . . . Now instead of simply deleting that ("did Ann Elias lie and did I attempt to unjustifiably gather information . . .") but again, that would be, it appears to me, would be something, if it is intimidation, it would be something that the Committee would have an interest in. But you didn't simply delete it. You changed it. You added considerably to it by making the point that we never intended to intimidate anyone. You went far beyond the entry with the second entry. My point is, let me just make the point and then ask you to respond: The passage that you deleted suggests that there might be diary entries related to the gathering of information about the women . . . And it suggests further that there may have been concern that Elias had perhaps not been truthful. . . . And then in the entry that you put in the Cormack transcript where the entry goes beyond that to an absolute "We never intended to intimidate anyone." Whereas in one there is an implication and in the second one you go beyond that. You kill that completely by saying you never intended to intimidate anyone.

A: Well, you bet. We didn't intend to intimidate anybody. . . . We were given 24 hours by the *Washington Post* to gather information . . . It was not to be part of the story but to judge the evaluation of the people that had complained . . . So, no, we didn't intend to intimidate, and that's why I put it in this way. If the press ever got this, I want them to see that. . . .

Q: . . . My question is, though: Why use the diary—which the diary should be basically an anecdotal record of what transpired under a given period of time—why use a diary entry to make that point? I mean, you could have deleted it. If you had deleted the passage, there wouldn't have been any reference to it, and you could have made a statement to the press, couldn't you, that said I never intended to intimidate anyone? But you put it in the diary in retrospect rather than—

A: Well we had said to the press on a number of occasions that we did not intend to intimidate. This wasn't a new statement. But you try to give this a preciseness that simply, in retrospect, cannot be given to it. . . .

AUDIOTAPE	CORMACK TRANSCRIPT

October 9, 1993

Stopped at Cathy's and gave her the tapes to transcribe. I said Cathy, do you think you can do seven tapes by Tuesday night? She said she didn't think so. She said when you're dictating, different machines, in airports, noise in the background and sometimes you speak low because you don't want people to hear, she said I know your voice as well as anybody, and I know your inflection. I could probably transcribe this faster than anybody else can ever transcribe it. But she said an hour's dictation doesn't just take just an hour's typing. You've got to go back and listen. She said I'll be lucky to do four tapes by Tuesday night.

Again, I went over to the condominium. I am just excited about seeing the progress and getting into it. I'm just looking forward to having a place of my own and playing with it and making it the way I want it. It's Roy Prosterman and land reform. If you own it you want to take care of it.

The deleted passage indicates that a few days after his deposition was interrupted and the Committee specifically requested to see his diaries on October 6, 1993, Senator Packwood delivered to Ms. Cormack *the* tapes, and asked her to finish seven of them by the following Tuesday. This passage tends to indicate that Senator Packwood retrieved his diary tapes from Ms. Cormack shortly after his deposition was interrupted and the Committee specifically asked to review his diaries, and that he returned them a few days later, on October 9.

Senator Packwood testified that he would not have seen this entry until later in October 1993, when it came out of Ms. Cormack's typewriter. He thinks that he would have taken the typed page back to Ms. Cormack and had her substitute the new language, or he could have dictated instructions to her on a tape, with yellow underlining on the typed page.

Senator Packwood stated that he would have wanted to take out the information that appeared in the audiotape because it was wrong. He did not take her seven tapes on this date; he only had a couple of tapes left, and one of them may have been a half-tape. He asked Ms. Cormack to do seven tapes by Tuesday night, but he did not want the diary to give the impression that he had taken seven tapes to her on this date.

Senator Packwood also guessed that the diary issue had exploded in the press by this time. Senator Packwood did not want the press to know that there were diary tapes because nobody, not even Ms. Cormack or his attorneys, knew that there were tapes. Senator Packwood later said that neither his attorneys nor Ms. Cormack knew he kept *backup* tapes, although obviously they knew that his diary was transcribed from tapes. He simply did not want the press to know about tapes, period.

Senator Packwood testified that this entry would have been transcribed by Ms. Cormack later in October, and he felt that he had the right to take something out that was wrong, when it was the first time he had seen the typed transcript. He did not believe that he was "forever stopped" from changing anything he ever dictated again after the deposition, and if he was seeing it for the first time, he was free to change it.

Senator Packwood could recall no particular reason that he added the information that appears in the Cormack transcript, but he stated that it was accurate.

AUDIOTAPE	CORMACK TRANSCRIPT

October 10, 1993

Talked to Cath about 8:30. She'd left a message. She said it had taken her about 11 hours to do a tape and a half. She isn't even to the election yet. She says she got—she can finish seven—seven tapes by Tuesday night. I told her do those first three tapes as soon as she can and finish up the other four as best she can.

Dictated through Sunday morning at 10:00, at 9:20 a.m.

I really didn't do much all day. I went out to Radio Shack, bought some things, went over and kind of looked at the apartment. I'm getting anxious to move in. If there was ever a day I just frittered away, and frittered it away enjoyably, it was today. I—paragraph.

I stopped over at the just to chat. They invited me to stay for dinner, but I really didn't want to because I was going to go to bed early.

did give me four different frozen soups she had made, a corn chowder, a turkey with rice, a black bean and something else. So I

Kind of a leisurely day. I got up, read the Post thoroughly. Again, even though they attack me I find the paper a good paper and one of the better papers in the country. Then I just went out for a walk, walked around the Cathedral, went over to the condo—I'm so anxious to move in. If there was ever a day I just frittered away, this was it. Enjoyed it but frittered it away.

Had some soup and went to bed.

took them home. Thawed out the
corn chowder, had it, and was in
bed by 7:30.

Dictated through Sunday
night, October 10.

The deleted passage indicates that Senator Packwood was
pressing Ms. Cormack to finish seven of the diary tapes, perhaps
the tapes he had delivered to her the day before. It also indicates
that as of this date, Ms. Cormack had only typed part of the
1992 tapes. This is consistent with the October 20, 1993 letter
from Senator Packwood's attorneys to the Committee, stating
that Ms. Cormack had only finished typing about half of the 1992
tapes by that point. The substituted passage is completely innocu-
ous, and contains no reference to the diaries.

Senator Packwood testified that he did not specifically recall
deleting this entry, but he could have, because it gives the
impression he gave Ms. Cormack seven tapes the day before,
which is incorrect. He stated that he took her one or two tapes,
the one that was in his machine when he gave her tapes in
August, and maybe one-half of another tape.

Entries Dealing with Campaign Activity
and Campaign Purposes.

AUDIOTAPE	CORMACK TRANSCRIPT
December 31, 1992	
The most important thing that happened was a phone call from FS-1. W-1, that Oregonian reporter, was calling her, follow-ing up on some alleged violations of ethics in letters that we sent	But the most important thing that happened during the day was that FS-1 called. She said a reporter named W-1 of the Oregonian had called her and he was on the trail of a story about alleged vio-

out in 1984 and 1985. He had heard from sources that FS-1 had quit because she refused to type a letter in the office on Senate equipment that was a fund-raising letter, so she quit over it. She blames Elaine totally for it. She doesn't blame me at all. She said we had done a mailing earlier in my travels to New England, but she said those mailings of course were all right. They were in response to invitations that I had to speak, and we were simply putting other functions together around them. Well, it's a good thing FS-1 doesn't know everything.

W-1 wanted to know how many pieces were done, how many man-hours did it take. It was not franked mail, not Senate stationery. He asked her, "Did you get a ruling from the Ethics Committee?" She said, "No, Ethics might have said it was okay." He then said, "Well, FS-2 apparently quit over the same thing, and, he says, "you and FS-2 quit at about the same time." FS-1 says, "No, we quit seven or eight months apart." He asked if FS-1 then went over to the campaign. She left in the summer of '84. She said no, she didn't go

lations of law or ethics or some-thing—some letters that had been sent out on official Senate stationery or on Senate time or something like that—and FS-1 quit. And FS-1 said she blames Elaine. **FS-1 said, "You know I don't like Elaine very well."** She said the New England letters we sent out were okay because we had been invited to speak. W-1 then wanted to know how many letters or how many man hours. She said, she wasn't sure. W-1 asked if we'd gotten a ruling from the Ethics Committee. FS-1 said she didn't know. W-1 then asked if FS-2 didn't quit about the same time. FS-1 said no. He'd been there seven or eight months and quit after FS-1 did. FS-2 then called FS-1 and FS-1 assumed FS-2 had told W-1 all of the information he had. W-1 said no, that his source is not a member of the staff. That he has called   , he has called and he may try   . FS-1 said Elaine might honestly think (inaudible) fired FS-1 for another reason because Elaine and FS-1 weren't getting along at all at this time. But FS-1 said, "   knew because when I was visiting   in back to work until she went to work for in '85.

Then FS-2 called FS-1. FS-1 assumed that FS-2 had told him all this, and FS-2 says no, he hadn't told him, that he had all the details when he called FS-2 three weeks ago. W-1 says the source was not a member of staff, and he has called   , , and he may try   . FS-1 said that no one would have known except Elaine and FS-1, because they worked on this in private in my office. She said, however,   would know, because   and FS-1 talked when I was visiting   in 1985, and FS-1 and   sat in the outer office and she told her the story. This is eight years ago, so why did she quit?   knows, but FS-1 didn't tell her, so she presumes   did.

W-1 asked if FS-1 knew   . FS-1 said only in the sense that she had heard of her, in the way she has heard of Jack Faust or Dave Barrows or   , as she calls   . FS-1 said she was quite critical of the Oregonian for even thinking of doing a

1985 she had told   about it and FS-1 knows that   knows but FS-1 didn't tell   so FS-1 presumes   did. W-1 asked if she knew   and she doesn't. FS-1 told W-1 she was mad at the Oregonian for doing the story and she did not want her name used under any circumstances. FS-1 then told me she had utterly no respect for Elaine and **she said, "Senator, I don't want to do anything to harm you but I don't like Elaine."**

story like this. She said FS-2 was
not going to allow his name to
be used or   name to
be used. FS-1 asked for the same
privilege but W-1 refused. FS-1
said, "Elaine does things the Senator doesn't know about, and
the Senator should not be
blamed for things he didn't
know about." FS-1 again said that
New England was okay. It was
not a fund-raiser.

*He asked her who the mailings
were being done for. FS-1 said she
couldn't remember, although he
has called her two or three times
and she does remember now it was
                , but she hasn't told
him that. Used his letterhead. There
was no enclosure that went with it.
W-1 asked about   and
some letter that included a coin.
Well, of course that was the shekel
letter, and that was sent out by our
direct mail house.*

*FS-2 left six months or so after
FS-1 left, allegedly for the same reason, a different letter. He said it was
an Israeli or a Jewish letter.* FS-1
said, I don't have a lot of
respect, in fact, I don't have any
respect for Elaine, but if you're
going after Elaine, you should
separate her from Bob Packwood," she said.

These entries discuss charges that appeared in the press in late 1992, to the effect that two staffers had quit Senator Packwood's office after being forced to do campaign work on Senate time. On March 25, 1993, the Committee asked Senator Packwood to respond to these published allegations. The sentences added to the Cormack transcript, to the effect that one of the staffers making these charges did not like Elaine Franklin, Senator Packwood's chief of staff, could be viewed as an attempt to ascribe a motive to the complaint being made by this staffer—the desire to "get" the chief of staff.

The deleted passages also indicate that there may in fact have been a campaign related mailing that was done from Senator Packwood's Senate office.

Senator Packwood's response appears after the next diary excerpt.

AUDIOTAPE	**CORMACK TRANSCRIPT**
January 1, 1993	
FS-1 says, "My quotes are positive to you, and if you let me use them, it would put you in a good light." I said, "FS-1, we're better off to have no quotes attributed to anybody. That's the only safe way to do anything." Well, W-1 called her back, said he had talked to his editor and it's okay to use FS-1's name because the name had come from third party sources, but he would be willing to say that she refused any comment. She wanted to	FS-1 says, "My quotes are positive to you and if you let me use them it would put you in a good light. I said, "FS-1, I'd rather not be in any light—good or bad. I'm tired of being in the light." Well, W-1 called her back and said he had talked to his editor and said it's okay to use her name because her name had come from a third party source, but he would be willing to say that she refused any comment. She wanted to know what to do. **I said, "FS-1, you said you**

know what to do, and I said, "When he calls back, tell him you don't want your name used under any circumstances." *I said, "FS-1, this is not going to help you. You will be regarded as a danger to employ." She says, "I know." I said, "What you should have said from the start is, I don't want to talk with you about this, and hung up."*

W-1 thinks that Elaine has stepped over the ethical and legal line many times, but he's having a hard time getting sources. He asked about Elaine's travel expenses. FS-1 said, "They're all legitimate. I used to do her travel expenses." he asked about what hotel did we stay at at Dorchester. He wanted to know what hotel we stayed at at Bandon. He said, "In reviewing the reimbursements, it seems the Senator spends a lot of time in Coos Bay." At least that's the way FS-1 interpreted it. FS-1 thought he meant a trip. I said, "Did he mean when you were there or does he mean currently?" FS-1 says, "Well, I'm not sure." Of course, what he could be thinking is, Elaine spends a lot of time in Coos Bay. FS-1 said she didn't get along with   , and she told W-1 to call   , in the hope that

wanted to help me but you don't mind getting Elaine. Please realize that anything you say to 'get Elaine' hurts me, professionally and personally."

*might say FS-1 is wacko. She did
get along with*   .

7:30, Elaine called. I filled her in
on the entire situation for about
10 minutes. She called me back
10 minutes later. In the interim
W-1, W-1, had called Julia
wanting a statement, and Julia
had called Elaine to find out
what to say. Elaine wants me to
find out if FS-1 confirmed that
was the reason that she quit. I
called FS-1 and she said yes, she
confirmed that was the reason.

Dictated through 10 minutes
to 8 o'clock, Friday night, January 1st, after talking with FS-1,
confirming the reason she quit,
but before I got back to Elaine.

Eight o'clock, I got back to
Elaine, told her that FS-1 confirmed that she had quit because
of the demand that she do the letters. *I said, "You've got two choices,
Elaine. You can stonewall this and
say these letters—this never happened, or you can say FS-1 was fired
because she wouldn't do other work,
or however you want to handle it."*

Dictated through 8:15, Friday,
January 1st, after telling Elaine
that FS-1 had confirmed that she
had quit because she was ordered
to do the political letter, but
before Elaine had called W-1.

I called Elaine and filled her in
on all of this. She called me back
ten minutes later. In the interim
W-1 had called Julia wanting a
statement and Julia had called
Elaine to find out what to say.
Elaine wants me to find out if
FS-1 confirmed that was the reason she quit. I called FS-1 and
she said, "yes."

Got back to Elaine and told
her that FS-1 claimed that she
had quit because of the demand
she do the letters. **Elaine said,
"Didn't she do political letters in
1980?" I said, "I assume so
because she was my personal
secretary all during that campaign." Elaine said, "Did she
ever complain about doing political letters?" I said, "No."**

Dictated through Friday, January 1, at 8:15 p.m.

The passages substituted on the Cormack transcript again portray the former staffer's motive in making the charges as a desire to "get" Elaine Franklin, Senator Packwood's chief of staff. The substituted passages reinforce this theme, by suggesting that the former staffer had done political letters before without complaining.

The deleted passages also indicate that there may be some validity to the former staffer's claims, and that Senator Packwood advised Ms. Franklin either to "stonewall" the claims, or to state that the former staffer was fired for other reasons.

Senator Packwood testified that he made the original entries to his diary audiotape at the same time that he was reviewing his diary tapes to find entries for his attorneys regarding the intimidation issue, during the end of December 1992 and early January 1993. While he was reviewing his tapes for his attorneys, the former staffer called him, and told him that the *Oregonian* had called her about the story. He had several conversations with her about it, and also with Ms. Franklin.

The Senator testified that at the time, he was being beaten by the press, and he was very concerned that this would result in another story. Senator Packwood provided several versions of how and when he changed these entries. He first testified that when he gave Ms. Cormack the tapes to use in transcribing excerpts from the fall of 1992 for his attorneys, he may have also asked her to transcribe these entries, during the Christmas recess.

Senator Packwood then testified that he thought he transcribed these entries himself during the Christmas recess, using his secretary's transcribing machine, because he wanted to see them in print. He then stated that he could not remember whether he transcribed the entries, or whether he asked Ms. Cormack to do so.

Senator Packwood further testified that he was not sure if he made the changes to these entries on the tape around the time of the Christmas break in 1992. He could not remember if he gave Ms. Cormack these entries to type, indicating which parts of the tape she was to type, or whether he ran these two days onto a separate tape and gave it to Ms. Cormack to transcribe, or whether he simply redictated the whole thing. Although he had earlier testified that he made the changes to these entries before he went back to Oregon and had the terrible experience with the press in January 1993, he later stated that he was not sure of that, and he probably would not have made the changes until he finished the tape that was in his machine. He then stated that he listened to this tape sometime when he was finished listening to this tape sometime when he was finished listening to the 1992 tapes, but that he did not wait until he was finished changing the 1992 tapes to change this one.

Senator Packwood then said again that at the same time he gave Ms. Cormack the tapes containing the fall 1992 excerpts, even before he was done dictating on this particular tape, he either gave her this entry to transcribe, or he looked at and redictated it, although he did not necessarily remember redictating it right then.

Senator Packwood testified that he made the bulk of the changes to these entries. They were unusual, because he wanted to see them in "whole cloth" first as to what the former staffer had said, and what Ms. Franklin had said about the story.

Senator Packwood testified that Ms. Cormack could have left portions of these entries out when she was transcribing, and that he did not want to say that he did it all.[48]

---

[48] Ms. Cormack testified that she would not have typed the first and third passages as they appear on the transcript, had she heard what was on the audiotape. Although it was possible that she skipped over the second passage, this entry did not fall into any of the categories that she was "boiling down" for the sake of time.

Senator Packwood also testified that these conversations with his former staffer, and the fact that the press was involved, caused him to start changing his 1992 diary tapes.

Senator Packwood testified that he did not know why he deleted the information from the audiotape, or why he substituted the entries to the Cormack transcript. There was no logic to the things that were left in and the things that were taken out. He stated that his mental state of mind in that period was just not rational, and he could not give a rational answer as to why he put things in and left things out.

Senator Packwood was asked why he added the three entries indicating that the former staffer did not like Ms. Franklin. He stated that the former staffer in fact hated Ms. Franklin and had told him this in telephone conversations around the time of the changes.

Senator Packwood could not recall advising Ms. Franklin either to stonewall this issue, or to say that the former staffer was fired for other reasons, as indicated in the entry on the audiotape. He was questioned as follows:

Q: Do you have any reason to believe this diary entry didn't reflect what you said to [chief of staff]?

A: I'm not going to get into this discussion about accuracy. I don't know. You're asking me when you dictate on the fly, when you dictate when you're tired, do you accurately reflect things? You may or may not. You may totally miss the accuracy, I don't know.

AUDIOTAPE	CORMACK TRANSCRIPT
January 4, 1993	
Went to dinner with Elaine at Mrs. Simpson's. She was very down but she was able to laugh.	Went to dinner with Elaine at Mrs. Simpson's. She was so down she was unable to laugh.

She is so incensed about the FS-2 and FS-1 charges that she lost her focus. Of course, these relate to her, and she wants to clear her name. She says, you're going to be all right, but I'm not employable. I said, you're employable with me. She goes, "Oh, God." I can see where the Oregonian is going next. They're going to try to prove we did all kinds of politics in the office. I had talked with Lynn, and she said, we didn't do any political fundraising in the office. We did some thank-you letters, and they fell into two categories. One, we thank everybody who perhaps came to one of the PAC fundraisers, and then we do an occasional letter if somebody sent money directly to the office, *but that what we did an immense amount of, was memos to the staff on research in the office about voting record and issues I needed in my debates forum and what not. No question about that.*

She is so incensed about the FS-2 and FS-1 charges that she's lost her focus. Of course these relate to her and she wants to clear her name. She says, "You're going to be all right but I'm not employable." I said, "You're employable with me." She goes, "Oh God." I can see where the Oregonian is going next. They're going to try to prove we did all kinds of politics in the office. I talked with Lynn and she said we were very careful about not sending out any fundraising letters from the office. **Anything she did she did on her time.** She said she did some minor thank-yous if somebody actually sent money to the office and she may have thanked people who came to special events **but she did them on her time. She said we were especially careful because we'd been warned by the Ethics Committee and [Former Ethics Committee Staff Director] to avoid office involvement.**

The deleted passages, entered in his diary at the time that the *Oregonian* was looking into charges that former staffers left his office after being forced to do campaign work on Senate time, indicate that Senator Packwood in fact did an "immense amount" of political work in his Senate office, in the form of memos and research about his opponent's voting record, and issues for debate. The substituted passages instead disclaim any involvement by anyone in his Senate office in political work, and portray his staff as being very careful to avoid such activity.

Senator Packwood testified that he thought he was responsible for the changes from the audiotape to the Cormack transcript; he could not imagine Ms. Cormack adding the material that appears in the Cormack transcript.[49] He stated that he would have made these changes in January, February, March, or April 1993, before he finished making changes to the 1992 tapes.

Senator Packwood stated that he probably would have added the language to the Cormack transcript to emphasize, if it got out in the press, that they were not heavily involved in politics in the office. And in fact, the former Ethics Committee Staff Director had come to his office to advise him. He would have deleted the corresponding entry in the audiotape because he would not want the press to see it.

He stated that he did not know, as it says in his diary, if they did an "immense" amount of research in the office about his opponent's voting record. They did some research, but "immense" may be an overstatement. The Senator testified as follows:

Q: Why would that be of concern to you?
A: Probably because we were doing politics in the office.
Q: Did you understand that that was permitted or not permitted?
A: I knew that we were not supposed to use the office—we used to think of it fundraising, not so much research, and that we tried to keep pretty clear of the office except for the occasional letters that you see [staffer] did. But most

[49] Nor could Ms. Cormack, who did not even know who the former Ethics Committee Staff Director was.

of it of our mail, most of our fundraising was outside the office, but the memos and research we probably did.

Q: Senator, I think you just indicated that you did do a good bit, maybe immense isn't the right word but you did a good bit of politics in the office.

A: Well, I think "research" is the correct term.

Q: Political research?

A: No. More voting research.

Q: Why would you need [opponent's] voting record and issues for any purpose other than in connection with your campaign?

A: Well, I said that.

Q: So it was in connection with your campaign that that information that research was being done?

A: We were hoping that he wasn't going to be our opponent but if he was, that was the purpose of.

Senator Packwood could not recall who in his office was doing the voting research, but he stated that his personal secretary would have typed any memos he did for his opponent research books.

AUDIOTAPE	CORMACK TRANSCRIPT
March 6, 1992	
I introduced [Senator X], who was the speaker that night, and he was excellent. No notes. Good humor. *He says, you know, the Republicans have got a nutrition program. It's help you get a job and have money in your pocket so you can go to the grocery store and buy food.*	I introduced [Senator X] who was the speaker that night and he was excellent. No notes. Good humor. He finished and and I and Elaine and [Senator X]— — and the guy traveling with [Senator X] met for

That is our nutrition program. He finished,   and I and Elaine and [Senator X]— —and the guy travelling with [Senator X], met for just 10 or 15 minutes. *[Senator X] again promised $100,000 for Party-building activities. And what was said in that room would be enough to convict us all of something. He says, now, of course you know there can't be any legal connection between this money and Senator Packwood, but we know that it will be used for his benefit.   said, oh, yes. God, there's Elaine and I sitting there. I think that's a felony, I'm not sure. This is an area of the law I don't want to know.* [Senator X] left. Elaine and I headed back to the motel.

just ten or fifteen minutes. **There was the usual argument—I suppose a more polite word for it would be discussion—of how much money the National Committee or Senatorial Committee or any committee was going to give the state party. I remember those arguments all my life. When I was county chairman it was how much was the state going to give the county. The lesser unit always wants the greater unit to give them money of some kind. Well, anyway, the discussion ended in a draw.** [Senator X] left and Elaine and I headed back to the motel.

The deleted passage indicates that another Senator, with Senator Packwood's knowledge, had agreed to direct $100,000 from a Republican Party Committee to be used to benefit Senator Packwood's campaign, and had discussed this with Senator Packwood in a meeting with Elaine Franklin and another person. This entry raises questions about the possible violation of campaign finance laws. Substituted in its place is an innocuous passage discussing campaign funding.

Senator Packwood testified that he deleted the information from the audiotape, and substituted the information that appears on the Cormack transcript. He stated that the entry on the audiotape was an instance where he did not want to embarrass a fellow Senator, and in fact the entry was wrong:

> This is no crime. Party building activities are perfectly legal and the Senatorial committee gives money to the party if the party puts up money for the Senate candidate. It cannot just be a passthrough where they give them 100 and they pass it on.

When he realized that the entry was wrong, Senator Packwood decided that it was not something he would want out in the press. He testified that he substituted the material that appears on the Cormack transcript just to fill up the tape.

Senator Packwood testified that the part of the diary entry reading "But he says now of course there can't be any legal connection between this money and Senator Packwood" is an example of a conversation that never occurred, because the other Senator would not have said that. Those were his [Senator Packwood's] words attributed to the other Senator, and they did not even reflect the essence of something that the other Senator said to him.

Senator Packwood testified that the meeting reflected in this entry actually took place. But beyond that, he stated that the entry was simply wrong. He testified that the conversation in fact reflected nothing that was illegal, that the entry was in jest, and that nobody in Senator X's position would take that kind of a risk.

AUDIOTAPE	CORMACK TRANSCRIPT

March 20, 1992
Elaine has been talking to me pri-
vately about independent expendi-
tures. Apparently the Automobile
Dealers are willing to do some

spending against AuCoin. Of course
we can't know anything about it.

       going to do it. We've
got to destroy any evidence we've
ever had of   so that we
have no connection with any independent expenditure. Elaine says that
Tim Lee is also willing to do an
independent expenditure, but I don't
know how we've ever given the
impression we have of no connection
to him.

We decided to not play up Hispanics
very much. We have a——not Hispanics, but coalitions generally, ethnic
coalitions. We have   .
       is Chairman of our
Hispanic Coalition. We need probably a black chair and several Asians,
and that's about it. But don't have
the group do very much. Just have
the names.

   We talked about The Oregon Cit-
izen Alliance. They have now
reserved an auditorium in June in
Salem to put an independent on
the ballot, but I am confident with
       I can beat
and the OCA. Nevertheless, they've
reserved an auditorium in Salem.

**We talked about independent
expenditures. I said I didn't
want to know about that and
none of us were to know about
that. We want independent
expenditures to be truly independent. Those who are going to
support us will support us.
Those who won't won't. Let's let
the chips fall where they may.**

The deleted entries suggest that Senator Packwood knew about possible "independent expenditures" by the Automobile Dealers and possibly Tim Lee, a former staffer, on his behalf, and that he intended to destroy any evidence of a link to the individual who would make the expenditures for the Auto Dealers. This entry raises possible questions about campaign finance improprieties.

The substituted entry is a self-serving passage portraying Senator Packwood as having no knowledge of any independent expenditures made on his behalf, and being above any involvement with or knowledge of any such expenditures.

Senator Packwood testified that he suspected that Ms. Cormack left out the first entry on this date, although he was not sure.[50] He thought that he would have taken out the paragraph about the coalition. He was sure that he deleted the paragraph about the OCA, as the OCA had been a major problem for him in his campaign. He stated that he had been terribly afraid that the OCA was going to put a candidate on the ballot against him in the 1992 election. The OCA also had a measure on the ballot on anti-gay rights that was the hottest issue he had ever seen on the Oregon ballot, and which was heavily editorialized by the *Oregonian*. He was not on their side on this issue, or the abortion issue or the compulsory school prayer issue, and the OCA was going to try to take a shot at him. His campaign did everything they could do to prevent this.

Senator Packwood's opponent in the 1992 election accused him of making deals with the OCA, and the press questioned him repeatedly about this. He did not want to have anything in his

---

[50] Ms. Cormack testified that the first passage was not the type of entry that she would have left out of the transcript as she was typing, although it was possible that she could have missed it as she typed the transcript. She did not believe she would intentionally have left it out.

diaries about the OCA. Senator Packwood agreed that there was not anything in this particular entry that would offend the OCA, but he stated that he had attempted to take out anything he could find about the OCA.

Senator Packwood was asked why he was concerned about the entries referring to the OCA when at the time that he took them out, in the spring of 1993, the election was over. He stated that at the time, he was beset by the press, which was looking for everything they could find about him from the time the story came out in the *Washington Post* about the allegations of sexual misconduct. He did not want the press reliving the election. The press was excoriating him, and he did not want to give them this information.

Senator Packwood stated that there was no particular reason that he substituted the information in the Cormack transcript about independent expenditures, other than that they may have been talking about it at the time. The subject was on his mind the same day that he was changing his tapes, and he wanted to fill the space on the tape.[51]

Senator Packwood testified that the industry group in general did not do any independent expenditures against his opponent. This particular group did not do anything for or against Senator Packwood, or for or against his opponent. He did not recall this conversation with Elaine Franklin about independent expenditures, or any conversation about the individual who was to make the expenditures and the industry group, or about Tim Lee and independent expenditures.

Senator Packwood was asked what he meant by the reference to destroying evidence connecting them to the individual who

---

[51] Senator Packwood stated that he added this information to the tape sometime between January and April of 1993.

was to make the expenditures, or to independent expenditures. He stated that if one were going to have coordinated independent expenditures, which is wrong, one would not want any evidence of association with anyone connected to the group that was doing independent expenditures. But they did not do any coordination of independent expenditures. They never had any evidence about the individual named and any potential independent expenditures, nor did they destroy any evidence related to this individual.

| **AUDIOTAPE** | **CORMACK TRANSCRIPT** |

October 6, 1992

Came back to the office and met with   from the National Rifle Association at three o'clock. *He showed me the piece the National Rifle Association is going to send out hitting   . God, is it tough! It starts right out: vote to toss out   and vote for Senator Bob Packwood. Toss out of Congress someone who believes he made a mistake when he supported your Second Amendment Right. Vote to toss out   .*

Then they quote when said Congressmen who were supported by the NRA were patsies. Or, if you had an endorsement by the NRA you were in an ideological straitjacket.

Then, the article in The Washington Post: Confessions of a Former NRA Supporter.

Came back to the office and met with   of the NRA. **I kind of like the guy but he is a bit of a braggart about how many races he sees the NRA winning and how solid is going to be the NRA's control in the House. He didn't talk so much about the Senate. He may be right by my intuition tells me the tide is turning against the NRA. With more and more crime I think you're going to see a situation where people will think gun registration is the answer. It isn't going to solve these problems. And I'm not sure what will but I don't think we want to try to take guns away from people. I think the second amendment defends that right. I'm happy to**

I cannot tell you how tough it is. They are going to send it to 90,000 members. And, he said if he has enough money he's going to send it out to 100,000 Oregon gun owners, or something like that. Now the question is: Are they going to do a second mailing just before the post-card about "get out and vote."

God, things are going in the right direction today. It's a month to go and there are going to be ups and downs, but we're up today.

Dictated through Tuesday, October 6th at four o'clock. And here, Cathy, I'm going to end.

hear   out and I'm happy to hear of his plans for the House races and I assume they will support me although they haven't said that for sure.

Again, the deleted passages indicate that Senator Packwood was meeting with the NRA and reviewing their efforts against his opponent. In the substituted passage, Senator Packwood distances himself from the NRA and their goals, and does not mention that he was counting on the NRA's support.

Senator Packwood testified that he was probably responsible for deleting the information from the audiotape and substituting the information that appears in the Cormack transcript, because he did not want the press to know about his negotiations with the NRA, and that he was talking with the NRA about the mailing they were going to send to their members. The entry that was substituted, which he says is accurate, was put in to fill the space, although it obviously would not fill the whole blank space left by the deletion.

Senator Packwood assumed that the meeting with the individual from the NRA actually took place, although he did not recall it. He could think of no reason why he would have recorded such a detailed summary of the meeting if it actually had not taken place.

Entries Referring to Senator Packwood's Negotiations with the Oregon Citizens Alliance During his 1992 Campaign

Senator Packwood testified that he deleted every reference to the Oregon Citizens Alliance which he could find, because this would be an explosive subject in Oregon. At least five such entries were deleted.

During his 1992 campaign, Senator Packwood was accused by the media of making a deal with the Oregon Citizens Alliance (OCA), a conservative group, that they would not run a candidate against him in return for certain promises. Senator Packwood consistently denied these accusations. Senator Packwood's diary tapes for 1992 and 1993 contain a number of entries discussing what could be characterized as negotiations with the OCA by others on Senator Packwood's behalf. These entries do not appear on the Cormack transcript, and in some cases, entries have been added that deny any deal was ever made with the OCA.

Senator Packwood testified that there never was a "deal" with the OCA, and that he added information to the Cormack transcript to emphasize that for the benefit of the press.

Entries Referring to Contacts with Committee Members by Senator Packwood During the Committee's Inquiry

There are a number of entries on the 1992 audiotapes, which do not appear on the Cormack transcript, referring to conversations by Senator Packwood with members of the Committee concerning the Committee's inquiry.

Senator Packwood testified that he deleted these entries from his diary tapes because he was afraid that if the press obtained them, they would suggest a "Republican conspiracy" in connection with the Committee's inquiry.

Entries About Senator Packwood Accepting Contributions to his Legal Defense Fund from Lobbyists

There are several entries in the 1993 diary tapes related to Senator Packwood's acceptance or solicitation of contributions to his legal defense fund from lobbyists visiting his Senate office. At least one of these entries gives the impression that a group contributed to his legal defense fund in order to get or stay in his good graces.

Senator Packwood stated that he attempted to remove any references to contributions to his legal defense fund by lobbyists, because the press would attempt to make corrupt, illegal, and immoral inferences from them about the way politics work. He stated that it is perfectly legal, ethical, and moral for a group, even one that has opposed you in the past, to come in and make a contribution.

Senator Packwood denied any improper linkage between his acceptance of contributions to his legal defense fund and the conduct of his official Senate duties.

Findings
Reliability of the Diaries

Senate Ethics Counsel finds that from 1969 through 1993, Senator Packwood kept detailed daily diaries. More specifically, for the diaries covering the period from January 1, 1989 through November 21, 1993, Senator Packwood recorded, often in minute detail, events in his professional and personal life, as well as his thoughts and feelings on a wide range of subjects, covering both his professional and personal life. Counsel finds that despite Senator Packwood's protestations about the unreliability of his diaries, these diaries were in fact an attempt by Senator Packwood to accurately record, from his perspective, events which he witnessed or in which he participated, and his thoughts and feelings about a variety of subjects.

While, as Senator Packwood points out, his recollection or assessment of events at the time may in some instances turn out to be inaccurate, or differ from the recollection of others, that does not mean that Senator Packwood did not set out to record events and perceptions as accurately as he could. Counsel finds that while Senator Packwood's diaries may not always be complete or accurate in every respect as a historical account of events, they are certainly accurate as a contemporaneous reflection of *his* perception of events, and his thoughts and feelings about a broad array of subjects.

Counsel notes that Senator Packwood made arrangements to leave his diaries to a historical trust. This fact, together with the sheer comprehensive nature of the diary entries, which record everything from Presidential briefings to the most mundane details of Senator Packwood's personal habits, is powerful evidence that Senator Packwood himself intended his diaries to be an accurate contemporaneous reflection of his perception of events, professional and personal, and his contemporaneous thoughts and feelings on many subjects.

Senate Ethics Counsel concludes that this contemporaneous record created by Senator Packwood is in fact reliable evidence of the events that it memorializes, as perceived by Senator Packwood at the time he recorded them, and of his contemporaneous thoughts and feelings.

Alteration of the Diaries

Senate Ethics Counsel finds that as of December 1, 1992, Senator Packwood was on notice that he was the subject of the

Committee's inquiry into allegations of misconduct. After that time, Senator Packwood had an obligation of trust to the Senate, irrespective of any legal obligation which might attach, not to alter or destroy *any* documents or evidence in his possession or control that could be relevant to the subject of the Committee's inquiry.

There is no dispute that substantial portions of the entries for Senator Packwood's 1992 and 1993 diaries did not make it from the original contemporaneous audiotape onto the transcripts typed by Cathy Cormack. Although a large number of these entries appear to have been skipped over, paraphrased, or otherwise changed by Ms. Cormack in her rush to complete the diaries in the late summer and early fall of 1993, Senator Packwood himself testified that he deleted from his audiotapes most of the entries where corresponding entries were substituted on the typed transcript.[52] Many of the entries falling into this category dealt with matters that were directly related to the Committee's inquiry or that raised questions about possible misconduct falling under the Committee's jurisdiction. Senate Ethics Counsel finds that Senator Packwood intentionally altered many of the diary passages that related to the Committee's inquiry or raised questions about possible misconduct within the

[52] Of course, if the Committee had the altered tapes from which Ms. Cormack transcribed the 1992 and 1993 diaries, it would be better able to pinpoint which entries Ms. Cormack skipped over, as they would still be on the tape, and which entries Senator Packwood deleted, as they would be missing from the tape, and which entries were altered after the transcripts had been typed. Despite his knowledge as of October 6, 1993 that the Committee wanted to see his diaries, and his receipt of a subpoena on October 21, 1993 for all of his diary tapes and transcripts, Senator Packwood never instructed Ms. Cormack not to continue her usual practice of erasing her copy after she finished typing it. Senator Packwood testified that he also erased his copy of the changed tape, keeping instead the original, unchanged diary tape.

Committee's jurisdiction, and that he did so after he was on notice that he was the subject of the Committee's inquiry.

Senator Packwood's Motivation for Making Changes to His Diary

Senator Packwood has testified that he took out entries from his 1992 and 1993 diary tapes because he feared that once they went to his attorneys, they would be leaked to the press. He testified that he did not act out of a desire to keep the deleted entries from the Committee, but that his sole motivation was to prevent entries that could be embarassing to himself or others from getting to the press through his attorneys. Several factors should be considered in evaluating this testimony.

First, if Senator Packwood were truly concerned about embarassing entries in his diaries leaking to the press, he could simply have deleted those entries. There was no need to substitute passages in their place, passages that were often self-serving or exculpatory. Indeed, in one instance, while he deleted a passage that would be highly embarassing to himself and others if it became public, he substituted in its place an entry that would have been equally embarassing to another staff member if it had become public. He offered no explanation for his substitution of entries, other than that it was the result of his compulsive habit of dictating.

The nature of the entries that Senator Packwood took out of his diary is also a strong indication that his motivation may not have been simply to keep entries from leaking to the press. A good number of these entries relate specifically to the subject of the Committee's inquiry—either the women involved, the issue of intimidation, or the progress of the Committee's inquiry. Indeed, Senator Packwood changed entries which related to the subject of intimidation of witnesses well after his own attorneys had instructed him to collect and forward entries related to the intimidation issue. Many of the remaining entries that were changed raise questions about other possible misconduct by Senator Packwood that would be subject to the Committee's jurisdiction. The nature of the entries deleted points to the conclusion that Senator Packwood set out to delete not only those possibly incriminating entries relating to the Committee's inquiry, but any entries that might trigger further inquiry by the Committee into other areas of possible misconduct.[53]

Further, Senator Packwood made no changes to his already-transcribed pre-1992 diaries, as he did to his untranscribed 1992–1993 tapes. This contrast in treatment between the pre-1992 diaries and the 1992–93 tapes is underscored by the fact that Senator Packwood deleted several passages in his 1993 diary tapes referring to his consensual relationship with a staffer, (S-1), and his concern that she might be trying to "build a case" against him. Yet he did not delete an entry in November 1989 which describes in explicit detail how he and the staffer had sex on his office floor, although the deleted entries make it clear that he knew when this incident took place.

Additionally, Senator Packwood stated that he was concerned that his diaries would be leaked once he turned them over to his

[53] While the deleted entries about the Oregon Citizens Alliance, which raise questions about his campaign tactics, do not appear to implicate Senator Packwood in any official misconduct, it is not clear whether this was not a matter of concern to senator Packwood at the time he made the changes to these entries, given the fact that he was also changing other entries related to the campaign, dealing with possible coordinated expenditures. Three other deleted entries related to dinner with his attorneys and meetings with a friend who was a judge do not appear to relate to any potential official misconduct. The fact that *not all* of the deleted entries related to the Ethics Committee's inquiry or possible misconduct, however, does not preclude the reasonable conclusion, supported by the clear weight of the evidence, that *many or most* of the deletions that Senator Packwood admitted he made appear to have been made with the Ethics Committee in mind.

attorneys. Yet the evidence indicates that with the exception of the October–November excerpts from 1992 dealing with the intimidation issue, his attorneys never asked him to turn over any significant portion of his diaries to them *in toto,* although he did provide them with selected entries from his diary during the course of 1993.[54] Indeed, his attorneys did not receive any of the diary, other than the selected excerpts that Senator Packwood provided to them, until after his deposition was interrupted in October 1993 when the Committee requested the diaries. At that time, they first received the diary transcript covering the years 1969 through 1991, followed by 1992–1993 transcripts as Ms. Cormack typed them.

Senator Packwood has emphasized to the Committee that he did not destroy the original audiotapes, and that if the Committee had gotten up to 1992 and 1993 in its original review of the diaries, he would have informed the Committee of the changes. He overlooks the fact that at the same time that Committee Counsel was reviewing the earlier years of the diary in October 1993, he was permitting Ms. Cormack to type transcripts for 1992 and 1993 *from the altered audiotape,* and was turning over to his attorneys transcripts prepared from these altered tapes. At that time, Senator Packwood knew that the Committee wanted to review his diaries through 1993. And even after he received the Committee's subpoena asking for diaries and tapes, he continued to have Ms. Cormack type from the altered audiotapes, which transcripts he provided to his attorneys.

---

[54] Once the Committee asked to review his diaries in October 1993, Senator Packwood gave his attorneys copies of the transcripts for 1992 and 1993 prepared from the altered tapes as Ms. Cormack typed it, to be reviewed by his attorneys and provided to the Committee. He did *not,* however, tell his attorneys that these transcripts had been typed from altered tapes. As late as October 20, 1993, Senator Packwood's attorneys wrote the Committee advising it that some of the transcript for 1992 would be forthcoming for the Committee's review.

Had he intended for the Committee to review a transcript prepared from the original, unchanged diary tapes, he would not have had Ms. Cormack typing from the altered audiotapes. It is also significant that Senator Packwood did not tell his own attorneys that the transcripts Ms. Cormack was typing, and that he was providing to them during this period after October 6, 1993, had been altered. Indeed, even as late as October 20, 1993, Senator Packwood remained silent as his attorneys informed the Committee that some of the transcripts for 1992, which unbeknownst to them had been typed from the altered tapes, would soon be available for review by the Committee.[55]

Senator Packwood has also emphasized that the Committee received the original audiotapes, and thus was not misled. It is true that, after a lengthy court battle, the Committee received the original audiotapes. The issue, however, is not whether the Committee eventually received evidence to which it was lawfully entitled,[56] but whether Senator Packwood intentionally created a second version of that evidence after he knew or should have known the Committee wanted it, and whether as part of that process he destroyed evidence. Any improper conduct occurred when Senator Packwood made the changes to his diaries or destroyed evidence as part of that process, regardless of whether the Committee eventually received the authentic version, or regardless of whether the Committee avoided the possibility of being actually misled, because it successfully obtained the originals.

---

[55] Moreover, if Senator Packwood made changes to his diaries for benign purposes, why did he not simply listen to the tapes and identify those changes for the Committee after he lost in Court, instead of leaving to the Committee the task of transcribing his tapes and comparing them to the Cormack transcript? He was specifically invited to do so by Senate Legal Counsel.

[56] Of course, all such evidence was *not* received by the Committee, because the altered tapes were destroyed.

The Timing of the Changes

For the purpose of determining whether Senator Packwood engaged in improper conduct, it is not necessary to make a specific finding regarding the timing of his changes to the diary. The timing of the changes, however, may reflect Senator Packwood's state of mind in making the changes.

The Committee's inquiry into allegations of sexual misconduct began December 1, 1992. On February 4, 1993 the inquiry was expanded to include possible witness intimidation. Thereafter, on March 29, and July 16, 1993 the Committee sent document requests to Senator Packwood requesting information and documents concerning these allegations. The information sought by these requests included information such as that contained in some of the diary entries altered by the Senator. Senator Packwood has testified that he began changing his 1992 audiotapes beginning in January 1993 and continuing through April 1993, and that later, in late July or early August 1993, he began changing his 1993 audiotapes. Thus, even if one accepts his testimony as to the timing of the changes, Senator Packwood was intentionally altering materials related to the Committee's inquiry after he knew or should have known that the Committee had sought or would likely seek these materials.

Thereafter, on October 6, 1993 at the interruption of his deposition the Committee requested specific periods in their entirety from his diary dating from 1969, specifically including the period from August 1989 thru October 6, 1993.

Senator Packwood has testified that he made most of the changes, with a few exceptions, in the first seven months of 1993, well before his deposition was interrupted in October 1993 and the Committee specifically requested his diaries. Senator Packwood's testimony in this regard must, however, be evaluated in the context of other evidence.

If the diary changes were made after the interruption of Senator Packwood's deposition on October 6, 1993, this could account for the fact that Senator Packwood only made changes on the untranscribed tapes for the years 1992 and 1993: once the Committee asked for the diaries, and Senator Packwood turned over the already typed transcripts through 1991 to his attorneys, he could not make any changes to those entries. But he still had the audiotapes for 1992 and 1993, most of which had not yet been transcribed.

Senator Packwood testified that he felt compelled to fill up the space left on an audiotape after deleting passages. However, an alternative explanation for the substitution of entries in the place of deleted entries could be that these changes were, in fact, made to the transcript *after* it was typed by Ms. Cormack. It does make sense that one would want to fill up a blank space after deleting entries from a typed transcript, in order to hide the fact that entries had been taken out. While some of the changes were made on the tapes themselves, since Ms. Cormack noticed the Senator's tape changes as she typed, she testified that in the two week period from mid-to-late October 1993, on more than one occasion, Senator Packwood brought back to her pages she had already transcribed that he had subsequently changed, and asked her to make those changes. She could not remember what time period these changes covered. While the Senator says he does not believe he changed any pre-deposition entries during this period, he testified that it is possible that he did change entries from either 1992 or pre-October 1993 as they came off Ms. Cormack's typewriter, *after* his deposition was interrupted on October 6, 1993 and *after* he received the Committee's subpoena on October 21, 1993.

Consistent with the evidence, one could reasonably conclude as follows: that after the Committee asked for his diaries on

October 6, 1993, Senator Packwood went to Ms. Cormack and retrieved the untyped tapes for 1992 and 1993, and mentioned the possibility of a subpoena as he did so;[57] that he deleted or changed some information from the audiotapes,[58] and returned them to Ms. Cormack a few days later;[59] that as he received the typed transcripts from her, and discovered that there was additional material that he needed to take out, he instructed Ms. Cormack to do so, filling up the blank spaces, or evening out the pages with benign or exculpatory information to disguise the deletions.

If one concludes that Senator Packwood made the changes during this time period, it is equally clear that Senator Packwood was intentionally altering materials related to the Committee's

---

[57] At her third deposition, over a year after the events in question, Ms. Cormack recalled that Senator Packwood picked up audiotapes from her in September 1993, not October. This is consistent with Senator Packwood's testimony. However, Senator Packwood's diary for October 9, 1993, indicates that he dropped off the tapes to Ms. Cormack on that date, and asked her to type seven of them right away, and another diary entry for October 10, 1993 also discusses her rushing to type the tapes. Both of these October entries were subsequently changed by Senator Packwood, and there are no similar entries in September. Correspondence from Senator Packwood's attorney, dated October 20, 1993, indicates that as of that date, Ms. Cormack had only typed about half of the diaries for 1992. This is consistent with Ms. Cormack's testimony, describing the two week period of mid-to-late October as part of the "crunch time," when she was pushing hard to complete the tapes.

[58] The Senator has testified that during December 1992 and 1993 as he was listening to the 1992–93 untranscribed tape. He believes he may have made notes of the location of embarrassing passages which he would not want to get into the hands of the press. If he had this information at hand, the Senator could quickly locate and delete or change the passages.

[59] Senator Packwood destroyed his copy of the changed audiotapes, and never instructed Ms. Cormack not to destroy hers, even after receiving the Committee's subpoena. Thus, it is impossible to make a full accounting of exactly which entries were deleted from the tape by Senator Packwood, which entries Ms. Cormack listened to but simply did not type, and which entries Senator Packwood added by making changes to transcript rather than tape.

inquiry when he knew or should have known that the Committee had sought or would likely seek these materials.

Counsel also notes that in his appearance before the Committee, Senator Packwood stated that he finally told his attorneys about the existence of the original backup audiotapes, and the fact that he had made changes to the 1992 and 1993 tapes, after he received the subpoena from the Department of Justice on November 19, 1993, because he thought the Department of Justice might need them.[60] However, the Committee's subpoena, which the Senator received almost a month earlier, specifically asked for diary transcripts and tapes for the years 1989 through 1993. Only days before he received the Department of Justice subpoena, when he was discussing with the Committee the possibility that he could resign and thereby avoid the Committee's subpoena, Senator Packwood told Senator McConnell, then the Committee's Vice Chairman, that he wanted a "window of opportunity" in which to destroy his diaries.[61] Such a window would have been created if the Committee's subpoena expired before the Department of Justice subpoena was served. However, the Department of Justice subpoena was served before he could resign. It is reasonable to conclude from this sequence of events that Senator Packwood was willing to resign if it meant that he could destroy his diaries, and that he only told his attorneys about the existence of original backup tapes, and that he had

[60] The Committee's subpoena of October 20, 1993 specifically asked for all tapes as well as transcripts. The Senator explained that the DOJ subpoena jogged him to action where the Committee subpoena had not because it involved a possible criminal issue and he did not know what that entailed. It is unclear why the Ethics Committee subpoena, approved by a 94 to 6 vote of his Senate colleagues, did not carry the same force with Senator Packwood.

[61] Senator McConnell immediately informed Senator Bryan (then Committee chairman) and Committee Counsel of this conversation.

altered the tapes for 1992 and 1993, when the destruction of his diaries was no longer an option.

Destruction of Evidence

Senator Packwood testified that he made changes to a duplicate copy of his diary tapes, and that he then made a copy of this changed duplicate to give to Ms. Cormack to type.[62] As she finished typing, she destroyed her copy, and he destroyed his, keeping instead the original, unaltered diary tape, which did not correspond to the typed transcript. If the Committee had access to the altered diary tapes, it would better be able to establish what deletions were made to the tapes by Senator Packwood, as these would not be on the tapes, as opposed to what entries were simply not typed by Ms. Cormack and, importantly, what changes were made by Senator Packwood to the transcript after it was typed.[63] Even accepting Senator Packwood's testimony about the timing of the changes to his diaries, he continued to allow Ms. Cormack to destroy her copy of the altered tapes, and he continued to destroy his, *after* the Committee asked to review his diaries, *and after* he received the Committee's subpoena, which specifically asked for all audiotapes as well as transcripts. All of the altered tapes must have been destroyed, since none were produced to the Court in response to the Committee's subpoena. Likewise, since no transcript pages marked by Senator

[62] Ms. Cormack did not complete her transcription of the altered tapes until at least November 9, 1993.

[63] This is significant because Ms. Cormack has testified that during the two week period in mid-to-late October 1993, when she was pushing to complete the diaries, on a few occasions Senator Packwood brought her diary pages she had already typed, with instructions on changes to be made to them. If the Committee had the altered tapes, this would help establish whether certain entries were changed after the Committee had asked to review his diaries on October 6, 1993, during this mid-to-late October period.

Packwood for changes by Ms. Cormack were provided to the Court, these must also have been destroyed by Senator Packwood and/or Ms. Cormack.

It is clear from the October 20, 1993 letter from Senator Packwood's attorneys to the Committee, stating that only half of the 1992 tapes had been typed and were ready for review by Committee counsel, and from Cathy Cormack's testimony that the two week period of mid-to-late October was part of the "crunch time" for typing the transcripts, that a significant number of altered tapes were transcribed, and the *tapes destroyed,* after the Committee specifically asked for the diaries, and *after* the Committee more specifically subpoenaed all diary tapes as well as diary transcripts. Thus, Senator Packwood created an altered version of his diaries wherein a significant number of the alterations related specifically to the Committee's inquiry or to matters within the Committee's jurisdiction, and then destroyed the evidence (the altered tapes) which was critical to a determination as to the purpose of the changes, which purpose the Senator has testified had no relationship to the Committee's inquiry.

Reliance on the Advice of Counsel

Senator Packwood has repeatedly stated that he felt free to alter his diaries during 1993 because his attorneys made the determination that the Committee was not entitled to them, and that, in making those changes, he relied upon the fact that his attorneys were not providing the Committee with any diary excerpts in response to the Committee's requests. Senator Packwood testified that his attorneys made the decision to withhold his diaries from the Committee in response to its document requests. Despite repeated questioning, he could not elaborate on precisely what his attorneys told him on this subject. Nevertheless, this claim, that his attorneys made the decision about what to provide to the Committee, is corroborated by Mr. Fitzpatrick of Arnold & Porter.

Senator Packwood, however, was not charged by the Committee with a failure to turn over his diaries to the Committee in response to its requests. The Committee charged Senator Packwood with intentionally altering his diaries after he knew or should have known that the Committee had sought or would likely seek them. Senator Packwood was certainly entitled to rely upon his attorneys' decision to withhold his diaries on the grounds of privilege, even if his attorneys' judgment was later proven to be incorrect. But Senator Packwood's attorneys did *not* advise him that it was permissible to alter his diaries, privileged or not. Indeed, his attorneys did not even know that he was altering his diaries until November 21, 1993, the day before they resigned. Senator Packwood cannot shift responsibility for the alteration of his diaries to his attorneys.

Moreover, Counsel notes that Senator Packwood began changing his diaries in January 1993, at least two months before he received the Committee's document request on March 29, 1993. Senator Packwood told the Committee that his attorneys made the decision not to turn over his diaries to the Committee sometime *after* the Committee's March 29, 1993 document request. Even accepting Senator Packwood's assertion that he felt free to change his diaries because of his counsel's decision not to turn them over to the Committee, there was no such advice to rely upon when he was changing the 1992 tapes during January, February, and most of March, 1993.

It should not be overlooked that Senator Packwood is himself a lawyer. He knew as early as December 1992, when his attorneys asked him for excerpts from his diaries touching on the intimidation issue, and as he provided them with other excerpts from the diary throughout early 1993, that his attorneys considered his diaries important to his defense to the extent they contained material relevant to the Committee's inquiry. It is certainly reasonable to expect that Senator Packwood could anticipate that the Committee might also want access to his diaries at some point. Indeed, an entry in Senator Packwood's original diary audiotape (which does not appear in the Cormack transcript, dated March 29, 1993 because the Senator deleted it), the same day that Senator Packwood received the Committee's document request, makes it clear that Senator Packwood was concerned that the Committee might get access to his diaries. Those diaries contained information that was directly relevant to the Committee's inquiry. Regardless of his attorneys' determination about what he could withhold from the Committee, Senator Packwood knew the importance of preserving the integrity of anything that might at some point become evidence in an ongoing inquiry, and the consequences of altering any such potential evidence.

Conclusions

Senate Ethics Counsel finds that Senator Packwood intentionally changed entries in his diaries that related to the subject of the Committee's inquiry, or to areas of possible misconduct that were subject to the Committee's jurisdiction, at a time when he was the subject of an inquiry into misconduct by the Committee, and when he knew or should have known that the Committee would likely seek or had sought those diaries as evidence in its inquiry.

It is not necessary to Counsel's finding of improper conduct to also find that Senator Packwood acted for the specific purpose of obstructing the Committee's inquiry. Such a determination is better left to other authorities, and Counsel defers to their eventual judgment on this matter. Counsel does find, however, that

Senator Packwood purposefully selected and changed entries in his diary tapes for 1992 and 1993 that he knew were relevant to the Committee's inquiry, and that could be incriminating to him, along with other entries that could result in Committee inquiry into other activity.

Senate Ethics Counsel finds that Senator Packwood's actions were contemptuous of and subverted the Senate's Constitutional self-disciplinary process. By delegation of authority from the Senate, the Committee is specifically empowered to obtain evidence from Members and others who are the subject of Committee inquiry, and it is entitled to rely on the integrity of such evidence. Indeed, the entire process is compromised and rendered wholly without value if persons subject to the Committee's inquiry, or witnesses in an inquiry, are allowed to jeopardize the integrity of evidence coming before the Committee.

Senate Ethics Counsel finds that Senator Packwood's actions constitute an abuse of his position as a United States Senator, are a violation of his duty of trust to the Senate, and constitute improper conduct reflecting discredit upon the United States Senate.

Counsel suggests that the matter of diary alteration is appropriate for referral to the Department of Justice for its attention pursuant to Committee Rule 8(a).

6

Evidence Regarding the Allegations of Soliciting Employment for Senator Packwood's Spouse

THE EVIDENCE RELATING to the issue of whether Senator Packwood may have inappropriately linked personal financial gain to his official position by soliciting or otherwise encouraging offers of financial assistance from persons having a particular interest in legislation or issues that he could influence is set forth below.[1]

STEVE SAUNDERS

Background

Steve Saunders worked for Senator Packwood from 1977 until 1981. From 1977 until January, 1979, he was the Director of Communications for the National Republican Senatorial Committee, which Senator Packwood chaired. From 1979 until 1981, he was the Staff Director of the Senate Republican Conference, which Senator Packwood also chaired. In May, 1982, he established his own consulting firm. He is currently the sole proprietor of an international trade consulting firm; a sculpture export

---

[1] This information was referred to the Department of Justice pursuant to Rule 8(a) of the Committee's Rules of Procedure on or about November 22, 1993. On June 28, 1995, the Department of Justice informed the Committee that it had declined criminal prosecution of the allegations related to job opportunities for the Senator's wife.

business, which markets the work of American sculptors in the U.S. and overseas; and a retail art gallery. He has been close friends with both Senator and Mrs. Packwood for roughly sixteen years. He is a registered foreign agent for the Mitsubishi Electric Corporation ("Mitsubishi").

The November 1989 Diary Entries

The most significant diary entries relating to Mr. Saunders are dated November 3 and November 6, 1989, respectively. The November 3 entry provides, in pertinent part, as follows:

> Saunders arrived and he and I went over to the Tortilla Coast or whatever that place is for beers. I drank two quickly and I said, "Steve, I need to talk about the purpose of the meeting." Steve said, "I think I know. You and Georgie are splitting." I said, "Well, I think we're going to separate and I kind of want to know if you could be of some help." He said, "In what fashion." I said, "I don't know how much your firm makes." He says, "We're doing $600 to $700 thousand a year now." I said I wonder if you can put Georgie on a retainer." He says "How much?" I said, "$7500 a year." He says, "$7500 a year???" I said, "Yeah." He said, "Consider it done." When he said 'yeah' I think he thought I was going to say a month. He said, "I'd be happy to do it." . . . But in any event, I've now got her $20,000. $7500 from Ron, $7500 from Steve, $5000 from[2]

Three days later, on Monday, November 6, 1989, Senator Packwood recorded the following in his diary:

[2] The fact of this meeting is supported by a letter dated November 6, 1989, in which Senator Packwood thanked Mr. Saunders for meeting with him. Mr. Saunders testified that he never received this letter.

At a request of Steve Saunders I stopped in at the Finance Committee to read two questions which I wanted asked of a man named Spero, the President of Fusion something or other. This guy's been carrying on a vendetta with the Japanese about patents for years, first in the Commerce Committee with Jay Rockefeller pushing it there and then in the Finance Committee with Jay pushing it again. It's funny. Fusion is in Maryland. I don't know what the connection is with West Virginia. Steve Saunders thinks that Jay is just genuinely concerned but he keeps pushing and pushing this issue so I said of course I'd go and ask the questions.[3]

A transcript of the November 6, 1989 Finance Committee hearing indicates that Senator Packwood briefly attended the hearing, read two questions he wanted asked of Mr. Spero into the record, and then left.[4] Documents produced by Mr. Saunders indicate that questions virtually identical to the ones asked by Senator Packwood at the hearing were submitted to a Finance Committee staffer by Mr. Saunders on November 6, 1989.[5] In other documents submitted by Mr. Saunders, he advised his client Mitsubishi that Senator Packwood was not originally scheduled to attend the hearing and rearranged his schedule at the last minute because Mr. Saunders asked him to appear.[6]

---

[3] This entry is supported by Senator Packwood's handwritten calendar of events, which reads "Finance for Saunders" on November 6, 1989 at 2:00 p.m.

[4] The two questions read into the record by Senator Packwood for Mr. Spero, which explore the differences between the U.S. and Japanese patent systems, appear on page 3 of the hearing transcript.

[5] Senator Packwood testified that while the questions could have been submitted by Mr. Saunders, he did not know that was the case at the time. He further testified that he does not recall having any discussion with Mr. Saunders at any time about the questions he had submitted for his consideration.

[6] Senator Packwood testified that he has no recollection of changing his schedule to attend the hearing. Mr. Saunders testified that he persuaded the Senator to make at least a brief personal appearance at the hearing.

Senator Packwood's Testimony:

At his deposition, Senator Packwood testified that on November 3, he had been drinking in the office before Mr. Saunders arrived. He stated that he drank a lot very quickly and was quite drunk, but he does remember going with Mr. Saunders to Tortilla Coast. He stated that he thinks they discussed Mr. Saunders hiring Mrs. Packwood, but he emphasized that this was a drunken evening for him.

Senator Packwood testified that he does not recall any of the specific conversation recorded in the November 3, 1989 diary entry. He stated that he thinks the meeting was held at his behest. The Senator stated that when Mr. Saunders and he and Mrs. Packwood had been in Asia the year before, he had discussed his marital situation with Mr. Saunders and he had offered to help. Referring to the November 3 entry, Senator Packwood stated that "whether I said exactly this or not, I think I asked him if he was prepared to sort of follow up on what he had said." Senator Packwood testified that he cannot recall whether they specifically discussed Mr. Saunders employing Mrs. Packwood prior to the November 3 meeting. Rather, he only recalls the offer to help, as the colloquy below demonstrates:

Q: Just to clarify, Senator, in terms of your discussions with Mr. Saunders, I believe you had said that you had had a conversation with Mr. Saunders prior to this time [Nov. 3] in which there was some discussion about employing Mrs. Packwood; is that correct?

A: That, I can't remember. Because I remember the gallery part. And whether it was before this or not—what I remember, Steve was a good friend. He knew about my marital troubles and had offered to help. Whether or not at that stage he says I'm opening an art gallery, I can't remember. But it was the offer to help that I recall.

Q: And when you say here I wonder if you can put Georgie on a retainer, as I understand your testimony, you simply can't recall whether you said that or not?

A: I don't recall any of the specific conversation.

Q: But given the context of what you described, I presume that it's possible that was said?

A: Well, what I remember is talking to him about a job. Beyond that, I can't remember.

Senator Packwood testified that he has no memory of any discussion at the November 3 meeting of the upcoming hearing on patents before the Finance Committee. Nor does he recall whether Mr. Saunders offered him any written materials in connection with the hearing on patents. He does not recall any discussion of Mitsubishi on November 3, although he was aware of Mr. Saunder's representation of Mitsubishi. The Senator testified that the Mitsubishi/Fusion issue was one that he had been working on for about 18 months as of November, 1989. He stated that he believed Fusion was inappropriately using Congressional hearings as a forum for complaining because they were unsuccessful in their commercial dispute with Mitsubishi.

Turning to the November 6, 1989 entry, Senator Packwood testified that he does not remember Mr. Saunders calling him to request that he attend the hearing. He testified that, "He [Saunders] may have called and said would you mind asking him [Spero] personally." When questioned further about the entry and why he attended the hearing, Senator Packwood responded as follows:

Q: Is that what you think you meant by "at a request of Steve Saunders?"

A: Well, I don't remember the phone call. I don't remember the questions, other than apparently they were questions I was going to submit, I would judge, the way this reads. And whether he called and said would you mind asking him personally or not, I don't know. This is a common thing that all of us do. If someone calls us up— apparently these are questions my staff did, but quite frequently you'll get questions from lobbyists that send you in questions and say will you go in and ask this.

Q: Would it be fair to say that Mr. Saunders is the one that brought the dispute between Mitsubishi and Fusion to your attention?

A: He may have been the one that initially brought it to my attention 18 months or so ago.

Q: Do you recall specifically whether it was him or someone with his organization?

A: No, I don't recall.

Q: And again, to the language at the very first sentence where you say "at a request of Steve Saunders," I believe you touched on this, but let me be sure I understand. Do you recall any type of written or telephonic communication from Mr. Saunders where he actually made the request for you to attend this committee hearing and ask these questions?

A: No, I don't. . . .

With respect to his handwritten calendar of events, which contains an entry that reads "Finance for Saunders," Senator Packwood denied that there was a connection between attending the hearing and Mr. Saunders:

Q: That would suggest that in your mind, there was a connection between attending that hearing and Steve Saunders; is that correct?

A: No. I think it is more likely that if he'd [Saunders] called me up and ask me to go ask the questions as opposed to my just handing them in and asking whoever was chairing the hearing that day, that I went up and asked the questions. Not that I was attending the meeting for him. This was an issue I'd been following for this long period of time. And I knew this guy Spero was going to be there, but I apparently had not intended to go to the meeting, but just turn the questions in and maybe Steve said please go ask them personally so I put this entry in.

Q: Do you believe you would have personally attended the hearing but for Mr. Saunders request?

A: That I can't remember now.

Q: So as I understand it, there wasn't a question as to whether you were going to have these questions asked, but rather a question if you would personally attend and ask the questions; is that correct, as opposed to submitting them in writing?

A: Yes, although "personally attend" doesn't necessarily mean stay at the meeting. . . .

Senator Packwood testified that he does not recall any discussion with Mr. Saunders about any type of connection or relationship between Mr. Saunder's hiring Mrs. Packwood and the questions that he wanted asked at the November 6 hearing. Nor was there any type of implicit understanding that there was a connection or relationship between his discussions with Mr. Saunders about hiring Mrs. Packwood and the questions he wanted asked at the November 6 hearing. In this regard, Senator Packwood testified as follows:

Q: . . . do you believe that there was a connection between your discussions with Mr. Saunders about employment opportunities for Mrs. Packwood and his request of you to ask certain questions at this hearing?

A: Absolutely not. Steve was a close friend, had been for a decade and a quarter. I'd travelled with him. I'd worked on this issue with him for 18 months, and I would have done this if I would have never met with him on Friday night.

Brief History of Senator Packwood's Involvement in the Japanese Patent Issue

In a letter dated November 16, 1993 to Mr. Brooks Jackson of CNN, Senator Packwood provided a history of his involvement in the Japanese patent issue. He explained that his interest in this issue began around June of 1988 when he was preparing for a hearing before the Senate Commerce Committee's Subcommittee on Foreign Commerce and Tourism. In preparation of this hearing, he stated that his staff had described the dispute between Fusion Systems and Mitsubishi and Mitsubishi's hope that the hearing would focus on larger policy issues. During the course of this hearing, Senator Packwood asked U.S. government officials how the U.S. patent system stacked up against the systems of other countries. He also requested an additional hearing to hear from U.S. companies who had some success working with the Japanese patent system.

In his November 16 letter, Senator Packwood goes on to state that on January 27, 1989, during the confirmation hearings on the nomination of Carla Hills to U.S. Trade Representative before the Senate Finance Committee, he asked Ms. Hills to speak with experts in the patent area before making any decisions on issues involving the Japanese patent office. Then, on February 28, 1989, the Commerce Committee's Subcommittee on Foreign Commerce and Tourism held its second hearing on the Japanese patent system. At this hearing, he again asked U.S. government officials whether the U.S. patent system or the Japanese patent system was more in line with the rest of the industrialized world.[7]

Senator Packwood concludes his letter by asserting that he has had a longstanding interest in intellectual property issues. He states that during the 1988–89 hearings, he kept hearing how the Japanese system was unfair and discriminatory. However, he discovered that the Japanese patent system was more in step with the rest of the industrialized world than the U.S. system. He states that his efforts were an attempt to ensure balance in the review of the patent issue.

Mr. Saunders's Testimony

Mr. Saunders recalls that in the 1980's, his firm was retained by Mitsubishi to advise it on various trade issues. In 1987 or 1988, his company began working with Mitsubishi's Washington lawyers, lobbyists and public relations advisors regarding a dispute between Mitsubishi and a Maryland company called Fusion. According to Mr. Saunders, Mitsubishi had been attempting to negotiate a settlement of a dispute with Fusion over patents in Japan for several years. The head of Fusion, a Mr. Spero, decided that he wanted to try to apply additional pressure on Mitsubishi to reach a favorable settlement. Spero engaged the interest of the office of the U.S. Trade Representative, which ultimately resulted in the Deputy U.S.T.R. telling Mitsubishi executives that they

[7] Senator Packwood's diary entry of February 28, 1989 confirms his attendance at this subcommittee hearing. At the end of the passage, Senator Packwood records, "I think we have laid to rest the Fusion problem." In explaining what he meant by "laying to rest the Fusion problem," Senator Packwood testified that, ". . . I wasn't going to let him [Spero] use the hearing process to try to get us to force the Japanese to give him something that he didn't deserve. I had hoped I guess on this day that we had finally killed it." In a background memo for this hearing dated February 27, 1989, one of the Senator's staffers notes that Senator Packwood was "brought into this issue by Steve Saunders, on behalf of Mitsubishi."

should settle their dispute with Fusion on terms favorable to Fusion because the issue had become political in the United States. Mr. Saunders claims that he advised Mitsubishi that in the case of a home-grown American entrepreneur fighting a Goliath Japanese company, the best Mitsubishi could hope to accomplish was keeping the record straight. It was decided that the best way to deal with the publicity generated by Mr. Spero's efforts was to present the facts about the functions of the Japanese patent system and the Mitsubishi/Fusion dispute to members and staff of the Senate Commerce and Finance Committees.

Mr. Saunders recalls that during 1988, various persons associated with the firms retained by Mitsubishi met several times with Senator Packwood and members of his staff. Mr. Saunders sat in on at least two of these meetings during 1988 and 1989, which were arranged by Mitsubishi's lobbying firm, Thompson & Co. Mr. Saunders got involved because it became apparent that they needed to contact Senator Packwood, who was a senior member of the Commerce Committee and a leading free trader. He stated that his firm became involved because there had been a history of poor relations between the Senator and Bob Thompson of Thompson & Co. Mr. Saunders stated that Senator Packwood became very interested in the differences between the U.S. patent system and the patent systems used by other countries, including Japan. The Senator was not interested in the details of the dispute between Mitsubishi and Fusion.

On November 3, 1989, Mr. Saunders stated that he and Senator Packwood had dinner at a Mexican restaurant on Capitol Hill. He testified that he believes Senator Packwood was impaired by the alcohol he consumed at this dinner, although he described the Senator as a "functional alcoholic." Mr. Saunders claims that they did not discuss business matters whatsoever, including the upcoming November 6 hearing. There was no discussion of Mitsubishi or Fusion or the patent issue. Rather, he maintains they only discussed their families and personal lives. He testified that the Senator asked him what he was doing in his business and Mr. Saunders told him about his plans to start a sculpture exporting business and an art gallery. He testified that the Senator asked him how much his business was making and Mr. Saunders told him "$600,000 to $700,000 a year."

Senator Packwood then told him that he and his wife were going to divorce. He testified that the Senator told him that he wanted to "simplify his life" and that he was "tired of carrying all these people (i.e., his wife and children)." Although there had been some discussion of divorce in Asia the year before, Mr. Saunders stated that there was no discussion of employment for the Senator's wife at that time. The Senator also told Mr. Saunders that he had not yet told his wife about his plans to divorce and asked him not to say anything to her. Mr. Saunders asked what Mrs. Packwood would do and the Senator responded that he did not know. Mr. Saunders recalls that Senator Packwood then stated that he was a little worried about Mrs. Packwood's future sources of income. He told Senator Packwood that he did not think he had any reason to worry because Mrs. Packwood had been operating a successful antique business for several years and was talented in the buying and selling of antiques.

Mr. Saunders recalls that he told Senator Packwood that he had been thinking about calling Mrs. Packwood to help him with his new venture of marketing American sculpture in Japan. At that time, Mr. Saunders was in the process of setting up his sculpture exporting business and was in the beginning stages of setting up his gallery. It had occurred to him that Mrs. Packwood would be valuable to him because he believed that Mrs. Packwood's skill in the antique business was easily transferable to the contemporary art business. He testified that he initiated the idea of Mrs. Packwood working for him and that the Senator did not suggest such an arrangement. Mr. Saunders stated that he did not think the Senator was trying to solicit an offer of employment for his wife during this dinner.

Mr. Saunders testified that he specifically asked whether the Senator had any ethical problem with the idea because he was a registered foreign agent, and the Senator said no. The Senator asked him to keep him informed of the status of his discussions with Mrs. Packwood.

Mr. Saunders recalls that Senator Packwood asked how much money his wife could earn working for him. He advised the Senator that this would depend on how much time she wanted to work and what type of wage or commission arrangement she wanted to negotiate. Senator Packwood asked if she could make at least $7,500 a year. Mr. Saunders said that he thought she could easily make $7500 a year, although it struck him as somewhat of an odd figure. Mr. Saunders does not recall ever discussing putting Mrs. Packwood on a retainer.

On the morning of the November 6, 1989 hearing, Mr. Saunders testified that he heard that Senator Packwood would not be able to attend due to scheduling conflicts. He called Senator Packwood and urged him to at least stop in at the hearing and read the questions that he had submitted into the record. Senator Packwood said he was unsure whether he could and asked whether he had received the questions. Mr. Saunders testified that he had submitted proposed questions for the Senator to ask at the hearing to a staffer named Rolf Lundberg. He does not recall having any discussions with the Senator about the Fusion issue after the November 6 hearing. Mr. Saunders testified that he never had any discussion with the Senator about attending the hearing or asking questions at the hearing in connection with the employment proposal for Mrs. Packwood.

Mr. Saunders recalls that he called Mrs. Packwood soon after his dinner with Senator Packwood to discuss his proposal. Over the next several months, Mr. Saunders spoke with Mrs. Packwood several times about the possibility of her helping him with the entity that would become his sculpture business and eventually, with his art gallery. Some time in March or April of 1990, they got together to discuss his proposal in detail. In June, 1990, Mr. Saunders arranged for Mrs. Packwood to attend several sessions of the International Sculpture Conference in Washington, D.C. to see whether she would feel comfortable with the contemporary art business. Mr. Saunders recalls that after attending the conference, Mrs. Packwood told him she was not comfortable with contemporary sculpture and felt it was too far removed from her field. She indicated that she would be willing, however, to arrange antique buying trips and gallery visits for visiting clients of his consulting firm and their wives if there were any opportunities for that kind of work.

By June of 1990, Mr. Saunders had heard from Mrs. Packwood that other friends had spontaneously offered her jobs. She was persuaded that most of the people making her offers were asked to do so by the Senator in order to reduce the potential demand for alimony. It was at this time that she indicated that she thought Mr. Saunders was being used by the Senator. In one of his last conversations with the Senator about this subject, Mr. Saunders testified that the Senator became extremely interested in how much money his wife could earn. The Senator then stated that the alimony settlement could bankrupt him. He also asked Mr. Saunders for a statement describing his job offer to be used at the divorce trial, but Mr. Saunders refused. Mr. Saunders stated that although he did not feel coerced by the Senator, he did feel manipulated.

Mr. Saunders testified that although his first conversation with Senator Packwood about Mrs. Packwood's possible role in helping him develop his art businesses and his telephone call to the Senator to request that he attend the hearing on the Japanese patent system occurred three days apart, there was no connection in his mind between the job offer and his work for Mitsubishi. He stated that Mrs. Packwood had been extremely close to his family at critical times in his family's life. He stated there was never an express or implied quid pro quo. He explained that the Packwoods were two friends going through an agonizing situation and he was trying to act as a friend. He explained that the Senator was a friend and that Mrs. Packwood was an even closer friend.

Other Diary Entries Referring to Mr. Saunders and Job Offers for Mrs. Packwood and Related Testimony

10/18/89

In addition to the two diary entries discussed above, there are other diary entries spanning the time frame from October 1989 through June of 1990 in which Senator Packwood makes various references to Mr. Saunders extending employment opportunities to Mrs. Packwood. On October 18, 1989, he recorded the following entry in his diary:

. . . I did have time to come back to the office, talk to Tim Lee and he says he'll be happy to put up $10,000 a year for Georgie. That's three out of three and I haven't even hit up or Steve Saunders. I've got to handle this carefully. I don't want in any way there to be any quid pro quo. There shall not be any quid pro quo. I'm not going to do anything for these guys that I would not do for them anyway. My hunch is I'll get something out of Saunders and out of   . I think I'll ask them for $5000 apiece and hold it in reserve and indicate to Georgie that if she'll say she can make $20,000 I'll make sure she gets another $20,000.[8] Then I'll come up with more and that will give me enough of an asset base to be able to buy a small two bedroom townhouse.

When asked to explain what he meant by the words "hit up," Senator Packwood testified that his "use of the phrase 'hit up' is to call somebody."[9] He went on to testify:

Q: Were you calling these people for a particular purpose?
A: I would have been calling them to see if they would provide some help for me with Georgie.
Q: When you say "help," do you mean income?
A: Yes. That wouldn't be quite the same with   , but go ahead.
Q: What did you mean when you said—
A: Hold on a second. All of these people, as you're well aware that I called were old friends. They had all in one form or another, discovered the possibility of separation, had indicated they wanted to help. And I don't want in any way for you to think the term "hit up" as in other than I'm going to call and see if they can be of help, following

---

[8] Senator Packwood testified that he is not sure what he meant by "hold it in reserve." He explained that he hoped Mrs. Packwood could make $20,000 in her own antique business. The other $20,000 refers to the collective amount from the various opportunities being offered by his friends. He further explained that "asset base" refers to the proceeds from the sale of their house. He acknowledged that to the extent Mrs. Packwood was able to earn more money, his responsibility in terms of alimony would be less.

[9] In an entry on the Cormack transcript dated November 21, 1989, and received by the Committee from Judge Starr after Senator Packwood's deposition, Senator Packwood recorded:

It's time now to accept the offers that I've solicited from Crawford and Steve and   . That will give her $20,000 right now. Then I'll talk to Cliff Alexander perhaps. . I wouldn't mind getting her to about $30,000 here without initially calling on Tim Lee and Bill Furman in Portland.

up on their suggestion that if anything was going to happen they would be of help.

Q: But the purpose of calling them was to talk about income or job opportunities or business opportunities for Mrs. Packwood?

A: Yes, to discuss that.

Senator Packwood also testified at length with respect to the quid pro quo reference in his diary:

Q: Were you at all concerned, Senator, about the propriety of having discussions with or making requests of persons who might have an interest in legislation, having discussions about job opportunities or business opportunities for Mrs. Packwood? . . .

A: These were old friends. I've been in politics a quarter of a century and would there be, I suppose, a thousand lobbyists you could go to and make this kind of a request? I assume there would be. I didn't go to them. I went to people that I had known, that were friends of mine, in some cases drinking buddies of mine, in all cases, all long standing friends.

I did not go to them because they were lobbyists and I did not ever do anything for them nor would I do anything for them that I would not have otherwise have done but for Georgie and I being separated, married or otherwise. And I saw nothing wrong with going to people that had been longstanding friends, personal friends and asking for help.

And especially when I made it very clear, and you've probably seen it somewhere before when I said there's to be no quid pro quo, not only here but in the memo to the marriage counselor, where there was to be no quid pro quo and she was to keep track of her hours and records. And if she could not perform value received, then she would not be paid. I did everything I could to make sure this was legal and ethical . . .

Q: . . . Were you concerned about a potential quid pro quo?

A: No, I was not concerned about a potential quid pro quo at all. I don't do business that way. I don't trade my votes for money and I was not going to do any quid pro quo.

Q: Why did you—do you know why you recorded these thoughts? They appear to reflect a concern about a quid pro quo.

A: You will find those thoughts all through my diary . . . It's nothing unique here. That is the way I think. . . .

Q: I appreciate that. My question, Senator, is in the context of talking about and having conversations with these persons about providing income to Mrs. Packwood, in that same passage or at the end of that passage, you make reference to you do not want there to be any quid pro quo, not wanting to do anything for these guys that you wouldn't do for them anyway. And I guess my question is: Why—do you know why you put those thoughts, why you recorded those thoughts—

A: As I said, you'll see this kind of entry all through my diary dealing with different people. Conversations, I've often said, are not necessarily accurate. Thoughts may be more accurate . . . I put this in here because these are my thoughts . . . I don't do business that way . . . So I put it in because that's the way—I can't remember on this particular one why I put it in. That's just the way I think. . . .

Q: . . . In general, why would you have expressed those thoughts in connection with discussions relating to persons about job opportunities for Mrs. Packwood?

A: Why would I express it that way? Any place else in the diary, where somebody's coming in and I say by God, that's not the way I do business. Because those are my thoughts. I don't do business that way, and this diary is full of thoughts.

Q: Is there a reason specifically that those thoughts, that is thoughts about quid pro quos, would have been included in discussions about business opportunities for Mrs. Packwood?

A: Only in the sense I was going to make sure there would be no quid pro quo. And I did not want to do anything that would be a quid pro quo.

12/16/89 THROUGH 1/18/90

On December 16, 1989, Senator Packwood again referred to Mr. Saunders in his diary, expressing a desire for him to call Mrs. Packwood and "indicate the money he [was] willing to spend on her."[10] Senator Packwood testified that he was hoping to eventually obtain approximately $20,000 for Mrs. Packwood with respect to the offers of employment. On January 7, 1990, Senator Packwood noted in general that "it is imperative that she be willing to accept some business. If she says she won't I'll still have to try to get her some and see what happens." On January 18, 1990, Senator Packwood again referred to Mr. Saunders:

I hit   up. He says 'yes.'   a close friend but not as close as Cliff. The same with Saunders, same with Ron. They just say bang, bang, bang—yes. But not Cliff. That means next week I've got to turn to Saunders and then to Crawford.

---

[10] Senator Packwood testified that he meant what Mr. Saunders would be willing to employ her for if she was willing to provide services of value.

Here, Senator Packwood testified that when he recorded "hit up," he meant asking him if he could talk Georgie into a job.

1/24/90

On January 24, 1990, Senator Packwood recorded three entries involving job offers to his wife. In the first of these entries, after mentioning that he wanted Mr. Saunders (as well as others) to call Mrs. Packwood about the job offer, he recorded the following:

> I'll get Saunders to do the same. Then I can't decide whether it is   or   Tim Lee, or Crawford. I don't think I'll go beyond that right now. I want her to have at least $20,000 in offers. Boy, I'm scating [sic] on thin ice here. I'm glad I put in writing to her . . . that I'll help her get business but she must give service for value and that this is and I used the word—this is not to be a bribe for me or gift to you and if you cannot perform the service, then your income or retainer will have to be reduced or eliminated. . . .

When asked about this entry, Senator Packwood responded as follows:

> Q: . . . What did you mean by "Boy, I'm skating on thin ice here?"
> A: You asked earlier, could anybody construe this to be—I don't know if you said unethical or illegal or something like that, and I answered you've seen what the press will construe to be illegal or unethical. It's perfectly allright [sic]. And I knew what I was doing was perfectly allright, or I thought I knew what I was doing was perfectly allright. And I checked it as best I could'' and I didn't want

anybody to construe it any differently than that. I didn't want the press to do something if this got out. . . .

Q: What did you mean by the reference "I'm skating on thin ice here?"

A: That's where the press can take something that's perfectly legal, legitimate, moral and ethical and try to turn it into something wrong.

Also on January 24, 1990, Senator Packwood noted in his diary that Mr. Saunders had contacted him regarding the job offer to Mrs. Packwood:

I talked to Steve Saunders. I was returning his call. He had talked to Georgie. She had returned his call. He said he had a business proposition for her and the first question was, "Did Bob put you up to this?" He said, "No." He was lying, but he said 'no.' He said, "I called him because it involves Epson. Epson-America, of course has their major plant in Hillsboro [Oregon] and I wanted to make sure there was no conflict of

---

11 Senator Packwood testified that he discussed the arrangement involving job offers to his wife with his friend Jack Faust, who is an attorney. He also discussed it with Jack Quinn, who the Senator described as a lawyer at Arnold & Porter and an expert in ethics rules. In his appearance before the Committee, Senator Packwood again referred to Mr. Quinn's advice and stated that Mr. Quinn had provided him a memo on the subject. Mr. Quinn's correspondence and accompanying memo to the Senator are dated June 25, 1990. Senator Packwood also initially suggested that he might have discussed the subject with Mr. Wilson Abney, formerly of the Senate Ethics Committee staff. He later clarified that he did not have any discussion with Mr. Abney about the job offers for Mrs. Packwood, although he did have discussions with him about the filing requirements if he and his wife were living separately but still married. This testimony is supported by an entry in his diary dated January 24, 1990 and an exchange of correspondence dated January 25 and February 6, 1990, respectively.

interest. Bob said 'no' and I said, 'Do you think Georgie would be interested?,' and he said, 'You'd better call her. I don't know . . .''

With respect to this entry, Senator Packwood testified that he does not recall this conversation. He stated that Mr. Saunders knew that Mrs. Packwood would be angry if she knew he was involved in the offer. The Senator testified as follows:

Q: Had you, in fact told him [Saunders] to do this?
A: I'd ask him to call . . . he at some stage said Bob, what can I do to help and we talked about his help and to that extent, after he'd asked first could I be of help, but he wasn't going to say to her Bob told me to do this or she would have been livid.

He also testified that he could not recall having any discussions with Mr. Saunders about Mrs. Packwood's qualifications for the job.

Mr. Saunders testified that in one of his early conversations with Mrs. Packwood, she may have asked whether her husband put him up to offering her a job. He testified that the Senator's reference to him lying in the January 24, 1990 entry is inaccurate.

4/13/90

On April 13, 1990, Senator Packwood recorded in his diary another conversation with Mr. Saunders relating to the job offer for Mrs. Packwood:

I got ahold of Steve Saunders and said it's time to put the proposal in writing also and Saunders says, "Well, let me tell you what the latest is. I talked with Georgie yesterday . . . she is interested in escorting these women around town on shopping tours—the wives of visiting dignitaries—but she absolutely does not want me to put anything in writing and for the moment she is not interested in any kind of venture with my . . . sculptor art exporting company or something like that . . ."

Senator Packwood testified that he does not recall why he wanted the proposal in writing. He stated that he does not know whether the proposal was ever reduced to writing. He stated that he has only a dim recollection of any discussion with Mr. Saunders about Mrs. Packwood escorting the wives of visiting dignitaries on shopping trips.

Mr. Saunders stated that he is unsure whether he came up with the idea of escorting the wives or whether Mrs. Packwood first came up with this idea. This proposal never materialized. There was no further discussion about any type of employment opportunity for her after June, 1990. He does not recall the Senator ever telling him to put the proposal in writing. He testified that he probably spoke with the Senator every time he spoke with Mrs. Packwood to report on his progress.

Senator Packwood testified that there was no discussion at any time with Mr. Saunders about the job offer to Mrs. Packwood in connection with him taking or refraining from taking any action in his capacity as a Senator. Nor was there any type of implied understanding that there was a relationship between the job offer to Mrs. Packwood from Mr. Saunders and the Senator taking any action in an official capacity.

Mrs. Packwood's Testimony

Mrs. Packwood testified that soon after she first met Mr. Saunders in roughly 1980, and even before she started her antiques business, she had purchased Teddy Roosevelt memorabilia for him. Some time between January and June, 1990, Mrs. Packwood testified that Mr. Saunders telephoned and asked whether she would be interested in helping a client find North American Indian antiques. She testified that this was not ongoing employment. She did not accept this proposal.[12] She stated that Mr. Saunders made a second proposal which involved buying sculpture and art for commercial establishments in the Orient. She testified that she believes it was proposed as "being a little ongoing anyway." She testified that she was not interested in this proposal and advised him accordingly.

Mrs. Packwood testified that Mr. Saunders made a third proposal in this time frame which involved escorting the wives of his Japanese clients to antique shows and shops. Mrs. Packwood testified that she had no contact with Mr. Saunders after he made this last proposal until after the divorce. Mr. Saunders later suggested that Mrs. Packwood work at the art gallery he was planning on opening if she were going to stay in town. By that time however, she had decided to move back to Oregon.

As to Mr. Saunders's knowledge of the other job offers, Mrs. Packwood testified that she believed she ". . . ought to warn" him that ". . . there's a lot of stuff going on here that you could get caught in a web of, about finding employment for me that I'm not instigating." She testified that Mr. Saunders wondered why the Senator was so interested in how much she could earn. She stated that she believed that Senator Packwood became coercive and manipulative and Mr. Saunders then backed off.

Commenting in general, Mrs. Packwood testified that she did not regard the proposals as job offers. She explained that she was

---

[12] Mr. Saunders testified that this trip was part of his effort to interest Mrs. Packwood in the sculpture business.

not job hunting and that she viewed them as some kind of "coercive behavior." She went on to state, "They [job offers] frightened me, but Bob Packwood frightened me in his behavior at that particular time anyway, so it was all part of a huge package of manipulation of me." When asked whether she believes the proposals would have been made to her but for her husband's status as a Senator, she testified as follows:

> The exception would be Mr. Saunders. [With regard to] the other proposals. There was no reason to make them. In all the years I've known Ron Crawford, Tim Lee and   , nothing ever arose in conversation or communication of any kind between me and them to do with my working outside my home, doing anything other than what I had been doing for 25 years. And it's too much of a coincidence that they all three came forward at approximately the same period in my life with these sudden, whatever you call them, offers.

Summary of Senator Packwood's Response to the Evidence

Senator Packwood asserts that Mr. Saunders is an old friend who had offered to help when he learned that the Senator was separating from his wife. The Senator claims that he was merely following up on Mr. Saunders' offer of assistance when he discussed jobs and income for Mrs. Packwood. He contends that he turned to Mr. Saunders because they were longstanding friends and not for reasons related to his official position.

With respect to the November 3, 1989 diary entry in which he records that he asked Mr. Saunders to place his wife on a $7500 retainer, Senator Packwood says that he was quite drunk on this date and has no recollection of any of the specific conversation that appears in this diary entry, although he does recall talking to Mr. Saunders about a job and asking him whether he was prepared to follow up on his offer of help. Senator Packwood maintains that he has no recollection of discussing the November 6 Finance Committee hearing at the November 3 meeting with Mr. Saunders.

Senator Packwood testified that the references in his diary about quid pro quos simply reflect a desire on his part that the job proposals be legally and ethically correct and that there be no quid pro quos between the job offers and his official actions. In this regard, he asserts that he checked with a lawyer named Jack Quinn about the legality of the offers.[13] He also argues that he never attempted to conceal the involvement of those persons extending job offers to his wife because this information was publicly discussed at his divorce trial. Additionally, he relies on correspondence that he sent to his wife where he states, in part, that the job offers should not be considered as either gifts to her or bribes to him and that she must be prepared to provide value in return for payment.

Senator Packwood stated that he has no recollection of Mr. Saunders asking him to personally appear and ask questions at the November 6 hearing. He also says he has no recollection of whether he would have personally attended the hearing but for Mr. Saunders's request that he do so. He states that his

[13] In his statement before the Committee, Senator Packwood again referred to Mr. Quinn and stated that before he started talking with persons about job offers, he spoke with Mr. Quinn about the subject and that Mr. Quinn sent him information about gratuities, bribery and gifts. Mr. Quinn's correspondence to the Senator is dated June 25, 1990, after the Senator had already coordinated the job offers for his wife. Moreover, in his letter, Mr. Quinn states that he needs to do more research and thinking on the subject. He then cautions, "In the facts at hand, we have to be concerned with the coincidence of your influence over financial opportunities made available to Georgie and the fact that there is an indirect benefit from them to you."

involvement in the issue of the differences between the American and Japanese patent systems dated back at least as early as June of 1988.

Senator Packwood denies any connection between the discussion of jobs and income for his wife with Mr. Saunders and any of his official acts.

Findings

Senate Ethics Counsel finds that Senator Packwood did in fact solicit or otherwise encourage an offer of personal financial assistance from Mr. Saunders, an individual representing a client with a particularized interest in matters that the Senator could influence.

Counsel finds that Senator Packwood and Mr. Saunders engaged in discussions about job offers and income for the Senator's wife at at time when Mr. Saunders was actively representing a client with a specific and direct interest before Senator Packwood's committees. Although both have testified that Mr. Saunders first extended a general offer of assistance and Senator Packwood then merely followed up, the weight of the evidence indicates that Senator Packwood's role in encouraging and coordinating job offers for his wife was significant. In fact, Ethics Counsel finds that the Senator's discussions with Mr. Saunders about job offers for his wife comprised part of a deliberate and systematic plan by the Senator to accumulate approximately $20,000 in job offers for his spouse in order to reduce his alimony obligation. Additionally, Counsel finds that Mrs. Packwood was not looking for a job at the time Senator Packwood engaged Mr. Saunders in discussion about providing a job offer to her.

Ethics Counsel finds that Mr. Saunders's general offer of help was extended after the Senator expressed concern about his wife's future sources of income once they were separated and divorced. Moreover, Ethics Counsel finds that the Senator's diary entries, recorded nearly contemporaneously with the events as they occurred, suggest that the Senator played a more active role than simply following up with Mr. Saunders, as evidenced by the Senator's use of language such as "hit up," place on "retainer," and "accept the offers that I've solicited." Further, Counsel finds that the Senator and Mr. Saunders discussed a specific dollar amount ($7500) at their November 3, 1989 meeting. Additionally, Counsel finds that Senator Packwood requested Mr. Saunders to provide a statement describing his job offer to be used at the divorce trial, but Mr. Saunders refused.

Ethics Counsel finds that Mr. Saunders and Senator Packwood did have a longstanding friendship rooted in the Mr. Saunders's prior status as an employee. Notwithstanding this friendship, Counsel finds that at the time they were discussing job offers and income for Mrs. Packwood, Mr. Saunders was representing Mitsubishi in connection with its patent dispute with Fusion. Counsel notes that Senator Packwood's involvement in the issue of differences between the patent systems of Japan and the United States dated back at least eighteen months prior to the November 6, 1989 Committee on Finance hearing and that he publicly pursued this issue on at least three prior occasions. Nonetheless, Counsel finds that Senator Packwood rearranged his schedule at the last minute to personally attend the November 6, 1989 hearing at Mr. Saunders's request, within three days of the meeting where a job offer for Mrs. Packwood was discussed. Additionally, Counsel finds that the questions asked by Senator Packwood at the hearing, directed to Fusion's president, were virtually identical to the questions submitted by Mr. Saunders on behalf of Mitsubishi.

Counsel finds that Mr. Saunders discussed employment with Mrs. Packwood at various times between November 1989 and

June of 1990. Counsel further finds that Mrs. Packwood never accepted his offer of employment.

TIM LEE

Background

Tim Lee worked for Senator Packwood for about a year in the mid-1970's as an intern on his Washington staff. In the 1989–1991 time frame, he owned a company called Superior Transportation Systems (STS), a trucking brokerage concern. He is currently the owner of a company called Logistics Resource Management, Inc. His company owns rail cars, markets rail transportation and provides transportation consulting services.

Regarding his fundraising role, Mr. Lee was the chairman of the largest single event of the Senator;s 1992 campaign, a breakfast with then-President Bush in 1991. He stated this function raised between $350,000 and $400,000 after expenses. Mr. Lee also arranged a fundraising event in Seattle in January or February 1991, which raised between $18,000 and 20,000.

Diary Entries Referring to Mr. Lee and Job Offers to Mrs. Packwood and Related Testimony
10/18/89
Senator Packwood's diary entries relating to discussions with Mr. Lee about employment opportunities for Mrs. Packwood span from roughly October 1989 through April of 1990. On October 18, 1989, Senator Packwood recorded the following entry:

I got back and decided to make some inquiries as to whether I could get Georgie some income . . . I then called Tim Lee and said, "Tim, could you somehow put Georgie on retainer for $10,000?" They thought they could do that . . . I did have time to come back to the office, talk to Tim Lee and Tim says he'll be happy to put up $10,000 a year for Georgie. . . .

Senator Packwood testified that he cannot remember what he meant by the word "retainer" in the diary entry. He does not recall discussing a specific dollar amount with Mr. Lee. He testified that Mr. Lee was very familiar with his marital situation and that he had been talking with Mr. Lee about a job for Mrs. Packwood. Senator Packwood testified that his total recollection of discussions with Mr. Lee about jobs for Mrs. Packwood had ". . . something to do with antiques and his wife." Senator Packwood could not recall when they first started talking about antiques because they ". . . had talked about it, obviously before, concerning his wife and things Georgie was buying. I can recall taking things out on the plane that she (Georgie) had bought and taking it out to him (Lee), things of that nature. I don't know when we started talking about antiques and when this occurred."

Mr. Lee testified that he learned of the Packwood's separation some time in February or March, 1990, although he was aware that Senator Packwood had contemplated divorce at least a year prior to the time of the actual separation. Mr. Lee does not recall having discussions with Senator Packwood prior to the time he learned of the separation about providing any type of financial support for Mrs. Packwood.

Mr. Lee testified that he does not recall receiving a call from Senator Packwood in which the Senator asked him to put Mrs. Packwood on retainer for $10,000, nor does he recall ever telling Senator Packwood that he would be happy to put up $10,000. a year for Mrs. Packwood. He testified that the only time that he spoke to Senator Packwood about compensation for

Mrs. Packwood was when Mr. Lee brought up the antiques business. He does not recall whether his took place in October 1989 or March or April of 1990 He testified that the subject of income for Mrs. Packwood arose when Senator Packwood began complaining about the hardships of a potential divorce in terms of educational expenses for the children and maintaining two households. Mr. Lee responded by bringing up the idea of an antiques business. Mr. Lee does not recall the Senator requesting or encouraging him to make job offers to Mrs. Packwood beyond initiating the conversations that the divorce would be expensive.

To the best of his recollection, the first conversation he had with the Senator about providing income to Mrs. Packwood did not occur until after Mr. Lee's wife had returned from an antique buying trip with Mrs. Packwood in October, 1989.[14] From that time until the date of his April 14, 1990 letter setting forth the proposal, Mr. Lee stated that he spoke with Mrs. Packwood about the venture on two or three occasions. During one of his conversations with Mrs. Packwood, she referred to other job offers. She indicated that Mr. Lee's offer was one that she would consider, implying that the others were not. Mr. Lee kept Senator Packwood apprised of his conversations with Mrs. Packwood. Mr. Lee testified that he made no attempt to conceal the fact that he was talking to the Senator about the venture from Mrs. Packwood.

Mr. Lee testified that although it was not explicit, he and the Senator understood that the income generated from the antiques venture for Mrs. Packwood would make it easier on both of the Packwoods. He testified that he believed the job offer was legitimate and potentially lucrative for him.

---

[14] Mr. Lee testified that prior to his wife's October 1989 trip with Mrs. Packwood, there had been general off and on conversations for years between him and his wife about ". . . doing something in antiques involving Georgie."

3/27/90

On March 27, 1990, Senator Packwood recorded the following entry in his diary relating to Mr. Lee:

> . . . I frankly don't intend this supplement to Georgie to last more than five years in any event. I'd also talked with Tim Lee today to reverify his $10,000 and $10,000 from Bill Furman for Georgie. She'll have basically $30,000 to $40,000 in income for five years so long as I remain in the Senate.

With respect to the reference about the supplement to his wife lasting only five years, Senator Packwood testified as follows:

A: Well, it's kind of like our budget process. I don't think I was thinking more than five years down the road and I thought if I could get her this money for five years—I didn't mean for it necessarily to end, I just wasn't thinking beyond five years.

Q: In the last sentence of that passage, you say, "She'll have basically $30,000 to $40,000 in income for five years so long as I remain in the Senate." Was the supplement, as you refer to it here, conditioned upon your remaining in the Senate?

A: No.

Q: Do you know why you would have used these words?

A: No, I don't.

Regarding the reference to Bill Furman, Senator Packwood testified that at some stage, Mr. Lee approached Mr. Furman about becoming a partner in the proposed antiques venture. Senator Packwood testified that he does not recall when he first spoke to Mr. Furman about the venture. He stated that he never directly approached Mr. Furman about the proposal. When asked what the reference to $10,000 in the diary entry meant, Senator Packwood testified as follows:

A: I can't remember specifically what it refers to, and I don't know when he pieced together bringing Bill Furman in and how he was going to make this arrangement on the antique business. I can't specifically say what it refers to, no.

Q: Do you know in general?

A: No. I'm assuming antique and I'm assuming his business. At this stage, Lynn [Lee's wife] had been back with us— this is 1990, isn't it?

Q: Correct.

A: Lynn had stayed with us and I remember Georgie had lined up a lot of antique shows . . . And what I remember specifically was Lynn had bought some things, I think I recall this, and turned around and sold them in Oregon rather handsomely, I think. And I'm thinking this is the business they're talking about but I can't remember if it's now. That's what I recall about the business.

4/12/90

On April 12, 1990, Senator Packwood again recorded an entry involving Mr. Lee and the job offer to Mrs. Packwood:

. . . I called Tim Lee because he had left a message which said he had made the contact. I got a hold of him and he said he'd spent an hour and a half talking to Georgie . . . Tim said he finally thought he made some headway and that she might be willing to consider a proposal that he had. I said, ". . . how are you going to make it legal?" He said, "Well, I'm going to suggest I put money into a business jointly to be run by Lynn (that's his wife) and Georgie. She would buy antiques and ship them out west and Lynn would sell them . . ." Tim says he'll put the entire $20,000 a year in himself—enough for Georgie to get $20,000 plus something extra for Lynn—but what she'll take out is what he would otherwise give her for an allowance so it's simply a wash. And he said he'll work out a deal with Bill Furman—some business arrangement with him—and Bill will simply give Tim more money in some kind of a business deal for what he would otherwise put into the business for Georgie. God, I'm glad I don't know this. I think it's legal allright. I would hate for it to get out but I've got that ethics letter that says what she earns while we're separated is not a violation of ethic1s. Now, I've got Tim and $20,000 . . .

When asked about his apparent concern over the legality of the arrangement, Senator Packwood testified as follows:

A: I just wanted to make sure it's legal. Again, I'm trying to make sure that everything that's going to happen here is legal.

Q: Were you at all concerned or did you have any information to suggest that it might not be legal?

A: No. I didn't have anything. You asked a lot earlier but I can't remember the words you used, when we were talking about the press. I was trying to bend over backwards to make sure that the job offers Georgie got were legitimate job offers for which she would perform services for value. That's what I meant. I want to make sure everything is legal.

Q: Senator, this says, again referring to the sentence we were just talking about, "I said . . . how are you going to make it legal" as a question, and I'm wondering was it at all questionable to you?

A: Again, I don't recall this conversation. I noticed down below I say—I think it's legal—I think it's legal allright. I don't recall specifically this conversation. I just recall wanting to make sure it was all right or things were all-right [sic]. It didn't matter if it was Tim or _____ or Steve. I wanted to make sure they were allright. . . .

Q: . . . You say, "God, I'm glad I don't know this. I think it's legal allright." What were you referring to there?

A: I haven't got the foggiest idea unless it makes reference to this up above where Tim is saying well, we'll do some-thing with my business relations to Bill, and then I say I guess that's legal. Again, I can't remember any of this conversation. I don't even want to know it. I just want to make sure what Georgie does, she performs for value is okay . . .

Q: . . . do you recall any reason you wouldn't have wanted to know what their arrangement was? In other words, this says "God, I'm glad I don't know this."

A: I didn't figure so long as what Georgie was going to be doing was legal, ethical, moral and anything else, I didn't think it made any difference how Tim worked out his arrangement with Bill Furman . . .

Q: . . . you record "I would hate for it to get out;" what do you mean there?

A: I don't know what I mean there. All I know is I appar-ently say I guess it's legal, allright. I don't know what I mean. I just want—I don't want anything that the press is going to take, that they're going to try to slant in some way that portrays it as wrong . . .

Mr. Lee does not recall telling Senator Packwood that he would put up the entire investment himself and that Mr. Furman would participate by giving him extra business. Nor does he recall discussing the legality of the arrangement with Senator Packwood. Mr. Lee does not recall having any concerns about the legality of the proposed venture. Mr. Lee recalls telling Senator Packwood that he anticipated Mrs. Packwood would receive a draw of $20,000. He intended for there to be enough money so that both Mrs. Packwood and his wife would receive at least $20,000 based on some sales projections he had done.[15]

4/15/90

Mr. Lee reduced his proposal to writing in a letter dated April 14, 1990.[16] Mr. Lee does not recall Senator Packwood making any changes to the letter. In a diary entry dated April 15, 1990, Senator Packwood recorded that he had met with Mr. Lee and Mr. Lee showed him the letter that he was sending to Mrs. Packwood detailing his proposal for an antiques business. Senator Packwood noted that Mr. Lee was going to offer Mrs. Packwood $20,000 to $25,000 a year plus 40% of the net profits and that Bill Furman was going to put up half of the money. Later the same day, Senator Packwood recorded an entry in his diary setting forth the status of his efforts to obtain job offers for his wife:

> Needless to say it gives me the final hook although I'm still feeling guilty . . . but at least we have the ducks lined up. at $5,000, Tim Lee and Bill Furman at $20,000, Steve Saunders at whatever adds to the total of $25,000 and I'll have Ton Crawford send her a letter that says, "Georgie, I'd be willing to talk with you about employment," perhaps having put in the letter in the magnitude of $7500 a year.

[15] These projections were based on the profits his wife had made on sales of items purchased in the east and conversations with his wife's family, who own an antique business. Mr. Lee does not recall discussing the details of his April 14 proposal with his wife.

[16] Senator Packwood testified that he cannot remember whether he suggested that Mr. Lee reduce his proposal to Mrs. Packwood to writing.

Senator Packwood testified that as of April 15, 1990, he thinks he had lined up each of the above individuals to provide job offers to Mrs. Packwood.

Mr. Lee testified that either just before or just after he drafted the letter to Mrs. Packwood, he asked Bill Furman if he would consider investing in the venture. He later changed this testimony and stated that he could have spoken to Mr. Furman about participating as early as October or November, 1989. Mr. Lee testified that Mr. Furman stated he would take a look at the proposal and that he thought it sounded good.[17] Mr. Lee does not recall having any conversations with Mr. Furman about sources of income for Mrs. Packwood other than the specific discussion about the antiques venture. Mr. Lee testified that he went to Mr. Furman because he was the only individual with whom he had a personal relationship who might be interested in the venture and who had the resources to participate.[18] Mr. Lee stated that he knew Mr. Furman had been a contributor to the Senator's campaign and that the Senator had been helpful in some of Mr. Furman's efforts.[19]

Legislative Matters of Interest to Mr. Lee

By way of background, Senator Packwood testified that he is a "deregulatory hawk." He explained that he played a major role in deregulating the trucking industry in 1980. He stated that

[17] Mr. Lee does not recall discussing the legitimacy of the antiques business with Mr. Furman.

[18] Mr. Furman would have been required to come up with either $25,000 or $50,000 to capitalize his half of the venture.

[19] Mr. Lee testified that he informed Senator Packwood of Mr. Furman's involvement right before or right after the letter was sent. He later testified that he could have told the Senator about Mr. Furman's involvement earlier. Mr. Lee does not recall Mr. Furman or Senator Packwood ever indicating that they did not want Mr. Furman's name associated with the venture.

when he became Chairman of the Finance Committee in 1981, he partially deregulated AT&T in the Senate and it died because of an antitrust judgment before the House acted. He explained that he deregulated freight forwarders, the merchant marine, railroads, buses—"Anything I could deregulate, I would." He explained that he arranged for Mr. Lee to testify in 1985 before a subcommittee of the Commerce Committee because he was having oversight hearings on whether truck deregulation was working and Mr. Lee was a "classic example" of the success of deregulation.

At the time Mr. Lee extended an employment proposal to Mrs. Packwood in April, 1990, he was the owner of a trucking brokerage firm, STS, Inc. In June of 1990, the Supreme Court issued its decision in a case called *Maislin Industries, U.S., Inc., v. Primary Steel, Inc.,* 497 U.S. 116 (1990) ("*Maislin*"). This decision had specific implications for Mr. Lee's business. Mr. Lee explained that *Maislin* upheld the common carrier doctrine. During this period, a number of large motor carriers were going out of business. *Maislin* allowed the bankrupt carriers to go back to shippers and bill them for the difference between what they agreed to charge on a contract basis versus what the common carrier tariffs stated. Scott Paper Company, one of Mr. Lee's largest clients, was sued by the trustee of the bankrupt carrier STS had been using. Although Mr. Lee's company agreed to hold Scott Paper harmless, Scott was nonetheless concerned about its future exposure.[20]

---

[20] In a memo from Mr. Lee to the Senator dated November 14, 1991, Mr. Lee arranged for a meeting between representatives of Scott Paper and Senator Packwood. In a diary entry dated November 15, 1991, the Senator noted that there was discussion at this meeting about Scott making a $3,000 contribution to him. Senator Packwood testified that he does not recall any discussion of the *Maislin* decision or the Negotiated Rates Equity Act or the job offer to Mrs. Packwood in connection with this meeting.

Senator Packwood testified that he does not know if he ever had discussions with Mr. Lee about the *Maislin* decision and its implications for Mr. Lee's business, although he stated that he ". . . did not like the *Maislin* decision. I wanted to get rid of the *Maislin* decision." He stated that Mr. Lee may have asked him to sponsor or cosponsor legislation to overturn or modify the decision. Senator Packwood explained that ". . . lots of people . . . were asking us to cosponsor it. I think all the shippers hated it. They were going to get stuck with these bankrupt truck lines' bills, for things they never knew they were responsible for." Senator Packwood testified that he did not have any discussions with Mr. Lee about the job offer for Mrs. Packwood in connection with or relation to him sponsoring or cosponsoring legislation that would remedy the impact of *Maislin* on Mr. Lee's business.

On July 30, 1990, the Commerce Committee, chaired by Senator Exon, passed the Negotiated Rates Equity Act ("NREA"), which would have had the effect of reversing the *Maislin* decision. Senator Packwood testified that he does not know whether he discussed this bill with Mr. Lee or not. He further testified that there was no connection or relationship between his vote, either in the Commerce Committee or on the bill itself, and Mr. Lee's job offer to Mrs. Packwood. Senator Packwood was one of ten co-sponsors of the bill. The bill languished in 1990 due to House inaction and was reintroduced in 1991. The bill passed the Senate in 1992, but died again after the House failed to act. The bill was reintroduced in 1993 and passed.

Mr. Lee testified that he does not recall ever discussing Scott Paper's concerns over *Maislin* with the Senator. In fact, he does not recall ever speaking to the Senator about *Maislin* or the NREA. To the extent he talked with the Senator about legislation, Mr. Lee testified that their conversations were limited to general comments along the lines of "deregulation would be good for my business."

The Status of Mr. Lee's Offer in August, 1990

In a letter dated August 1, 1990, Mr. Lee advised Senator Packwood that Mrs. Packwood had informed him she was not interested in his proposal at that time. Mr. Lee wrote back to her and explained that his offer was ". . . an open one and one that you may pursue with me at a time of your chosing[sic]."[21] Senator Packwood testified that he does not recall speaking with Mr. Lee about Mrs. Packwood's response to the job offer. Nor does he recall whether he requested Mr. Lee to again offer the job to her or hold the offer open. He acknowledged that had Mrs. Packwood accepted this offer, it would have had a positive financial effect for her and thus, a positive impact for him, assuming the judge hearing the divorce case would have considered it.

Senator Packwood testified that he did not, at any time, have any discussion with Mr. Lee about the job offer to Mrs. Packwood in connection with him taking or refraining from taking any action or position in his capacity as a Senator. Nor was there any implicit agreement with Mr. Lee about the job offer in connection with him taking any official action or position.

Mrs. Packwood's Testimony

Mrs. Packwood testified that she started her antiques business in 1983 with a friend. She bought the partnership in 1984 and has continued on her own since that time. When living in Washington, D.C., her activities related to the antiques business con-

---

[21] As of February 6, 1991, Mr. Lee continued to hold open his offer of employment to Mrs. Packwood. Senator Packwood does not recall any specific conversations with him about the job offer at this time.

sisted of the following: participating in antique shows four to twelve times a year; managing a stall in an antique mall on a fairly consistent basis; and filling special orders for people who wanted unusual gifts.

Mrs. Packwood testified that her husband asked her to have Businessman one's wife stay with them in the fall of 1989 so that Mrs. Packwood could take her antiquing. She does not recall discussing with Mr. Lee's wife the possibility of opening some type of business together. She does not believe she has spoken with Mr. Lee's wife since her visit in the fall of 1989. She testified that it was clear to her that whatever Mr. Lee was doing with respect to an antiques proposal was separate from his wife.

Mrs. Packwood testified that she does not recall ever speaking to Mr. Lee about her antique business prior to late 1989. Referring to Mr. Lee's reference in the April 14 letter to her son's schooling, she stated that there must have been some conversation about paying for her son's education; "I presume when I spoke to him [Mr. Lee] that I was terribly worried about how to keep my son in school so he was offering to help the Packwoods out." She does not recall any specific discussions with Mr. Lee about her financial situation. She testified that she told each person who contacted her on the telephone to put their proposal in writing.

Mrs. Packwood testified that at the time she received Mr. Lee's proposal, she did not know where she was going or what she was doing, or how she could take on any kind of offer of employment. She testified that she did not believe Mr. Lee's proposal was necessarily an offer of employment because there was no elaboration of how the proposal would take place. The proposal did not seem like "anything solid" to her.

Mrs. Packwood testified that she suspected that her husband was behind Mr. Lee's offer. In fact, she stated that Mr. Lee may have indicated that Senator Packwood asked him to extend the offer, but she does not recall anything more specific. She testified that she was disturbed about the job offers because she thought it was "extremely cruel and unethical behavior" to treat a spouse in this way. She stated that because Mr. Lee later testified in the divorce proceedings as a witness for the Senator, she believes that he did not offer the proposal for her benefit. She last remembers speaking with Mr. Lee during the divorce trial. There was no mention of the business at that time. She does not believe she knows Mr. Furman.

Summary of Senator Packwood's Response to the Evidence

As in the case of Mr. Saunders, Senator Packwood testified that Mr. Lee is a longstanding friend who offered to help when he learned the Packwoods would be separating. Again, the Senator says he was merely following up on the offer of assistance. He asserts that he turned to Mr. Lee because of their friendship and not for reasons related to his official position.

Senator Packwood stated that his total recollection of discussions with Mr. Lee about jobs for Mrs. Packwood had ". . . something to do with antiques and his wife." He does not recall when they first started talking about the venture because Mrs. Packwood had been purchasing antiques for Mr. Lee's wife on an informal basis prior to their discussions about the venture.

With respect to his diary entry dated October 18, 1989, where he records that he asked Mr. Lee to place his wife on a retainer, Senator Packwood says he cannot remember what he meant by the word "retainer." Nor does he recall discussing a specific dollar amount with Mr. Lee. With respect to his diary entry dated March 27, 1990, where he discusses his contacts with various persons regarding jobs for his wife and records that his wife will have $30,000 to $40,000 in income "so long as [he] remains in the Senate," Senator Packwood denies that the income for his wife was conditioned upon his remaining in the Senate. Senator Packwood maintains that the his references to the legality of the proposed venture are simply expressions of his determination that the arrangement be legal and do not reflect a concern or question about the legality of this undertaking.

Senator Packwood said that he does not know whether he ever spoke with Mr. Lee about the Supreme Court's decision in *Maislin* and its impact on Mr. Lee's livelihood, although he acknowledged that Mr. Lee may have asked him to sponsor or cosponsor legislation to overturn or modify the decision. Similarly, Senator Packwood maintains that he does not know whether he discussed the NREA with Mr. Lee. Senator Packwood denies that there was any connection between his discussion of the antiques venture or income for his wife with Mr. Lee and his official actions, including his position on the NREA.

Findings

Senate Ethics Counsel finds that Senator Packwood did in fact solicit or otherwise encourage an offer of personal financial assistance from Mr. Lee, an individual who, although not a lobbyist, had a particularized interest in matters that the Senator could influence.

Counsel finds that Senator Packwood and Mr. Lee had conversations about jobs or income for the Senator's wife during a period when Mr. Lee had a specific and direct interest in a matter before one of Senator Packwood's committees. Although both have testified that Mr. Lee first extended an offer of help and Senator Packwood then followed up, the weight of the evidence again suggests that Senator Packwood's role in encouraging and coordinating job offers for his wife was significant. In fact, Ethics Counsel finds that Senator Packwood's discussions with Mr. Lee about jobs and income for his wife comprised part of a deliberate and systematic plan by the Senator to accumulate approximately $20,000 in job offers for his spouse in order to reduce his alimony obligation.

Additionally, Counsel finds that Mrs. Packwood was not looking for a job at the time the Senator engaged Mr. Lee in discussion about providing a job offer to her.

More specifically, Ethics Counsel finds that although Mrs. Packwood previously had purchased antiques for Mr. Lee's wife on an informal basis, the subject of income for Mrs. Packwood arose only after the Senator began complaining to Mr. Lee about the hardships of a potential divorce in terms of educational expenses for the children and the cost of maintaining two households. Moreover, Ethics Counsel finds that the Senator's diary entries, recorded nearly contemporaneously with the events as they occurred, suggest that the Senator played a more active role than simply following up with Mr. Lee's offer, as evidenced by the Senator's use of language such as place on "retainer," trying to "get Georgie some income," gaining the "final hook," and having the "ducks lined up." Further, Counsel finds that the reference in the Senator's diary that his wife will have an income "supplement" so long as he remains in the Senate suggests that he may have believed there was a connection between his ability to encourage job offers for his wife and his official position.

Ethics Counsel finds that Mr. Lee and Senator Packwood did have a longstanding friendship dating back to the time that Mr. Lee was one of the Senator's employees. Counsel also finds that throughout his career, Senator Packwood has consistently advocated deregulation of the trucking industry and his position with respect to the NREA was consistent with his deregulatory philosophy. Notwithstanding this friendship and Senator Packwood's views on deregulation, Counsel finds that during the time they were discussing the antiques venture for Mrs. Packwood, Mr. Lee had a particularized interest in trying to remedy the impact of the Supreme Court's decision in *Maislin,* which had specific adverse implications for his business. Counsel also finds that by virtue of his position on the Committee on Commerce, Science and Transportation, Senator Packwood was in a position to influence the outcome of this issue.

Counsel notes that Mr. Lee outlined his proposal to Mrs. Packwood in writing on April 14, 1990 and then advised her in writing in August 1990 and again in February 1991 that his offer remained open. Counsel also notes that the *Maislin* decision was issued in June of 1990 and the NREA passed the Committee on Commerce, Science and Transportation in late July, 1990. Counsel also notes that Senator Packwood signed the bill as one of several cosponsors in September of 1990. Ethics Counsel further notes that Mr. Lee testified at the Packwood's divorce trial on behalf of the Senator in January, 1991, describing his job offer to Mrs. Packwood. Counsel finds that Mrs. Packwood never accepted this offer of employment.

BILL FURMAN

Background

Bill Furman is the President of Greenbrier Companies of Lake Oswego, Oregon. Greenbrier is in the railcar manufacturing business through a subsidiary company called Gunderson, Inc. It is also in the business of leasing railcars and intermodal containers and trailers. Mr. Furman testified that he first met Senator Packwood in the early 1980's through a mutual acquaintance.

Mr. Furman has participated in two fundraising events for Senator Packwood. The first was the event with then-President George Bush organized by Mr. Lee in Oregon in 1991. Greenbrier also cosponsored a fundraising event in San Francisco earlier the same year (1991). More than $50,000 was raised at this event.

Diary Entries Referring to Mr. Furman, Job Offers to Mrs. Packwood, Greenbrier's Legislative Interests and Related Testimony
11/8/89

It appears that the first mention of Mr. Furman in Senator Packwood's diary in connection with a job offer to Mrs. Packwood occurred on November 8, 1989 with the following entry:

> He [Mr. Lee] said that [his wife], in staying with Georgie, said that two days was enough. That Georgie just leaned and leaned and leaned on her and talked about divorce—talked about   . That Georgie is terribly worried about money . . . Tim and Bill Furman, the President of Greenbrier (sp?), are prepared to do anything for Georgie. Bill says, "What do we need? $40 or $50 thousand year from me? Count on it. . . ."

Senator Packwood testified that he recalls almost nothing by way of discussions with Mr. Furman about his involvement in the proposal. He went on to state that he does not recall Mr. Furman being involved in the venture this early in time. He first recalls Mr. Furman being involved in the spring of 1990, at the time of Mr. Lee's letter to Mrs. Packwood.

11/9/89

The next diary entry relating to Mr. Furman being involved in the job offer to Mrs. Packwood is dated November 9, 1989:

Mike Kelly and I got to the Bill Furman breakfast . . . And it was nothing but to thank me for what I had done on Trailer Train(?)[22] and the investment tax credit—whatever it was I got for them in the tax reform bill—and of course Furman has said he'll join Tim Lee in helping keep Georgie solvent. . . .[23]

When asked about this entry, Senator Packwood testified that he does not remember this conversation. As to Mr. Furman's motivation in offering to help his wife, Senator Packwood responded as follows:

Q: . . . Was it your understanding that Mr. Furman's involvement in the job proposal for Mrs. Packwood was as an expression of gratitude or thanks for what you had done for his company earlier on?

A: Well, again, it's funny. I don't have any recollection of this conversation either. This is one and the previous one, it just does not ring a bell to me at all that it ever occurred. Maybe Bill Furman can remember it better, or Tim if he was there. But no, I did not assume it would have been gratitude. I would like to think that when you succeed in helping an Oregon company in keeping it going and a thousand jobs, that you've succeeded in doing something that the state appreciates but again, I don't recall this and I certainly don't recall gratitude.

Q: In other words, in your mind, was there a connection between Mr. Furman's appreciation for what you had done for him and for his company, and his participation in the job offer for Mrs. Packwood?

[22] Senator Packwood corresponded with the ICC regarding Trailer Train on a number of occasions.

[23] This breakfast meeting is referenced in a letter dated November 13, 1989 from Mr. Furman to Senator Packwood in which Mr. Furman states, in part, "I hope you know you can count on me for the future."

A: No. My experience with Mr. Furman, and some of it's more recent, he is a pretty canny businessman and what he gets into, he gets into it on the assumption he's going to make money. I certainly didn't assume it was pure gratitude for what I had done in keeping the jobs in Oregon.

With respect to the Trailer Train issue mentioned in the diary entry, Mr. Furman explained that Trailer Train (now known as TTX Company) is owned by a large number of railroads and operates a pool of freight cars in the United States. He explained that at the time of the diary entry, Trailer Train was applying to the ICC for an extension of its pooling authority. This authority would include antitrust immunity for purchasing and pooling, enabling the railroads to collectively pool their purchasing power. Greenbrier and others in the industry were concerned about the length of that authority and the power that was being vested in Trailer Train and thus supported a Department of Justice ("DOJ") initiative to have a formal hearing at the ICC to review the extension and approval of authority.

Greenbrier approached members of the Oregon delegation, including Senator Packwood, to support the DOJ initiative and to urge them to write the ICC to request that they review this matter. Senator Packwood, as well as other members of the Oregon delegation, wrote letters supporting the request for review. Mr. Furman testified that he met with Senator Packwood on this issue at least once and the meeting probably took place in 1987. The purpose of the meeting was to familiarize the Senator with the issue and ask for his support. He also recalls a breakfast with Senator Packwood where the subject was discussed. Mr. Furman testified that the ultimate outcome of the issue was difficult to ascertain and did not clearly satisfy any of the interested parties. Trailer Train received authority for pooling, but for a shorter term than they were requesting and with some limitations.

4/15/90

Senator Packwood again recorded a reference to Mr. Furman in an April 15, 1990 diary entry which refers to a meeting between Mr. Furman, Mr. Lee and Senator Packwood and a discussion about the proposal for Mrs. Packwood:

> . . . Bill Furman is going to put up half the money. He and his partner own all of Greenbrier . . . Tim and I and Bill went to dinner at Standfords, right across from where their office is, and Bill told me about a new rail car they're designing . . . Anyway, he said, "Bob, there's no quid pro quo. You've done so much for my company and done so much for this state and I just want to do anything I can to make your continued existence in politics possible." I said, "Well, this may be the difference in my being able to run for reelection in 1992 and run for the Presidency in 1996.

Senator Packwood testified that he does not recall this conversation with Mr. Furman. He explained, ". . . At this stage, is this an amalgam of my thinking, and this is a conversation that did not occur or a conversation that occurred totally differently and I put it in this fashion? I don't know. I don't recall this conversation. . . ."[24]

When shown the April 15, 1990 diary entry, Mr. Furman stated that he recalls having a meeting on a weekend and going to Stanfords, although he thought it was for lunch, not dinner. He does not recall Mr. Lee showing the Senator a letter referring to the antiques proposal, nor does he recall any discussion of the proposal. As to the diary attributing to him a comment

[24] In a letter dated April 19, 1990, four days after this diary entry, Senator Packwood wrote a brief note to Mr. Furman in which he stated, "Thanks so much for all of your help. I won't forget it. Sunday night was delightful . . ." Senator Packwood testified that he does not know what he was referring to in this letter.

about there being no quid pro quo, Mr. Furman testified that it would not have been unusual for him to tell the Senator that he supports him and that he thinks he has done a good job for Oregon, but these types of comments would not have been in connection with the antiques proposal for Mrs. Packwood. He stressed that he does not ever recall talking about financing a business for Mrs. Packwood with the Senator.[25] Later in his deposition, he testified that such a conversation with the Senator did not take place. He does not recall discussing a new type of railcar with the Senator, but it would not have been unusual to describe what his company was doing.

5/2/90

Senator Packwood again refers to Mr. Furman in a diary entry dated May 2, 1990:

> Met with Bill Furman, Jim Beale, and   who works for Greenbrier (sp?) in some capacity. Furman of course is eternally appreciative to me. He says that but for what I did for him in '86 with the transition rules he'd be out of business. Now he's prosperous beyond imagination and gives me the entire credit. He's going to put up half the money Tim Lee's putting up for Georgie's business. . . .

Senator Packwood testified that there was no connection in his mind between Mr. Furman's appreciation or gratitude for what the Senator had done with the transition rule in 1986 and Mr. Furman's participation in the venture for Mrs. Packwood. He does not recall discussing any substantive legislative matters at this meeting.

[25] Nor does he recall ever discussing the antiques proposal with Mr. Lee in Senator Packwood's presence.

With respect to the May 2, 1990 diary entry, Mr. Furman testified that he recalls attending a breakfast with the Senator around that date. He does not recall discussing the antiques proposal at this meeting. He testified that they had thanked Senator Packwood for his support on a number of issues in the past, but the references to being "eternally appreciative" and "prosperity beyond imagination and giving him the entire credit" is ". . . not at all anything that we would have said or did say." He stated that he does not know how Senator Packwood could have come away with the impression that he was involved in financing the proposal, unless it came from Mr. Lee. He stated that he never actually agreed with Mr. Lee to finance a business involving Mrs. Packwood.

Regarding the transition rule mentioned in the diary entry, Mr. Furman explained that in 1986, his company sought relief from certain provisions of the Tax Reform Act. Greenbrier had entered into several transactions that predated the act. Certain provisions of the act would have applied retroactively to these transactions and as a result, several large orders would have been cancelled. Greenbrier was successful in obtaining a transition rule which corrected the situation. Greenbrier's lobbyist testified that the transition rule was secured by approaching Senator Packwood and members of his Finance Committee staff and submitting a proposed transition rule. Mr. Furman testified that they were very pleased with the transition rule because it ". . . literally saved quite a lot of the jobs . . . certainly several hundred people." Mr. Furman did not meet with Senator Packwood on this issue, but he did meet with one of his staffers after the transition rule was obtained to express his appreciation.

5/31/91

On May 31, 1991, Senator Packwood recorded an entry in his diary describing a meeting with Mr. Furman and another unidentified person in his office in which Mr. Furman was asserting that long trucks should be kept off the highways. Senator Packwood testified that he does not recall any discussions with Mr. Furman about the long or "giant" truck issue. Senator Packwood testified that he did not agree with Mr. Furman's position on this issue.[26]

Mr. Furman testified that the long truck or LCV (Long Combination Vehicle) issue was a major concern for Greenbrier. Greenbrier was part of a national coalition of transportation companies involved in rail transportation. As a member of this coalition of railroad suppliers, Greenbrier's specific role was to assist the railroad industry in stopping the proliferation of LCV's on the highways. Greenbrier's lobbying firm met with all members of the Oregon Congressional delegation, including Senator Packwood, in this effort. There was eventually legislation in 1992 that was known as the "iced tea legislation"—the Intermodal Surface Transportation Act—which stopped the proliferation of LCV's. Mr. Furman met personally with Senator Packwood on this issue at least once. Mr. Furman testified that Senator Packwood was not particularly helpful. Mr. Furman described him as "relatively neutral, looking at both the trucking arguments and the rail arguments."

Senator Packwood testified that there was no discussion with Mr. Furman at any time about the job offer to Mrs. Packwood in connection with him taking or refraining from taking any official action. Nor was there any implicit understanding or agreement that Senator Packwood would take some official action in connection with or relation to Mr. Furman participating in the venture.

---

[26] In a letter dated June 24, 1991, Senator Packwood thanked Mr. Furman for keeping him up to date on Greenbrier's efforts in opposing "giant trucks in Oregon." Senator Packwood testified that he and Mr. Furman were on different sides of this issue.

Mr. Furman's Testimony Regarding Mr. Lee

In describing his business relationship with Mr. Lee, Mr. Furman explained that Mr. Lee's company STS was a railcar customer of Greenbrier. Greenbrier also leased and financed railcars for Mr. Lee personally. Greenbrier currently has about fifty railcars loaned or leased to Mr. Lee. Mr. Furman described Mr. Lee as an important customer.

Mr. Furman testified that Mr. Lee talked to him about lending him some money in connection with a business that his wife was considering in association with Mrs. Packwood. This conversation took place subsequent to the Packwood's separation. Mr. Furman does not recall speaking with Mr. Lee's wife about the proposal. Mr. Furman testified that Mr. Lee told him that his wife and Mrs. Packwood had worked together over the years buying and selling antiques and would become involved in the antiques business in some way. Mr. Furman testified that he does not specifically recall the amount of money Mr. Lee mentioned, but that $50,000 might be a good approximation of the upper limit.

Mr. Furman testified that it was his impression that Mr. Lee was talking about a loan as opposed to an investment. He stated that Greenbrier had loaned Mr. Lee's company money on several occasions. Prior to this time, however, Mr. Furman does not recall ever making any loans to Mr. Lee that were unrelated to the trucking business. Mr. Furman testified that he responded to Mr. Lee's request by telling him that it was an interesting proposition and that if Mr. Lee would prepare some sort of memorandum, he would consider it. When asked whether Mr. Lee indicated why Mrs. Packwood would be involved, Mr. Furman stated that Mr. Lee explained that he and his wife were good friends with the Packwoods and that they were concerned about what Mrs. Packwood was going to do for a living. There was no indication from his conversation with Mr. Lee that Mr.

Lee's concern about Mrs. Packwood had originated with Senator Packwood.

Mr. Lee did not prepare a business plan or any type of writing on the proposal for Mr. Furman. Mr. Furman only recalls discussing this subject with Mr. Lee on one occasion. Mr. Furman testified that as far as he was concerned, the proposal just kind of died. When asked about Mr. Lee's April 14, 1990 letter to Mrs. Packwood, Mr. Furman testified that he had never seen this letter before. He testified that he was not aware at the time that Mr. Lee actually extended any type of proposal to Mrs. Packwood. Mr. Furman testified that he did not know Mrs. Packwood and never spoke with her about Mr. Lee's proposal.

Summary of Senator Packwood's Response to the Evidence

Senator Packwood testified that unlike the other persons with whom he had discussions about jobs and income for his wife, Mr. Furman is not a longstanding friend. The Senator recalls almost nothing by way of discussions with Mr. Furman about his involvement in the antiques proposal. In fact, Senator Packwood says that Mr. Lee approached Mr. Furman about participating in the venture without the Senator's knowledge. Despite diary entries to the contrary, Senator Packwood does not recall Mr. Furman being involved in the venture in November, 1989. Rather, he does not recall Mr. Furman being involved until the spring of 1990.

Moreover, despite several diary entries that appear to indicate otherwise, Senator Packwood testified that there was no connection between Mr. Furman's appreciation for what the Senator had done for his company and his participation in financing the venture. In fact, Senator Packwood denies any connection between any of his official actions and Mr. Furman's participation in partially financing the antiques venture for his wife.

Findings

Although the level of direct contact was not as extensive with Mr. Furman as it was for some of the others with whom he had discussions about jobs and income for his wife, Ethics Counsel finds that Senator Packwood did in fact encourage an offer of personal financial assistance from Mr. Furman, an individual with particularized interests in matters that the Senator could influence and in fact, had influenced in the past.

Ethics Counsel finds that Senator Packwood and Mr. Furman were not longstanding friends. Moreover, Counsel finds that Senator Packwood did not initiate contact with Mr. Furman. Rather, Counsel finds that Mr. Furman was recruited to participate in financing the venture by Mr. Lee. Although Counsel notes that Senator Packwood may not have been aware at the outset that Mr. Lee was going to enlist the assistance of Mr. Furman, Counsel finds that Senator Packwood was aware of Mr. Furman's possible participation as early as November 1989 and that he acquiesced in this participation.

Despite his testimony to the contrary, Counsel finds that the Senator's diary entries, recorded nearly contemporaneously with the events as they occurred, suggest that there was at least some connection between Mr. Furman's participation in financing the venture and the Senator's official position. Counsel finds that in discussing Mr. Furman's willingness to assist in the antiques venture for his wife, the Senator repeatedly refers to Mr. Furman's appreciation for official actions taken by the Senator that benefitted his company. For example, in his diary entry dated November 9, 1989, the Senator records that he attended a breakfast sponsored by Mr. Furman which ". . . was nothing but to thank me for what I had done on Trailer Train and the investment tax credit—whatever it was I got for them in the tax reform bill—and of course Furman has said he'll join Tim Lee in helping to keep Georgie solvent. . . ." In his diary entry dated April 15, 1990, the Senator records a meeting among Mr. Lee and Mr. Furman and himself and states in part that ". . . Bill Furman is going to put up half the money . . ." and Mr. Furman said, "Bob, there's no quid pro quo. You've done so much for my company and done so much for this state and I just want to do anything I can to make your continued existence in politics possible. . . ." And, in a diary entry dated May 2, 1990, the Senator records a meeting with Mr. Furman and states in part, "Furman of course is eternally appreciative to me. He says that but for what I did for him in '86 with the transition rules he'd be out of business. Now he's prosperous beyond imagination and gives me the entire credit. He's going to put up half the money Tim Lee's putting up for Georgie's business. . . ."

Counsel finds that Mr. Furman had specific and direct interests in a number of legislative matters at various times that the Senator could influence by virtue of his positions on the Committee on Finance and the Committee on Commerce, Science and Transportation, including (but not limited to) the 1986 transition rule discussed above, the Trailer Train issue, and the LCV issue.

Counsel notes that Mr. Furman denies speaking directly to the Senator about the venture and further denies actually agreeing to provide the financing. Counsel, however, is persuaded to the contrary by the Senator's April 15, 1990 diary entry recording a discussion between the two of them about the matter, and also by a letter from the Senator to Mr. Furman dated April 19, 1990 in which the Senator states in part, "Thanks so much for your all of your help. I won't forget it. Sunday night was delightful . . ."

Counsel finds that Mr. Furman did not speak directly to Mrs. Packwood about his participation. Counsel further finds that Mrs. Packwood was not aware of Mr. Furman's involvement in the venture.

RON CRAWFORD

Background

Ron Crawford first met Senator Packwood in 1968 during the recount of his first election. Mr. Crawford described the Senator as one of his best friends. Mr. Crawford's consulting business is called F.P. Research Associates and he is a registered lobbyist. There is also a fundraising component to his business, but that is handled by his son.

In Senator Packwood's 1992 campaign, Mr. Crawford's firm was involved in raising money from PAC's around the country.[27] Mr. Crawford has been active in fundraising in every one of Senator Packwood's campaigns. In 1991–92, Senator Packwood's reelection campaign paid Mr. Crawford's firm approximately $60,000 for fundraising, consulting and event management.

Mr. Crawford is a registered lobbyist for the National Cable Television Association and the American Bus Association and has been so since the early 1980's. At the time of his deposition, he had recently registered as a lobbyist for the Sturm Ruger Company. He has a ten year business relationship with this company. At the time of his deposition, he also recently had become a lobbyist for the National Restaurant Association. He has previously represented Shell Oil[28], the American Iron and Steel Institute,

[27] In a diary entry dated October 8, 1991, Senator Packwood recorded the following: "The advantage Ron brings to me in the Washington PAC scene is that much of his income is dependent upon his relationship with me." Senator Packwood testified that he does not know how much Mr. Crawford earns or how much of his income is dependent on him.

[28] On September 13, 1989, Senator Packwood recorded an entry in his diary that Mr. Crawford was in to see him on behalf of Shell Oil. He noted the following conversation: "He [Crawford] said, 'I know how much you hate the oil companies.' I said, '. . . I still hate the oil companies but I'll do you a favor.'" Senator Packwood testified that ". . . whenever anybody comes in like this and if you're going to do something anyway, you let them think it's a big favor."

General Motors, the Pharmaceutical Manufacturer's Association[29], Caribbean Marine, and Northrop as a registered lobbyist.[30]

Diary Entries Referring to Mr. Crawford and Job Offers for Mrs. Packwood and Related Testimony
10/18/89

On October 18, 1989, in the context of discussing the persons he was contacting or contemplating contacting about income for his wife, Senator Packwood first recorded an entry in his diary referring to Mr. Crawford and job offers for his wife:

> . . . Talked to Ron Crawford. He'll put up $7500 a year for Georgie. That's three out of three and I haven't even hit up or Steve Saunders . . .

When asked whether he asked Mr. Crawford to extend a job offer to his wife, Senator Packwood testified that he believes that Mr. Crawford first broached the subject rather than him asking Mr. Crawford to extend the job offer. He testified that he does not recall the circumstances as to how this subject arose. He explained, "This is one of those where you talk with somebody three and four times a day and you have dinner with them twice a month and you are so closely interlinked with them, you can't conceivably recall who said what when." He further stated that he does not know how they came upon the figure of $7500 a year.

[29] On July 11, 1990, Senator Packwood recorded in his diary that two representatives of Abbott were into see him and noted, "But Ron wanted me to meet with them because they want to retain Ron because, as Ron says, "People hear that you're tough to get to and they know I can get to you." I said, "Well, that's a happy relationship for all of us." Senator Packwood testified that he is delighted to see Mr. Crawford's clients because Mr. Crawford does not mislead him.

[30] Mr. Crawford recalls two issues of interest to Northrop: 1) the sale of F-20 aircraft to Jordan and 2) funding for the B-2 bomber. In both cases, Senator Packwood voted against the positions advocated by Northrop.

Mr. Crawford testified that he had discussions with Senator Packwood about the Senator's concerns about his children and wife and the political implications of a separation and divorce a few months before the Senator separated from Mrs. Packwood in January of 1990. Mr. Crawford testified that Senator Packwood may have expressed concern about the financial impact of a divorce, but he cannot really recall. He does recall talking about the expenses of a divorce with the Senator.

Mr. Crawford testified that he does not recall Senator Packwood ever asking him to provide his wife with income or employment. Rather, he stated that he offered to help Mrs. Packwood. He stated that he was concerned for both Senator and Mrs. Packwood because of the divorce. He testified that at the time, he was trying to enhance his master list of names of contributors by collecting more information about them so that he would potentially have names available around the country to assist him in his lobbying efforts. He testified that he was also trying to think of things that might be helpful to Mrs. Packwood. He stated that he knew things were going to be tough for the Packwoods financially and this proposal would be a way that she could help him and he could help her.[31]

Mr. Crawford testified that he is confident that he discussed this proposed employment with Senator Packwood, but he does not recall the circumstances. He thinks he made a comment along the lines of: ". . . well, I've got some stuff that I'd love to have somebody like Georgie do." He does not recall Senator

[31] Mr. Crawford testified that this has been an ongoing project since 1989 or 1990 and that he has hired college students on a part-time basis to accumulate this information. He stated that he is still accumulating this information with one part-time college student. He testified that he does not believe he hired people to perform this job prior to the time he made the proposal to Mrs. Packwood. He subsequently amended his testimony to state that he believes he did hire a college student to perform this job before extending the proposal to Mrs. Packwood.

Packwood ever mentioning a specific amount of money he wanted Mrs. Packwood to earn. He testified that Senator Packwood may have come to the $7500 a year figure because Mr. Crawford must have told him that he thought Mrs. Packwood could work on a part-time basis and that   could pay her between $400 and $600 a month. However, they never got to a point where they discussed dollars in concrete terms because Mrs. Packwood never called him back to explore the job offer. Mr. Crawford testified that he telephoned Mrs. Packwood on two or three occasions but did not actually speak to her, leaving messages on her answering machine. Mr. Crawford testified that he must have told the Senator that he was unable to reach Mrs. Packwood and that the Senator may have suggested that Mr. Crawford write her a letter.

1/18/90

Senator Packwood again referred to Mr. Crawford in a diary entry dated January 18, 1990. In this entry, Senator Packwood described the success he had had to date in obtaining offers of employment for his wife:

> . . . It's funny. I hit   up. He says 'yes.' a close friend but not as close as Cliff. The same with Saunders, same with Ron. They just say bang, bang, bang—yes. But not Cliff. That means next week I've got to turn to Saunders and then to Crawford.

Senator Packwood testified that the discussions about job offers for his wife did not happen with military-like precision. He stated, "It was all merging and I was kind of trying to come up with this total of $20,000 if I could."

3/27/90

On March 27, 1990, Senator Packwood again referenced Mr. Crawford in his diary in connection with a job offer or income to Mrs. Packwood:

. . . Finally Ron Crawford rescued me and we went off to dinner at the Phoenix Park. In his usual optimistic fashion he went over the [Senate] races he thought we would win . . . I told him I thought he was unduly optimistic but I thought we could pick up the Senate in '92. Crawford goes, "Shit." He says, "I need the money." I said, "Well, if you're going to support Georgie in the style to which I'd like her to become accustomed . . ." and he laughed. He says, "Yeah, I'll guarantee the $7500 for five years. And he said, "If you're Chairman of the Finance Committee I can probably double that." We both laughed. I don't intend to do that. I frankly don't intend this supplement to Georgie to last more than five years in any event. I'd also talked to Tim Lee today to reverify his $10,000 and $10,000 from Bill Furman for Georgie. She'll have basically $30,000 to $40,000 in income for five years so long as I remain in the Senate.

Senator Packwood testified that Mr. Crawford's job offer to Mrs. Packwood was in no way conditioned upon or contingent upon him remaining in the Senate or serving as Chairman of the Finance Committee. He explained the above entry as follows:

That remark is one between two guys that are drinking and said in jest in this sense. You know what happens when parties change control and all of a sudden all of the lobbying groups that are Republican, clients come in. When the Democrats are in control, the clients go again. That is said in jest. I never had any intention of that. He didn't have any intention of that and it was purely a humorous remark between us. Again, I want to give the same caveat to all of these conversations, but I just want to say that we both laughed . . . Any of these conversations that have quotation marks, and especially if I'd been drinking, is suspect.

A page from Mr. Crawford's calendar indicates that he met and had dinner with Senator Packwood on March 27, 1990. He does not recall any discussion with Senator Packwood on March 27 about employment or income for Mrs. Packwood. He testified that Senator Packwood did not ask him to send a letter to Mrs. Packwood offering employment and specifying $7500 a year as income. Nor does he recall Senator Packwood ever discussing the $7500 as a figure he hoped Mr. Crawford would be able to provide. He stated that he was only trying to help a family that he and his wife loved dearly.

4/15/90
Senator Packwood again made reference to Mr. Crawford in connection with a job offer to his wife in a diary entry dated April 15, 1990:

> . . . but at least we have the ducks lined up.   at $5,000, Tim Lee and Bill Furman at $20,000, Steve Saunders at whatever adds to the total of $25,000 and I'll have Ron Crawford send her a letter that says 'Georgie, I'd be willing to talk with you about employment,' perhaps having put in the letter in the magnitude of $7500 a year.

Senator Packwood testified that he cannot recall whether it was his suggestion or recommendation to Mr. Crawford to reduce his job offer to Mrs. Packwood to writing. Nor does he recall whether he suggested any language to go into such a writing. In fact, he testified that he is not sure he ever saw the letter until after it was sent.

6/6/90

On June 6, 1990, Senator Packwood recorded in his diary another contact with Mr. Crawford involving the job offer to his wife:

> Had a phone call with Ron Crawford and I told him to re-call Georgie and make the offer . . .

Senator Packwood testified that he may have mentioned an offer from Mr. Crawford to his wife and she indicated that she preferred not to talk to him. The Senator testified that he does not believe Mrs. Packwood and Mr. Crawford ever actually communicated.

Mr. Crawford testified that he had never previously spoken with Mrs. Packwood about working for him. Nor had she ever expressed an interest in working with his firm. Mr. Crawford testified that Senator Packwood did not ask him to go back again and try to contact her when she did not respond. Mr. Crawford does not recall any discussions with the Senator after he advised him that he had not heard from Mrs. Packwood. He testified that his offer of employment was to help Mrs. Packwood. He did not have any discussions with Senator Packwood about whether the job offer would help him as well.

The evidence indicates that Mr. Mr. Crawford did, in fact, send a letter to Mrs. Packwood dated June 13, 1990. In this letter, Mr. Crawford indicated that he wanted to ". . . discuss what I believe could be several business opportunities that you might be interested in." Although his letter mentions "several business opportunities," Mr. Crawford testified there was only one. He never received a response from Mrs. Packwood and he has not spoken to her since before the divorce. When asked what his understanding was of the nature of the job being offered by Mr. Crawford. Senator Packwood explained that his wife had a great political background in that she had managed his 1962 and 1964 legislative campaigns and travelled around the state with him in 1968, 1974 and 1980. He testified that he believes she would have been a great consultant or campaign manager.

Legislative Matters of Interest to Mr. Crawford
Cable Regulation

Regarding specific legislative matters of interest to Mr. Crawford's clients, a Commerce Committee vote took place on June 7, 1990 to re-regulate the cable industry, six days before Mr. Crawford sent his written employment proposal to Mrs. Packwood. Senator Packwood cast the lone dissenting vote on this bill. In explaining this situation, Senator Packwood testified as follows:

[It was] . . . an outrageous, foolish bill . . . My staffer wrote the bill, the Cable Deregulation Act of 1984. And over fierce opposition, we deregulated cable prices and we said in exchange to cable what we want is more channels and better programming. And we got it in spades and then this damn bill came along to re-regulate it. It was a step backward. I hope we undo it. I'm going to try and undo it. And that is the background of that vote.

He testified that he never had any discussions with Mr. Crawford about the job offer to Mrs. Packwood in connection with his position on this piece of legislation, which he described as "adamant." Mr. Crawford testified that he may or may not have spoken to Senator Packwood about this bill, but he stated that he seldom talked to Senator Packwood on cable issues because for the most part, he knew where the Senator was coming from.

On September 27, 1990, Senator Packwood noted in his diary that Mr. Crawford was in to see him with a representative of the cable industry. The Senator recorded that they wanted his advice as to whether they should let a cable bill come up for consideration or attempt to stop it. Senator Packwood noted that he advised them to try and stop it. Senator Packwood testified that he does not recall any discussion with Mr. Crawford at this time about the status of the job offer. He further testified that he did not need to be lobbied on this matter because the cable industry's position was identical to his. He explained that this was a re-regulatory bill and that he and others wanted to filibuster it to the end of the session if possible. He testified that he cannot recall whether they held the bill or it came up, although he was successful in eventually killing the bill.

The Gun Lobby

Later in the September 27, 1990 diary entry referenced above, Senator Packwood recorded that Mr. Crawford stayed on to discuss the National Rifle Association. He noted that, ". . . Ron is big, big with the National Rifle Association." Senator Packwood testified that he meant that Mr. Crawford is active in the NRA and "owns a lot of guns." He stated that he does not think Mr. Crawford represents the NRA. Mr. Crawford testified that he does not do work for the NRA, although "he talks to them intermittently."

Senator Packwood testified that Mr. Crawford brought the issue of exempting custom gunsmiths from a firearms excise tax on behalf of the NRA to his attention. Staff memos indicate that Senator Packwood and his staff focused on this issue between February and April, 1991. In April of 1991, Senator Packwood introduced a bill exempting custom gunsmiths who make less than 50 firearms per year from the firearms excise tax. Senator Packwood testified that there was never any discussion with Mr. Crawford about the job offer to Mrs. Packwood in connection with his position on this particular piece of legislation.

Miscellaneous

Mr. Crawford testified that in the 1989–90 time period, his client the American Bus Association was concerned with the three cent diesel fuel tax exemption. His only contact with Senator Packwood or his staff on this issue would have been to simply confirm that it was not a problem. His client the American Iron and Steel Institute was interested in the issue of voluntary restraints in 1989–90. Senator Packwood opposed their position. Mr. Crawford does not recall meeting with Senator Packwood on this issue, although he did meet with staff.

Appointment of Mr. Crawford's Wife to the ITC

In addition, Senator Packwood played a major role in helping Mr. Crawford's wife, Carol Crawford, become appointed to the International Trade Commission in 1991. Senator Packwood testified that he was her primary supporter in her bid to become a member of the ITC. When asked whether there was ever any discussion with either Mr. Crawford or his wife about his support for her for the ITC position in connection with Mr. Crawford extending a job offer to Mrs. Packwood, Senator Packwood testified, "There never is any linkage at any time in my dealings with Ron or Carol and a job for Georgie."

Mrs. Packwood's Testimony

Mrs. Packwood testified that she and Senator Packwood had been friends with Mr. Crawford and his wife in the past, although Senator Packwood saw them much more frequently than she did. She testified that she did not return any of Mr. Crawford's telephone calls and never had any discussion with him about his proposal. She learned why Mr. Crawford was calling from her husband. She stated that she would not have been interested in business opportunities with him unless they involved her "already in place" antique business. Mrs. Packwood explained that she felt very uncomfortable with the whole situation, particularly with Mr. Crawford and his wife, because she believed they had been "aiding and abetting" the break-up with her husband. As a result, she did not want to have anything to do with Mr. Crawford, who she did not regard as a friend.

Summary of Senator Packwood's Response to the Evidence

Senator Packwood asserts that Mr. Crawford is an old friend who first broached the subject of extending a job offer to his wife. The Senator maintains that he was merely following up on Mr. Crawford's offer of assistance when he discussed jobs and income for Mrs. Packwood. He states he does not recall the circumstances as to how this subject arose. He testified he turned to Mr. Crawford because of their longstanding friendship and not for reasons related to his official position.

With respect to his October 18, 1989 diary entry where he records that Mr. Crawford will "put up" $7500 a year for his wife, Senator Packwood claims he does not know who said what when with respect to the job offer for Mrs. Packwood. He contends that he does not know how they arrived at the figure of $7500 a year. With respect to his March 27, 1990 diary entry where he records that his wife will have $30,000 to $40,000 in income for five years from the offers he has secured "so long as I remain in the Senate," Senator Packwood claims that Mr. Crawford's job offer was in no way conditioned upon or contingent upon him remaining in the Senate or serving as Chairman of the Committee on Finance.

Regarding his April 15, 1990 diary entry where he records that he will have Mr. Crawford send his wife a letter about employment, Senator Packwood maintains that he does not recall whether he suggested that Mr. Crawford reduce his job offer to writing. Other than Mr. Crawford's June 13, 1990 letter to Mrs. Packwood in which he invites her to explore "business opportunities" with him, Senator Packwood does not believe Mr. Crawford and his wife actually spoke about Mr. Crawford's job offer.

Senator Packwood notes that his lone dissenting vote on a bill before the Committee on Commerce, Science and Transportation to re-regulate the cable industry six days before Mr. Crawford sent his written employment proposal to Mrs. Packwood was entirely consistent with his deregulatory philosophy and his earlier positions with respect to deregulation of the cable industry. He asserts that he never had any discussions with Mr. Crawford about the job offer to Mrs. Packwood in connection with his position on matters affecting the cable industry. Similarly, he states that he never had any discussion with Mr. Crawford about the job offer to Mrs. Packwood in connection with his bill to exempt custom gunsmiths from a firearms excise tax in 1991, although he acknowledges that Mr. Crawford brought this issue to his attention. Additionally, although he acknowldges that he was the primary supporter of Mr. Crawford's wife in her bid to become a member of the ITC, Senator Packwood denies any linkage between his support of her and the job offer to his wife.

Findings

Senate Ethics Counsel finds that Senator Packwood did in fact solicit or otherwise encourage an offer of personal financial assistance from Mr. Crawford, an individual representing clients with particularized interests in matters that the Senator could influence.

Counsel finds that Senator Packwood and Mr. Crawford conducted discussions about jobs and income for Mrs. Packwood at a time when Mr. Crawford was representing clients with specific and direct interests in matters that Senator Packwood could influence by virtue of his positions on the Committee on Commerce, Science and Transportation and the Committee on Finance. Although both have testified that Mr. Crawford first offered to help and Senator Packwood then followed up, the weight of the evidence suggests that Senator Packwood's role in encouraging and coordinating job offers for his wife was significant. In fact, Ethics Counsel finds that Senator Packwood's discussions with Mr. Crawford about job offers and income for his wife comprised part of a deliberate and systematic plan by the Senator to accumulate approximately $20,000 in job offers for his spouse in an attempt to reduce his alimony obligation. Additionally, Counsel finds that Mrs. Packwood was not looking for a job at the time the Senator engaged Mr. Crawford in discussion about providing a job offer to her.

Ethics Counsel finds that Mr. Crawford's offer of assistance was extended after the Senator expressed concern about the costs associated with a divorce. Moreover, Counsel finds that the Senator's diary entries, recorded nearly contemporaneously with the events as they occurred, suggest that the Senator played a more active role than simply following up with Mr. Crawford, as evidenced by the Senator's use of language such as "hit up," "accept the offers that I've solicited," instructing Mr. Crawford to

". . . re-call Georgie and make the offer," and "I'll have Ron Crawford send her a letter . . ." about employment.

Ethics Counsel finds that Mr. Crawford and Senator Packwood did have a longstanding friendship dating back to 1969. Notwithstanding this friendship, Counsel finds that at the time they were discussing job offers and income for Mrs. Packwood, Mr. Crawford was representing a number of entities, including the National Cable Television Association, with particular interests in matters that the Senator could influence. Counsel notes that Senator Packwood has consistently supported deregulation of the cable industry and that his vote in June of 1990 was entirely consistent with his deregulatory philosophy.

Moreover, despite their friendship, Counsel finds that there is evidence to suggest that there was some connection between Senator Packwood's official position and his relationship with Mr. Crawford. For example, in a diary entry dated October 8, 1991, Senator Packwood records, "The advantage Ron brings to me in the Washington PAC scene is that much of his income is dependent upon his relationship with me." In an entry dated July 11, 1990, he records ". . . Ron wanted me to meet with them because they want to retain Ron because, as Ron says, "People hear that you're tough to get to and they know I can get to you." On March 27, 1990, while discussing the job offers he had coordinated for his wife, the Senator recorded that his wife would have an income "supplement" so long "as I remain in the Senate." And, on September 13, 1989, Senator Packwood recorded the following conversation when Mr. Crawford was in to see him on behalf of a client: "He [Crawford] said, 'I know how much you hate the oil companies.' I said, 'Ron, I still hate the oil companies but I'll do you a favor."

Counsel finds that Mr. Crawford extended his offer of employment in writing to Mrs. Packwood in a letter dated June

13, 1990. Counsel further finds that Mrs. Packwood did not accept this offer.

CLIFFORD ALEXANDER

Background

Clifford Alexander is the president of a corporate consulting firm. He stated that his firm's work principally involves work force inclusiveness or increasing opportunities in the work force for minorities and women. His firm also performs lobbying in a number of different areas. Another aspect of the services provided by his firm is corporate social responsibility. He first met the Packwoods twenty-five years ago. They became close friends and he and his wife have continued their relationship with Mrs. Packwood. The same is not true with the Senator, coinciding with the time of the Packwood's separation.

Diary Entry Referring to Mr. Alexander and Job Offers for Mrs. Packwood and Related Testimony
1/18/90

On January 18, 1990, Senator Packwood recorded the following entry in his diary relating to Mr. Alexander and a job for his wife:

A quick lunch with Cliff. It was a nice friendly lunch. He said, "Is there anything I can do?" I hit him up to give a job to Georgie, but he said, "Gosh, we've got that ICI client. It wouldn't look good." I said, "It doesn't matter if we're separated." Well, Cliff said . . . and this was after he was bragging about all the money he had, how much they're making, how much he's setting aside, what kind of trust he has for the

313

kids and that he needs to work five more years until he can retire comfortably on his investments and income for the rest of his life, but not enough money for Georgie. It's funny. I hit   up. He says 'yes.'   a close friend but not as close as Cliff. The same with Saunders, same with Ron. They just say bang, bang bang—yes. But not Cliff. That means next week I've got to turn to Saunders and then to Crawford.

Senator Packwood testified that he recalls telling Mr. Alexander and his wife that he had separated. He stated that he recalls talking to Mr. Alexander about providing a job offer to Mrs. Packwood. In this regard, the Senator testified that in this particular case, ". . . I approached him if he could be of some help." When asked whether his conversation with Mr. Alexander proceeded along the lines described in the diary entry, Senator Packwood testified as follows:

A: I don't remember his reference to ICI. What I remember, and I was kind of disappointed because he had—Cliff is a wonderful guy and a buoyant guy, and from time to time he would tell me how successful he was doing . . . And he was making very good money, and we were close friends and I remember I was disappointed when he said he couldn't help. Do I remember this specific conversation? No. Do I remember the ICI reference? No. But I remember I was kind of hurt by it.

Q: But you do recall asking him to provide a job for Mrs. Packwood; is that correct?

A: Yes. I guess I would have thought of all the people I could go to that was close, close friends that could have helped, it would have been Cliff.

Q: Do you recall what his response was?

A: Well, I don't recall him—I see ICI here. I don't remember him mentioning that. I just remember the hurt when he couldn't do it—wouldn't do it.

Q: But you don't recall a specific reason or explanation that he offered as to why he couldn't do it?

A: No.

Mr. Alexander's Testimony

Mr. Alexander testified that he learned of the Packwood's separation some time in 1990. Regarding the January 18, 1990 diary entry, Mr. Alexander testified that he does not recall having lunch with the Senator. He does not recall Senator Packwood asking him to provide a job to his wife, although he said this could have happened. He stated that had there been a need, Mrs. Packwood would have approached him directly. He stated that he would not have mentioned the ICI client in the way noted in the diary. Instead, he would have simply said no. Mr. Alexander does not recall talking to the Senator about a trust for his children and the fact that he needed to work five more years until he could comfortably retire. In fact, he testified that he does not have any trusts set up for his children and he does not plan to retire. He does not recall any discussion with Senator Packwood in which the Senator indicated that it would help their financial situation if his wife were able to find a job. He testified that he never helped find her a job.

Mr. Alexander testified that he does not recall any other occasion when Senator Packwood said anything about his wife needing a job. He stated that Mrs. Packwood did mention that she had been approached about employment, but he does not recall any names she may have mentioned. He testified that there may have been discussions with her about Senator Packwood's role in persons approaching her about job opportunities, but he does not recall any specifics.

Legislative Matters of Interest to Mr. Alexander

During the 1989 to 1991 time period, Mr. Alexander was retained by the Investment Company Institute ("ICI"), the national trade association for the mutual fund industry, to advance ICI's position on several legislative matters. Some of these matters included securing permanent repeal of the 2% floor on miscellaneous itemized business deductions; securing repeal of the 30/30 rule that applied to mutual funds; and opposing the Securities Transfer Excise Tax ("STET"). Mr. Alexander testified that he communicated with Senator Packwood or his Finance Committee staff on a number of occasions during the 1989–1991 time period in order to advocate ICI's position on these issues.

Mrs. Packwood's Testimony

Mrs. Packwood testified that she never had any indication from Mr. Alexander that he had been asked by the Senator to try and find her some type of employment.

Summary of Senator Packwood's Response to the Evidence

Senator Packwood's response to the evidence related to his contact with Mr. Alexander is unique in that this is the only case where Senator Packwood admits that he initiated the request for help as opposed to following up on an offer of assistance. Here, Senator Packwood acknowledges that he approached Mr. Alexander to see if he might be able to help with a job for his wife. Senator Packwood notes that Mr. Alexander was an old and good friend.

With respect to his January 18, 1990 diary entry in which he records that he had lunch with Mr. Alexander and "hit him up to give a job to Georgie," Senator Packwood recalls telling Mr. Alexander that he had separated from his wife and he recalls talking with him about providing a job offer for Mrs. Packwood. He recalls asking Mr. Alexander to provide a job for Mrs. Packwood and being disappointed and hurt when his close friend refused to help. The Senator does not recall Mr. Alexander making mention of the appearance problem that might be created because of his representation of a client called ICI.

Findings

Senate Ethics Counsel finds that Senator Packwood did in fact solicit or otherwise encourage an offer of personal financial assistance from Mr. Alexander, an individual representing a client with particularized interests in matters that the Senator could influence.

Counsel finds that Senator Packwood's discussion with Mr. Alexander about job offers for his wife comprised part of a deliberate and systematic plan to accumulate approximately $20,000 in job offers for his spouse in an attempt to reduce his alimony obligation. Counsel also finds that Mrs. Packwood was not looking for a job at the time Senator Packwood asked Mr. Alexander to provide a job offer to her.

Counsel finds that Mr. Alexander and Senator Packwood did have a longstanding friendship dating back to the time that the Senator arrived in Washington, D.C. Notwithstanding this friendship, Counsel finds that at the time Senator Packwood requested Mr. Alexander to provide a job offer to his wife, Mr. Alexander was representing ICI, a client who had specific and direct interests in matters that the Senator could influence by virtue of his position on the Committee on Finance. More specifically, ICI had a particular interest in issues such as the STET, the 30/30 rule, and final repeal of the 2% floor on miscellaneous itemized deductions. Further, Counsel finds that there is evidence in the Senator's January 18, 1990 diary entry to suggest that Mr. Alexander raised the potential appearance problem caused by his representation of ICI with the Senator and that the Senator dismissed this concern.

Counsel finds that Mr. Alexander never extended an offer of employment or income to Mrs. Packwood. Counsel further finds that Mrs. Packwood was not aware that the Senator had requested Mr. Alexander to provide her employment. Counsel notes that Mr. Alexander does not recall the Senator asking him to provide a job to his wife, although he admits the possibility of such a request.

FURTHER FINDINGS REGARDING
SOLICITATION OF JOBS

Counsel finds that Senator Packwood's efforts to obtain employment for his estranged spouse in an attempt to reduce any future alimony payments did not involve any *quid pro quo* and that he did not agree to receive or accept any financial benefit "for or because of any official act." As is clear from Senate precedent, however, conduct which does not rise to such an egregious level may, nonetheless, be improper.

With respect to his contacts concerning possible employment of his spouse with the five individuals discussed above, Senate Ethics Counsel finds that Senator Packwood engaged in a series of interconnected activities which linked his personal financial gain to his position as a United States Senator.

Counsel also finds that, notwithstanding the willingness of friends to be of assistance, Senator Packwood's role in encouraging and coordinating job offers for his wife was the predominant force responsible for such offers in this case. Counsel further finds that Senator Packwood conceived of, undertook and executed a deliberate and systematic plan to enhance his personal financial position in a manner which was greatly reliant for its success upon his position as a United States Senator and the legislative interests of those whom he solicited or encouraged. In this regard, Counsel notes the power inherent in the position of a United States Senator and the natural desire of persons and groups with substantial interests in legislation to have access to and ingratiate themselves with those whose decisions can significantly affect those interests.

Ethics Counsel finds that Senator Packwood's conduct in these activities reflects an abuse of his United States Senate office and constitutes improper conduct which has brought discredit upon the Senate.

7

Findings of Violations as Noticed
and Specified in the
Committee's Resolution

As TO THE violations noticed in the Committee's Resolution of May 16, 1995, Senate Ethics Counsel incorporates the findings set forth in Sections IV, V, and VI, above, as summarized below:

A. Senator Packwood abused his United States Senate office by improper conduct which has brought discredit upon the United States Senate, by engaging in a pattern of sexual misconduct between 1969 and 1990.

B. Senator Packwood engaged in improper conduct which has brought discredit upon the United States Senate, by intentionally altering diary materials that he knew or should have known the Committee had sought or would likely seek as part of its investigation.

C. Senator Packwood abused his United States Senate office and engaged in improper conduct which has brought discredit upon the United States Senate, by inappropriately linking personal financial gain to his official position, in that he solicited or otherwise encouraged offers of financial assistance from five persons who had a particular interest in legislation or issues that he could influence.

Respectfully Submitted,

Victor M. Baird
Chief Counsel

Linda S. Chapman
David M. Feitel
Staff Counsel

Publisher's Appendix

The following extract from Senator Packwood's diary, as supplied to the Senate Select Committee on Ethics, was not contained in the Ethics Counsel Report, but was included in Volume 3 of the ten-volume Documents Related to the Investigation of Senator Robert Packwood on pages 13–15. It contains, in the words of the Ethics Counsel, "a graphic description of Senator Packwood and the staffer making love in his Senate office." The Counsel adds that the staffer in question, when interviewed by the Ethics Counsel staff, "would not answer questions about whether she was ever the subject of any unwanted sexual advances by Senator Packwood." The staffer is called "S-1" in the diary but is otherwise unidentified.

Tuesday, November 21, 1989

[. . . .]

At 4:00 I had pictures with a couple of interns and Bob Eisenbud, that wonderful guy on the Commerce Committee who has helped us so much. And then about 4:30 we had a staff party. It started slow and got bigger. None of the professional Finance Committee came but the clericals came. We drank for about an hour and a half and played charades. At about 7:00 we began to dwindle and drift except for, finally, S-1. And we sat in the office. She is a sexy thing. Bright-eyes and hair and that ability to shift her hips.

We gradually drank and talked and she finally . . . I was on my side of the desk . . . and she reached her hand across and she said, "Do you love her that much?" I said, "Yeah, I do." She says, "I hope she knows how lucky she is." And I said, "S-1, I hope I know how lucky I am."

Now we're back, four or five hours later. Funny. The evening went on. We drank. I finally said to her, "S-1 would you like to dance?" She says, "I'd love to." So I slipped around the side of this gigantic desk and we danced. Boy, she wrapped her arm around my neck—and simply put it into me—it was a romantic song of some kind, but I knew and she knew what we were both thinking. Finished that song. Another slow and romantic one started and we danced again and I kissed her, and she says, "Do you really love her that much?" I said, "S-1, I love her that much." She held me even closer and she said, "Thanks." I said, "What does that mean?" She says, "I've been set upon by so many guys who said they loved me when I knew they didn't, and it's a privilege and pleasure to be held by one who isn't trying to con me." Well. I won't bore you with all of the details of the evening. S-1 and I made love, and she has the most stunning fig-ure—big breasts. She's not my kind of woman in that sense of the ____ —

They stand at attention. You can certainly tell man from woman. But just as I was about to insert I said, "S-1 I love ____ ." She said, "Senator, from the time I went into politics I've been trying to figure how I can get to work for you. So I started with this ____ (sp?) who is a slime and then I had the opportunity to go to work for ____ and I thought I'll go to work for ____ because that will get me in Washington and in Washington I'll be in close proximity and somehow I'll get to your office because that's what I want to do." I said, "S-1 bullshit." She says, "It wasn't really planned that directly but I believed in your issues and I heard you speak once and you didn't know it, but I wanted to be with you." She says, "You have no idea the hold you have over people." I said, "What is it?" She says, "Well, I think it's you hair—the way combs it." And we both laughed. She said, "I'm not sure if I know what it is." I said, "S-1 I don't know what it is at all." She said, "There's simply an attraction. I don't know what the other word is." Now bear in mind this is an hour and a half after we've made love and we're still both nude and lying on the rug. What I didn't know until later—get this—is that and   were still there in the outer office and they simply left us alone. I had locked the doors thank God, but by Noon tomorrow,   will know S-1 was with me for the better part of the evening.

Well,   came in. It's funny. S-1 and I were in there for three hours. Made love once. Got up and danced after we made love, lied back down on the floor, had another glass of wine—the wine was in the office. I rather enjoyed it in the sense it wasn't wham bam, thank you ma'am, but we finally got up and got dressed and she left, and then, only then, did and   appear from way down the hall and I think they had made sure they were way down the hall. So I said, " come in." She said, "I'm going to leave." I said, "It's worth your staying." I told her the situation about the divorce and separation. She stayed for 45 minutes and she was the normal, unemotional   except I was intrigued. She was a bit critical of Elaine in terms of Elain's management style. She said, "Elaine involves herself in all of these issues and interjects herself and we don't quite feel we have a free reign." I said, "Less than   , less than   ?" She said,

"Well, in a different sense." I said, "God,   involved
herself in all those damn women's issues." She said, "Well, that
was her issue." She said, "Elaine involves herself in stuff she
doesn't know about—more than she should." Hmmm. It was a
critical comment. She took off.

        's in Oregon with open arms awaiting me. And
is pissed.